MW01166772

PAWSITIVELY CLEMSON

TASTES OF THE TIGERS

A Clemson Cookbook

Naturally Fresh
Dressings, Sauces & Dips

This cookbook is a collection of favorite recipes, which are not necessarily original recipes.

The *Pawsitively Clemson* cookbook is officially licensed through the Clemson University licensing department and the Collegiate Licensing Company of Atlanta, Georgia. The University licensing program is designed to protect the integrity and ensure the proper use of the University name and logos. In order to administer the program, formal licensing procedures are established that allow Clemson University to benefit from the commercial use of both the registered name and the logos. The Clemson University licensing program is also designed to establish a cooperative relationship with licensees to assist them in developing a marketplace demand for "officially licensed Clemson products." The Clemson University licensing program began in 1982 as a result of increased requests to use University marks.

Copyright© 1998
IPTAY Scholarship Fund, "Pawsitively Clemson Cookbook"
P.O. Box 1529, Avenue of Champions
Clemson, SC 29633
(864) 656-2115 fax: (864) 656-0415

Library of Congress Number: 98-093499
ISBN: 0-9665499-0-2

Designed, Edited, and Manufactured by
Favorite Recipes Press
an imprint of

FRP

P.O. Box 305142
Nashville, Tennessee 37230
1-800-358-0560

Book Design: David Malone
Project Manager: Judy Jackson
Art Director: Steve Newman

Manufactured in the United States of America
First Printing: 1998   20,000 copies

Contents

Tiger twirler Brandy Perry escorts Jane Robelot, a 1982 Clemson graduate and co-anchor of "CBS This Morning," onto the field at the 1997 Homecoming game. Jane dotted the Tiger "i" and got a wedding proposal on the "Paw"vision scoreboard! She said, "Yes!"

Acknowledgments

The IPTAY Scholarship Fund acknowledges and thanks the following for their help in the production of this cookbook.

Co-Editors

Nancy M. Bennett
Nancy B. Cathcart

IPTAY Directors' Wives/Friends:
Jimmy Carol Avent
Joyce Bussey
Ava Campbell
Betty Dalton
Lib DesChamps
Ellen Dye (deceased)
Louise Edwards
Gale Golightly
LeeAnn Henderson
Julia Holcombe
Eva Holmes
Retta Hughes
Joan Kennerty

Kathy Lawhon
Robin Mahony
Anne Marchant
Rosemary McGee
Diane McLamb
Mary Jane Patterson
Margaret Reaves
Claudia Sanders
Nancy Matthews
Ila Jo Tice
Garland Timmerman
Lillian Walker
Debbie Whelchel

Bob Brooks & Naturally Fresh® Products
George Bennett, Executive Director, IPTAY
Bobby Robinson, Athletic Director
Clemson Athletic Administrators
Clemson Sports Information Office
Tara Stevenson and The Orange & White
Foster Cathcart, '51, Alumni Volunteer of the Year, '97-98
IPTAY Staff

and IPTAY representatives and members, along with Tiger alumni and fans, who graciously donated their favorite recipes to *Pawsitively Clemson*.

Special thanks also go to the Clemson coaches, athletes, trainers, tutors, managers, staff, and their families. Their selfless dedication in working to ensure that Clemson Athletics and IPTAY are unmistakably the very best is sincerely appreciated.

We wish to welcome new 1998 IPTAY Directors Mary Ann Bigger and Dr. James E. Bostic.

Introduction

Clemson College first opened its doors in 1893 as a small land-grant college. Thomas Green Clemson, son-in-law of John C. Calhoun, inherited the land and was convinced by Ben Tillman, then governor of South Carolina, to give the land to establish an agricultural and mechanical college. It opened with 466 students.

Clemson fielded its first football team in 1896. Unpaid professor W. M. Riggs, who had played at Auburn, and R. N. Bowman, for whom Bowman Field is named, coached that first team to wins over Furman and Wofford and a loss to South Carolina. There were 21 players.

The following year a full-time coach was hired, M. W. Williamson, who finished with a 2-2 record. J. A. Payton coached the next year to a 3-win, 1-loss season.

Because of a lack of funds, Riggs became the coach again in 1899, winning four games and losing two, to Georgia and Auburn. Clemson's football team came from hardy stock, most working on their parents' farms. They wore canvas uniforms and no headgear. Their orange and purple striped jerseys and stockings resembled tigers, which became the Clemson mascot.

After the 1899 season, at a meeting on December 7, participants created the football aid society; the 132 people there pledged $372.50. Its sole purpose was to aid the football program and secure a coach for the 1900 season. Dr. Riggs again looked to Auburn for a coach and chose John Heisman. In the four years that Heisman coached here, he compiled a record of 19-3-2. This made him the most successful coach in Clemson history.

Clemson football entered a dark period, losing more than it won until Josh Cody and then Jess Neely arrived. It took Neely seven years, until 1938, to build up the program and accomplish his winning record of 4-1. His last year was amazing. They went to their first bowl game in 1939, playing Boston in the Cotton Bowl and winning 6-3.

In 1931 Neely, with the help of Captain Frank Jervey, Assistant Coach Joe Davis and Captain Pete Heffner, discussed ways to get alumni to finance the football team. Captain Jervey volunteered to write letters to influential alumni. One went to Dr. Rupert H. (Rube) Fike, a cancer specialist in

Atlanta and a 1908 graduate. He decided that $10 was the magic number to ask from each Clemson alumnus and friend, under the slogan "I Pay Ten A Year." The purpose of the Clemson Order of IPTAY "shall be to provide annual financial support to the athletic department at Clemson and to assist in every other way possible to regain for Clemson the high athletic standing which rightfully belongs to her." By the end of 1935, there were 183 members; when Neely left in 1939, IPTAY had over $20,000 in its treasury.

Neely left, and Frank Howard took over as head coach. After three losing seasons, he urged IPTAY to raise football scholarship dollars. They did, and by 1948 Howard, with an 11-0 season, finished with Clemson's first unbeaten and untied record since 1900.

Dr. Fike retired as President of IPTAY, after serving 20 years. IPTAY's leadership was revamped to include a Board of Directors consisting of nine people. Today the Board consists of nine District Directors and all former IPTAY presidents. Their duties are to generate interest and funds for the IPTAY Scholarship Fund.

President and Mrs. Bob Edwards with Bob Hope

There are now 750 IPTAY representatives and 19,451 IPTAY members. George Bennett, current IPTAY Executive Director, reported that total money pledged for 1998 is $9,143,045, the first time IPTAY has hit the $9 million mark.

Although the football program has the largest budget, a total of 570 athletic scholarships in 19 sports are allocated through IPTAY. IPTAY and athletic funds are also used for the band, cheerleaders, academic scholarships, and many other needs of the University.

A Special Tiger Thank You

In 1967 Atlanta-based Eastern Foods, Incorporated, opened with a $10,000 investment, a handful of employees, and a 4,000-square-foot warehouse. Thirty-one years later, the company approaches $100,000,000 in sales, operates from a 250,000-square-foot state-of-the-art facility, and employs more than 330 people across the country. Founded by current Chief Executive Officer Robert H. Brooks, the company began by selling airlines a vegetable-based non-refrigerated coffee creamer. Although Eastern Foods no longer produces the product, coffee creamers launched the company.

Bob Brooks

The 1960 Clemson graduate's chance encounter with two strangers who informed him of a scholarship program at Clemson begins the story of this hard-working head of Naturally Fresh® Foods and Hooter's of America. In addition, Brooks has developed and is actively involved in an extensive sports organization that includes auto racing, professional golf, and a golf course.

Buoyed by a Clemson loan scholarship and a strong work ethic acquired from his upbringing on a Sweet Home, South Carolina, farm, Brooks today leads a half-billion dollar organization.

Applying his degree in dairy science, Brooks entered the dairy business as an intern in Gastonia, North Carolina, before moving into dairy sales with a company in Rock Hill, South Carolina. Broadening his career, Brooks joined an Iowa food processing company as an Atlanta sales engineer in 1961. During that time, the Army drafted Brooks to active duty for the Berlin crisis.

After military duty, Brooks joined a Philadelphia food formula company. Over the next five years he saved $10,000 and became an entrepreneur. In 1967 Brooks developed the non-dairy creamer and formed Eastern Foods, which served primarily the airline industry. Over time, Eastern Foods began to focus on a more diverse food business and discontinued the original creamer product. Each product package invites customers to call or write Brooks if not completely satisfied with a Naturally Fresh product.

By 1980 Eastern Foods began producing preservative-free foods. The Naturally Fresh line included dressings, sauces, and dips. Later, Jackaroo® Meat Sauces and Naturally Fresh Mountain Spring Water, along with oil and vinegar products, joined the company's lineup. All of the products are made at Eastern Food's College Park, Georgia, plant (near Atlanta). Products are shipped on company-owned and operated refrigerated trucks to Eastern Foods' 21 distribution centers. In addition, Brooks heads Hooter's of America, with more than 220 restaurants in 40 states and seven countries.

To help promote his enterprises, Brooks sponsored NASCAR driver Alan Kulwicki. The 1992 Winston Cup champion was killed on April 1, 1993, in an airplane crash that also took the lives of Brooks' 26-year-old son Mark, pilot Charlie Campbell, and Sports Marketing Director Dan Duncan. Not long after the accident, Brooks endowed Clemson's Robert H. Brooks Performing Arts Center, which includes the 1,000-seat Mark Brooks Auditorium. In addition, Brooks invested $2.5 million to fund the Brooks Sports Science Institute at Clemson. The institute's programs concentrate on all aspects of sports.

And sports occupies an important part of Brooks' business life as well. After Kulwicki's death, he formed the Hooter's Pro Cup Series under the United Speed Racing Alliance (USAR) group.

Brooks also owns Whitewater Golf Course south of Atlanta and sponsors the National Golf Association (NGA) Hooter's tour for aspiring golf pros. In 1997 eleven alumni from that group qualified for the U.S. Open. In addition, Brooks owns a hotel in Lakeland, Florida. He also owns the USA International Speedway in Lakeland, the Peach State Speedway in Jefferson, Georgia, and the Tri-County Speedway in Hudson, North Carolina.

Attributing the success of Eastern Foods to hard-working employees, Brooks offers employees an opportunity to share in company profits.

IPTAY and the Clemson University Athletic Department thank Bob Brooks and Eastern Foods for underwriting *Pawsitively Clemson*.

Tailgating and Appetizers

TAILGATE PARTY

Vicki's Artichoke and Crab Spread

16 ounces cream cheese, softened
2 tablespoons sherry
1 tablespoon Worcestershire sauce
2 (14-ounce) cans artichoke hearts, drained and chopped
1 pound crab meat, chopped
1 small onion, finely chopped
½ cup chopped slivered almonds or pecan pieces
2 to 3 tablespoons grated Parmesan cheese

Combine the cream cheese, sherry and Worcestershire sauce in a bowl; mix well. Stir in the artichokes, crab meat and onions. Spoon into 9-inch pie plate or 6x10-inch baking dish. Sprinkle with the almonds and Parmesan cheese. Bake at 350 degrees for 20 to 25 minutes or until thoroughly heated. Serve with toasted baguette slices. Yield: 32 servings

Victoria Grubbs Cox (Mrs. Walter Cox III)

Walter Cox at the Peach Bowl

Artichoke Dip

2 (14-ounce) cans artichoke hearts, drained and chopped
1 cup mayonnaise
½ cup grated Parmesan cheese

Combine artichoke hearts, mayonnaise and Parmesan cheese in a bowl; mix well. Spoon into a 9-inch pie plate or 6x10-inch baking dish. Bake at 350 degrees for 10 to 15 minutes or until thoroughly heated. Serve with assorted crackers. Yield: 16 servings

Joy O. Skelton (Mrs. Bobby Skelton)

Bean Dip

2 (15-ounce) cans refried beans
½ envelope taco seasoning mix
1 cup sour cream
1 cup shredded sharp Cheddar cheese
Texas Pete hot sauce to taste

Combine the beans, taco seasoning mix, sour cream and cheese in a bowl; mix well. Season with hot sauce. Remove to a baking dish. Bake at 375 degrees for 20 minutes or until bubbly. Garnish with sliced black olives and tomatoes. Yield: 16 servings

Meg Newton (Mrs. Robby Newton)

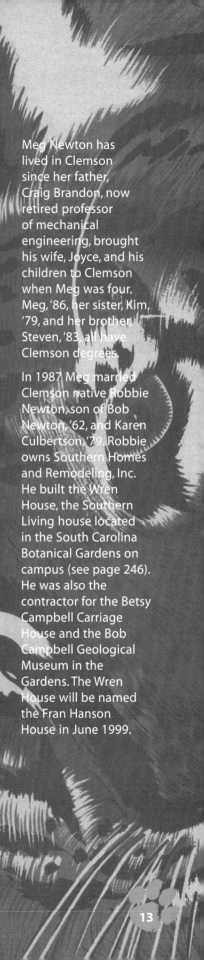

Meg Newton has lived in Clemson since her father, Craig Brandon, now retired professor of mechanical engineering, brought his wife, Joyce, and his children to Clemson when Meg was four. Meg, '86, her sister, Kim, '79, and her brother, Steven, '83, all have Clemson degrees.

In 1987 Meg married Clemson native Robbie Newton, son of Bob Newton, '62, and Karen Culbertson, '79. Robbie owns Southern Homes and Remodeling, Inc. He built the Wren House, the Southern Living house located in the South Carolina Botanical Gardens on campus (see page 246). He was also the contractor for the Betsy Campbell Carriage House and the Bob Campbell Geological Museum in the Gardens. The Wren House will be named the Fran Hanson House in June 1999.

Al and Connie Hancock served this appetizer for the Atlanta Board of Directors Annual Christmas Party. Al is a 1952 Clemson graduate.

IPTAY Caviar

2 (15-ounce) cans black-eyed peas, drained
1 (15-ounce) can hominy, drained
2 medium tomatoes, chopped
1 green bell pepper, chopped
1 yellow onion, chopped
5 green onions, chopped
½ cup minced fresh parsley
1 clove of garlic, minced
8 ounces Naturally Fresh Italian Herb Vinaigrette Dressing

Combine the peas, hominy, tomatoes, green pepper, onion, green onions, parsley and garlic in a bowl. Add the dressing; mix lightly. Refrigerate, covered, until chilled. Serve with tortilla chips or assorted crackers. Yield: 48 servings

Connie Hancock (Mrs. Al Hancock)

Al and Connie Hancock welcomed the Board into their home at Christmas.

Clemson Caviar

2 (15-ounce) cans black-eyed peas, drained
1 (15-ounce) can white hominy, drained
2 medium tomatoes, chopped
1 medium green bell pepper, chopped
4 green onions, chopped
1/2 cup chopped onion
1/2 cup minced fresh parsley
1 jalapeño pepper, seeded and chopped
2 cloves of garlic, minced
1 (8-ounce) bottle Italian dressing

Combine the peas, hominy, tomatoes, green pepper, green onions, onion, parsley, jalapeño pepper and garlic in a bowl. Add the dressing; mix lightly. Refrigerate, covered, for at least 2 hours. Serve with tortilla chips. Yield: 48 servings

Cathy Mathias

Cheese Ball

1 (4-ounce) jar extra sharp Old English cheese spread
16 ounces cream cheese, softened
1/2 cup bleu cheese, crumbled
1 cup chopped pecans, toasted
1 tablespoon Worcestershire sauce
1/2 teaspoon cayenne
1/4 teaspoon salt
1/8 teaspoon garlic juice (optional)

Allow the Old English cheese to stand at room temperature until softened. Mix the Old English cheese, cream cheese, bleu cheese, half the pecans, Worcestershire sauce, cayenne, salt and garlic juice in a bowl. Shape into 1 large ball or 2 smaller balls; roll in the remaining 1/2 cup pecans until evenly coated on all sides. Refrigerate, covered, until ready to serve. Serve with assorted crackers. Notes: For best results, do not use reduced-fat cream cheese. Use your hands to mix together the cheese ball mixture. The body heat from your hands will help to soften the cheese for easier blending. If desired, add 1/2 cup minced fresh parsley to the remaining 1/2 cup pecans before coating the cheese ball(s). Cheese ball(s) can be stored in the refrigerator for up to 2 weeks.
Yield: 20 to 25 servings

Sarah S. Boulware (Mrs. Louis M. Boulware)

Tiger Paw Cheese Ball

6 ounces cream cheese, softened
2 pounds Velveeta cheese, cubed
1/2 pound pecans, finely chopped
1 clove of garlic, minced
1 tablespoon Worcestershire sauce
2 teaspoons cayenne
Paprika

Combine the cream cheese, Velveeta cheese, pecans, garlic, Worcestershire sauce and cayenne in a bowl; mix well. Shape into a ball. Roll in paprika until evenly coated on all sides. Refrigerate, covered, until ready to serve. Serve with assorted crackers.
Note: For easier mixing, use your hands to combine the cheese ball ingredients. Yield: 24 servings

Lillian Hudson (Mrs. Bill Hudson)

Bill Hudson and granddaughter

Chipped Beef Cheese Ball

8 ounces cream cheese, softened
1 (4-ounce) jar dried beef, finely chopped
1 medium onion, chopped
1 medium green bell pepper, chopped
1 cup shredded sharp Cheddar cheese
Chopped walnuts or pecans

Mix the first 5 ingredients in a bowl. Shape into a ball. Roll in walnuts. Refrigerate, covered, for 30 minutes. Yield: 8 to 10 servings

Robin Lay

Cheese Straws

1½ pounds sharp Cheddar cheese, shredded, softened
1 cup margarine or butter, softened
3 cups sifted flour
1 teaspoon salt
2 teaspoons baking powder
¾ teaspoon cayenne

Cream the cheese and margarine in a mixer bowl. Add the flour gradually, beating at medium speed until blended. Blend in the salt, baking powder and cayenne. Press the dough through a cookie press onto lightly greased cookie sheets to make individual (4-inch) straws. Bake at 300 degrees for 15 minutes or until very lightly browned. Remove to a wire rack to cool. Yield: 50 to 75 servings

Betty Sharpe (Mrs. Bob Sharpe)

Mexican Corn Cheese Dip

1 (11-ounce) can Mexicorn
1 cup mayonnaise
1 cup shredded Monterey Jack cheese with jalapeño peppers
½ cup grated Parmesan cheese
8 to 16 jalapeño pepper slices

Mix the undrained corn, mayonnaise and cheeses in a bowl. Spoon into a 9-inch pie plate. Top with jalapeño peppers. Bake at 350 degrees for 30 minutes or until lightly browned and bubbly. Serve with tortilla chips. Yield: 24 servings

Beverly Hutto

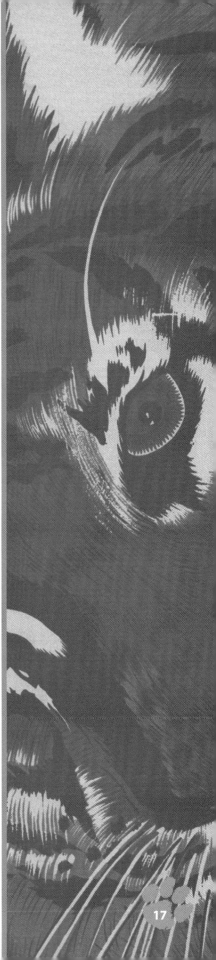

Tailgating and Appetizers

Cream Cheese and Chutney

8 ounces cream cheese, softened
1 teaspoon Worcestershire sauce
½ to 1 teaspoon curry powder
½ teaspoon salt
¼ teaspoon Tabasco sauce
3 bacon slices, cooked and crumbled
3 tablespoons chopped pecans, toasted
Chutney

Combine the cream cheese, Worcestershire sauce, curry powder, salt and Tabasco sauce in a bowl; mix well. Refrigerate, covered, overnight. Shape into a ball; flatten slightly. Top with the bacon, pecans and desired amount of chutney. Refrigerate, covered, until ready to serve. Serve with assorted crackers. Note: You may substitute 3 tablespoons imitation bacon bits for the cooked bacon slices. Yield: 8 servings

Betty Clausen (Mrs. Hugh Clausen)

Betty and Hugh Clausen

Tailgating and Appetizers

Shrimp Paste

3 (4-ounce) cans salad shrimp
Juice of 1½ lemons
¼ teaspoon black pepper
⅛ teaspoon cayenne
2 cups (about) mayonnaise
Onion juice or onion powder

Drain and rinse the shrimp under cold running water; drain well.
Place the shrimp in a bowl; mash with a fork or your fingers. Add
the lemon juice; mix well. Stir in the black pepper and cayenne.
Blend in the mayonnaise. Season with the onion juice to taste.
Refrigerate, covered, overnight. Serve with assorted crackers.
Note: If desired, serve as a sandwich spread. Cut bread slices into
rounds with a biscuit cutter. Spread each round with the Shrimp
Spread and top with an olive slice. Yield: 24 servings

Lou Willimon (Mrs. Gene Willimon)

Former IPTAY Director Gene Willimon (left), current Director
George Bennett (center), and former Director Allison Dalton

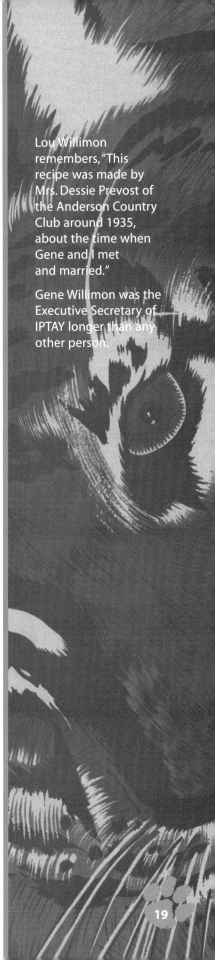

Lou Willimon
remembers, "This
recipe was made by
Mrs. Dessie Prevost of
the Anderson Country
Club around 1935,
about the time when
Gene and I met
and married."

Gene Willimon was the
Executive Secretary of
IPTAY longer than any
other person.

Harriet's Pickled Shrimp

3 pounds cleaned shrimp, cooked, deveined
1 large onion, sliced into rings
1 cup catsup
1 cup vinegar
½ cup olive oil
2 tablespoons prepared mustard
1 tablespoon sugar
1 tablespoon Worcestershire sauce
1 teaspoon celery seeds
⅛ teaspoon cayenne
⅛ teaspoon dillweed
⅛ teaspoon garlic powder
Salt and black pepper to taste
3 bay leaves

Layer the shrimp and onions in a large glass jar or bowl. Combine the catsup, vinegar, olive oil, mustard, sugar, Worcestershire sauce, celery seeds, cayenne, dillweed and garlic powder in a blender container; blend until smooth. Season with salt and black pepper. Pour over the shrimp mixture; top with the bay leaves. Refrigerate, covered, until ready to serve. Serve with wooden picks or assorted crackers. Note: This recipe will stay fresh for at least a week in the refrigerator. Yield: 10 servings

Cindy DesChamps (Mrs. Carroll Green DesChamps II)

At the DesChamps tailgate

Doc Harder's Pickled Shrimp

2 to 3 pounds shrimp
1 tablespoon salt
2 cups vegetable oil
1 cup vinegar
1 teaspoon salt
1 teaspoon dry mustard
1/4 teaspoon sugar
Ground white pepper
Red onion slices
Lemon slices

Add the shrimp to a large pot of boiling water that has been seasoned with 1 tablespoon salt. Boil 3 minutes or until the shrimp turn pink. Drain the shrimp; cool. Remove the shells and veins from the shrimp. Combine the oil, vinegar, 1 teaspoon salt, dry mustard and sugar in a bowl. Season with the white pepper to taste. Fill several jars with alternating layers of the shrimp, onions and lemons. Fill the jars with the oil mixture; cover with the lids. Refrigerate for at least 2 days, shaking the jars frequently.
Yield: 10 servings

Dr. Byron and Lillian Utsey Harder

Crabbies (or Shrimpies!)

1/2 cup margarine, softened
1 (4-ounce) jar Old English cheese spread
2 teaspoons mayonnaise
1/2 teaspoon garlic salt
1/2 teaspoon seasoned salt
1 (7-ounce) can crab meat (or tiny shrimp), drained
6 to 8 English muffins, split in half

Combine the margarine, cheese spread and mayonnaise in a bowl; mix until well blended. Stir in the garlic salt, seasoned salt and crab meat. Spread generous amounts of the crab meat mixture onto the muffin halves. Place on a baking sheet. Cover and freeze. When ready to serve, remove the desired number of muffin halves from the freezer and broil 5 to 7 minutes or until lightly browned and bubbly. Cut in half or into quarters to serve. Note: Use a pizza cutter to easily cut the broiled muffins. Yield: 8 to 10 servings

May Grosland McDowell Cox (Mrs. Frank Cox)

Dr. Byron Harder, '64, has been associated with Clemson athletics for over 26 years. When not treating the athletes' aches and pains, he enjoys shrimping around his beachfront getaway on Edisto Island. Friends know to expect his delicious Pickled Shrimp when they are invited to his hilltop home overlooking the Clemson campus. His talented wife, Lillian Harder (better known as Mickey), is the Director of the Brooks Center for the Performing Arts at Clemson.

The Harder family are ardent sports fans, particularly of basketball, where they were seen cheering for their son, Bill, '97, a member of the "Slab Five."

Pimento Cheese Spread

1 small onion
1 pound sharp Cheddar cheese, shredded
1 cup mayonnaise
1 (4-ounce) jar diced pimentos, drained

Grate the onion; reserve both the onion and the juice. Combine the onion, onion juice, cheese, mayonnaise and pimentos in a bowl; mix until smooth and creamy. Refrigerate, covered, until ready to serve. Serve at room temperature with French bread slices or assorted crackers. Note: This spread will keep fresh in the refrigerator for about 1 week. Yield: 4 to 6 servings

Beverly Hafer

Beverly Hafer and friends before the game

Tailgating and Appetizers

Vegetable Bars

2 (8-count) packages crescent roll dough
8 ounces cream cheese, softened
1 cup mayonnaise
1 (1-ounce) package ranch dry salad dressing mix
2 cups (about) broccoli florets
2 cups (about) carrot chunks
2 cups (about) cauliflower florets

Unroll the crescent dough into rectangles. Place on a nonstick baking sheet; press the edges and seams of the dough together to form a crust. Bake at 350 degrees for 10 minutes or until lightly browned. Remove to a wire rack to cool completely. Combine the cream cheese, mayonnaise and dressing mix in a bowl; mix well. Spread evenly over the cooled crust. Place the broccoli, carrots and cauliflower in a food processor; process until chopped. Sprinkle over the cream cheese mixture. Refrigerate, covered, until ready to serve. Note: Use a pizza cutter to easily cut the appetizer into bars. Yield: 32 servings

Heidi Penley, wife of Coach Larry Penley

The Penley family

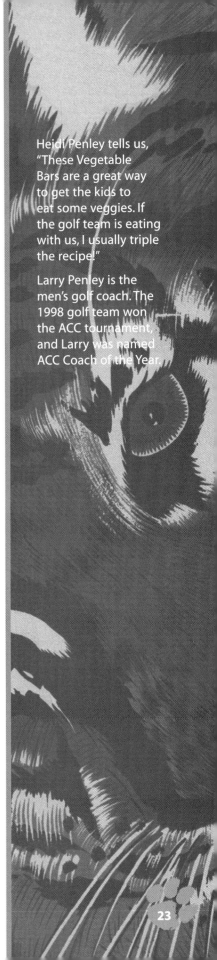

Heidi Penley tells us, "These Vegetable Bars are a great way to get the kids to eat some veggies. If the golf team is eating with us, I usually triple the recipe!"

Larry Penley is the men's golf coach. The 1998 golf team won the ACC tournament, and Larry was named ACC Coach of the Year.

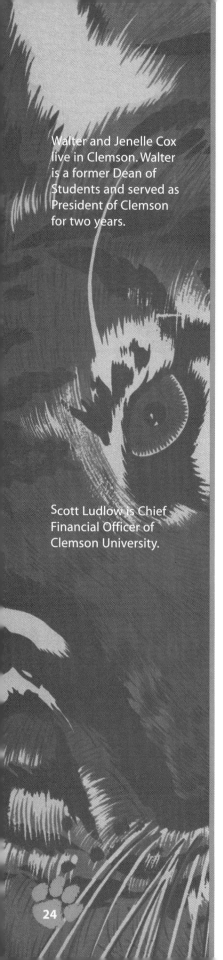

Vegetable Sandwich

1 onion, chopped
1 cucumber, chopped
1 tomato, chopped
1 cup chopped celery
1 cup chopped green bell pepper
2 teaspoons salt
1 envelope unflavored gelatin
2 cups mayonnaise

Combine the onion, cucumber, tomato, celery, green pepper and salt in a bowl; mix lightly. Drain well, reserving the liquid. Pour the drained liquid into a small saucepan. Add the gelatin; cook over low heat, stirring occasionally, until the gelatin is dissolved. Add the mayonnaise; mix well. Add to the vegetables; mix lightly. Refrigerate, covered, until set. Serve as a spread on bread slices.
Yield: 24 servings

Jenelle Garett Cox (Mrs. Walter Cox, Jr.)

Vegetable Pizza

2 (8-count) packages crescent roll dough
16 ounces cream cheese, softened
¾ cup salad dressing
1 (1-ounce) package ranch dry salad dressing mix
1 cup broccoli florets
1 cup cauliflower florets
1 cup chopped green bell pepper
1 cup radish slices
1 cup shredded carrots
1 cup shredded Cheddar cheese

Unroll the crescent dough into rectangles. Place on a lightly greased baking sheet; press the edges and seams of the dough together to form a crust. Bake at 375 degrees for 7 to 10 minutes or until lightly browned. Remove to a wire rack to cool completely. Mix the cream cheese, salad dressing and dressing mix in a bowl. Spread onto the crust. Chop the vegetables into very small pieces. Layer on top of the cream cheese mixture. Sprinkle with the Cheddar cheese. Refrigerate, covered, until ready to serve. Cut into squares before serving. Yield: 24 servings

Denise Ludlow (Mrs. Scott Ludlow)

Tailgating and Appetizers

Upside-Down Pizza Squares

2 pounds ground beef
1 (32-ounce) jar spaghetti sauce
1 cup shredded mozzarella cheese
1 cup shredded Cheddar cheese
4 eggs
½ cup milk
1 cup all-purpose baking mix

Cook the ground beef in a skillet until browned, stirring occasionally; drain. Place in a 9x12-inch baking dish. Cover with layers of the spaghetti sauce and the cheeses. Beat the eggs and milk in a bowl. Add the baking mix; mix well. Spoon evenly over the cheese to cover. Bake at 350 degrees for 30 to 45 minutes or until golden brown. Cut into squares. Use a spatula to flip over the squares onto serving plates and serve, meat-side-up.
Yield: 12 servings

Rosemary Dominick

Snackel

1 (16-ounce) bag small pretzels
1 (12-ounce) box Crispix cereal
1 (12-ounce) bag oyster crackers
2 (6-ounce) bags Parmesan flavor goldfish crackers
1 (7-ounce) box original flavor Munch'ems crackers
1 (12-ounce) can peanuts
2 (1-ounce) packages dry ranch salad dressing mix
1½ cups vegetable oil

Insert 2 paper grocery bags into a plastic grocery bag. Add the pretzels, Crispix, oyster crackers, goldfish crackers, snack crackers and peanuts. Combine the salad dressing mix with the oil in a bowl; pour over the cracker mixture. Close the bags and shake vigorously to coat all of the ingredients evenly with the dressing mixture. Let stand overnight to allow the paper bags to absorb the excess oil. Store in an airtight container. Yield: 32 servings

Sylvia Peters (Mrs. John Peters)

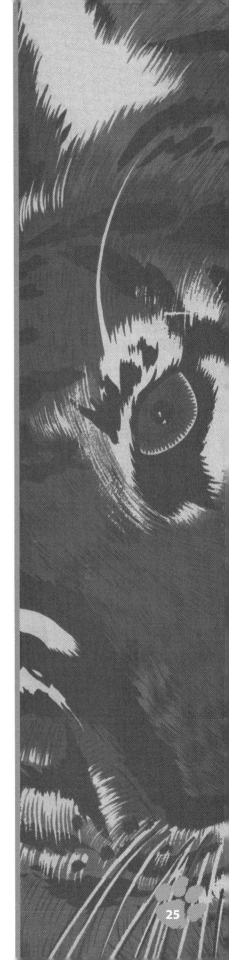

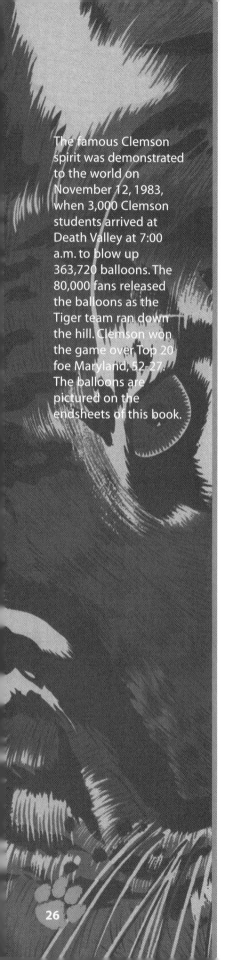

Ham Delights

1 cup melted margarine
1 medium onion, finely chopped
3 tablespoons poppy seeds
3 tablespoons prepared mustard
1 teaspoon Worcestershire sauce
2 (7-ounce) packages small party dinner rolls
1 pound thinly sliced ham or turkey
12 ounces Swiss cheese, sliced

Combine the margarine, onion, poppy seeds, mustard and
Worcestershire sauce in a bowl; mix well. Split the rolls in half.
Spread the margarine mixture evenly onto the roll halves. Top the
bottom halves of the rolls with the ham and cheese; cover with the
top halves of the rolls. Wrap the sandwiches in foil. Bake at 400
degrees for 10 minutes or until the cheese is melted.
Yield: 40 sandwiches

Marianne Sease

Spinach Balls

1 (10-ounce) package frozen chopped spinach
3 eggs, slightly beaten
1 cup herb-seasoned stuffing mix
1 medium onion, chopped
½ cup chopped water chestnuts
½ cup grated Parmesan cheese
1 teaspoon garlic salt
¼ teaspoon thyme
¼ teaspoon pepper

Cook the spinach according to package directions; drain well and
pat dry with paper towels. Combine the spinach with the eggs,
stuffing mix, onion, water chestnuts, cheese, garlic salt, thyme and
pepper in a bowl; mix well. Shape into bite-sized balls. Place on
nonstick baking sheets. Bake at 350 degrees for 20 minutes.
Note: Unbaked spinach balls freeze well. Yield: 60 to 70 balls

Frances Davenport (Mrs. Thomas Davenport)

Tailgating and Appetizers

Tiger Burgers

½ pound ground beef
2 tablespoons chopped onion
1 jalapeño pepper, chopped
Salt and freshly ground black pepper
2 American or Cheddar cheese slices
1 hamburger bun, split
Mayonnaise
Prepared mustard
Lettuce
Tomato slices

Divide ground beef into 2 equal portions. Flatten each portion between 2 sheets of waxed paper to form a thin, round patty, about 6 inches in diameter. Top one patty with onions and jalapeño peppers; season with the salt and pepper to taste. Cover with the cheese slices and second ground beef patty. Pinch the edges of the 2 patties together tightly to seal. Grill or broil 2 minutes on each side or until done. Serve on a heated bun spread with mayonnaise and mustard. Top with lettuce and tomato. Yield: 1 serving

Foster Cathcart

Tomato Sandwich

2 white or whole wheat bread slices
Mayonnaise
2 tomato slices
2 tablespoons finely chopped onions
2 tablespoons finely chopped pecans

Spread bread slices with mayonnaise. Sprinkle one bread slice with the onions; sprinkle the remaining bread slice with the pecans. Top one of the bread slices with the tomatoes; cover with the second bread slice. Refrigerate, covered, until ready to serve. Note: You may remove the crusts from the bread and peel the tomatoes before slicing, if desired. Yield: 1 serving

Mary Katherine Littlejohn

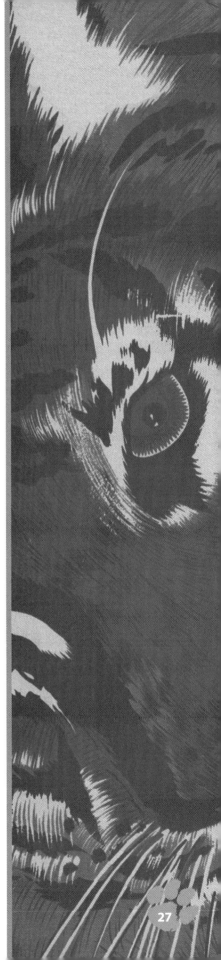

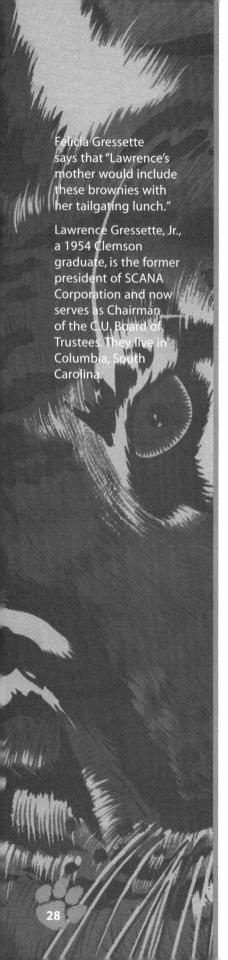

Brownies with Icing

½ cup margarine, softened
1 cup sugar
2 eggs
2 (1-ounce) squares chocolate, melted
½ teaspoon vanilla extract
1 cup flour
⅛ teaspoon salt
1 cup chopped nuts
1 cup sugar
¼ cup unsweetened cocoa
¼ cup milk
2 tablespoons margarine

Beat ½ cup margarine and 1 cup sugar in a mixer bowl until light and fluffy. Add the eggs, one at a time, beating well after each addition. Blend in the melted chocolate and vanilla. Add the flour and salt; mix well. Stir in the nuts. Spread into a greased and floured 9x13-inch baking pan. Bake at 350 degrees for 20 minutes or until a wooden pick inserted into the center comes out clean. Remove to a wire rack. Combine the remaining 1 cup sugar, cocoa, milk and 2 tablespoons margarine in a saucepan. Bring to a boil over low heat. Boil 1 minute or until thickened. Remove from the heat; cool. Pour over the warm brownies. Note: After cutting the brownies into squares, top each square with a miniature marshmallow, if desired. Yield: 24 servings

Felicia Gressette
(Mrs. Lawrence Gressette, Jr.)

Felicia and Lawrence Gressette

Chocolate Swanns

1 box milk chocolate chunk brownie mix
¾ cup firmly packed brown sugar
¾ cup chopped pecans
3 tablespoons melted margarine or butter

Prepare the brownie mix according to the package directions. Spread into a greased 9x13-inch baking pan. Combine the brown sugar, pecans and margarine in a bowl; sprinkle over the batter. Bake at 350 degrees for 25 minutes or a until a wooden pick inserted into the center comes out clean. Remove to a wire rack to cool before cutting into squares. Store in an airtight container. Note: These brownies freeze well. Yield: 24 servings

Bobbi Swann (Mrs. Joseph D. Swann)

Gingersnaps

4 cups flour
4 teaspoons baking soda
2 teaspoons cinnamon
2 teaspoons ginger
½ teaspoon salt
1½ cups shortening
2 cups sugar
2 eggs
½ cup light molasses
Sugar

Combine the flour, baking soda, cinnamon, ginger and salt in a bowl; mix well and set aside. Beat the shortening and 2 cups sugar in a mixer bowl until light and fluffy. Add the eggs, one at a time, beating well after each addition. Blend in the molasses. Gradually add the combined dry ingredients, beating until well blended. Refrigerate, covered, 1 to 2 hours or until well chilled. Shape the dough into 1-inch balls and roll in additional sugar. Place the balls on nonstick cookie sheets. Place the cookie sheets on the bottom oven rack and bake at 350 degrees until the balls spread out, about 3 minutes. Move the cookie sheets to a higher oven rack and continue baking until the cookies are set, about 6 minutes. Remove to a wire rack to cool. Yield: 4 dozen

Sarah Ellen Thomas Cox (Mrs. J.W. "Bill" Cox)

Bobbi Swann is the wife of Joe Swann, a 1963 Clemson graduate and a member of the Clemson Board of Trustees. Their son and daughter are also Clemson graduates.

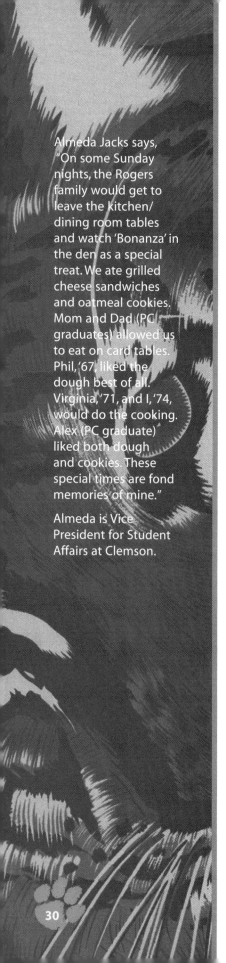

Oatmeal Cookies

1 cup shortening
1 cup granulated sugar
1 cup firmly packed brown sugar
2 eggs
2 tablespoons water
2 teaspoons vanilla extract
2 cups flour
1 teaspoon baking soda
3 cups oats, rolled

Beat the shortening, granulated sugar and brown sugar in a mixer bowl until light and fluffy. Add the eggs, one at a time, beating well after each addition. Blend in the water and vanilla. Gradually add the combined flour and baking soda. Add the oats; mix well. Drop tablespoonfuls of dough onto nonstick cookie sheets. Bake at 350 degrees for 10 to 12 minutes or until golden brown. (Do not overbake.) Remove to a wire rack to cool. Note: Cookies may be shaped into balls instead of dropping the dough into mounds onto the cookie sheets. Yield: 4 to 5 dozen

Almeda Jacks (Mrs. Putt Jacks)

Praline Cookies

¼ cup plus 3 tablespoons butter or margarine, softened
1¼ cups firmly packed brown sugar
1 egg
1 teaspoon vanilla extract
1 cup plus 2 tablespoons flour
¼ teaspoon salt
1¼ cups pecan halves

Beat the butter and brown sugar in a mixer bowl until light and fluffy. Blend in the egg and vanilla. Add the flour and salt; mix well. Drop tablespoonfuls of dough, 2 inches apart, onto ungreased cookie sheets. Press 1 pecan half into the top of each spoonful of dough. Bake at 350 degrees for 10 minutes or until golden brown. (Do not overbake.) Remove to a wire rack to cool. Yield: 3 dozen

Lucy Coleman

Grandmother's Tea Cakes

1 cup butter, softened
2 cups granulated sugar
2 large eggs
7 cups (about) flour
1 teaspoon baking powder
1 teaspoon salt
¼ cup milk
1 teaspoon vanilla extract
Colored granulated sugar

Beat the butter and 2 cups granulated sugar in a mixing bowl until light and fluffy. Add the eggs, one at a time, beating well after each addition. Combine 6 cups of the flour, the baking powder and salt in a separate bowl. Add to the butter mixture alternately with the combined milk and vanilla, mixing with an electric mixer at medium speed until well blended. Stir in enough of the remaining flour to form a stiff dough. Divide the dough into 4 or 5 balls. Place on a nonstick cookie sheet covered with floured waxed paper. Refrigerate, covered, overnight. Remove the balls from the refrigerator. Let stand at room temperature about 20 minutes. Place the dough on a lightly floured surface. Roll out as thinly as possible, using as little flour as possible. Cut the dough into desired shapes and place, 2 inches apart, on a greased baking sheet. Sprinkle with the colored sugar; press the sugar lightly into the dough. Bake at 350 degrees for 8 to 10 minutes or until lightly browned. Remove to a cooling rack to cool completely. Store in an airtight container. Note: For best results, each ball of dough should only be rolled out twice. Any leftover dough should be discarded. Yield: 6 to 7 dozen

Paul Quattlebaum
Trustee Emeritus

First Friday Parade began in 1974 and has become a Clemson tradition. The parade is held on the Friday before the first home football game.

Brunch, Breads and Beverages

BRUNCH TIME

Baked Apples with Irish Cream

2 tablespoons sugar
1 tablespoon chopped walnuts
1 tablespoon chopped raisins or other dried fruit
½ teaspoon cinnamon
4 baking apples, cored
½ cup butter
½ cup Irish cream liqueur

Combine the sugar, walnuts, raisins and cinnamon in a small bowl. Place the cored apples in a lightly buttered baking dish. Fill the apple centers with the fruit and nut mixture. Cut the butter into quarters. Place a butter quarter on top of each apple. Cover the dish with foil. Bake at 350 degrees for 25 to 30 minutes or until the apples are tender. Remove from the oven and let cool for 5 minutes. Place each apple on a dessert plate. Pour 2 tablespoons of the liqueur over each one. Serve immediately. Yield: 4 servings

Betty Miley

Eggs Sardou

2 (9-ounce) packages frozen creamed spinach
8 canned artichoke bottoms
8 poached eggs
2 cups prepared hollandaise sauce

Cook the creamed spinach according to the package directions. Heat the artichoke bottoms in a saucepan until warm; drain well. Place ¼ of the spinach on each of 4 serving plates. Top each with 2 artichoke bottoms, 2 poached eggs and ½ cup hollandaise sauce. Serve immediately. Note: Use hollandaise sauce mix to make this recipe even easier to prepare. Yield: 4 servings

Nancy Cathcart (Mrs. Foster Cathcart)

Nancy and Foster Cathcart

Foster and Nancy were honored as the 1997–98 Outstanding Alumni Volunteers of the Year at Clemson University.

Huevos Rancheros de Amigos

1 large onion, chopped
1 large green bell pepper, chopped
3 ribs celery, chopped
1 clove of garlic, minced
3 tablespoons olive oil
1 to 2 cups vegetable juice cocktail
1 (10-ounce) can tomatoes with green chiles
1 (8-ounce) can tomato sauce
1 (6-ounce) can tomato paste
Salt and pepper to taste
12 eggs
Corn or flour tortillas, warmed

Sauté the onion, green pepper, celery and garlic in the olive oil in a large skillet until tender. Add 1 cup vegetable juice cocktail, tomatoes with chiles, tomato sauce and tomato paste. Cook over medium-low heat for 30 minutes, stirring occasionally. Season with salt and pepper. Add enough of the remaining 1 cup vegetable juice cocktail to season to taste. Break the eggs into the vegetable mixture. Cook, uncovered, for about 5 minutes or until the eggs are poached. Serve the eggs and vegetable mixture on warm tortillas.
Yield: 6 servings

Nancy Cathcart (Mrs. Foster Cathcart)

Brunch, Breads and Beverages

Breakfast Brunch Casserole

1 pound hot pork sausage
1 pound mild pork sausage
2 medium onions, chopped
4 cups cooked rice
4 cups crisp rice cereal
8 ounces sharp Cheddar cheese, shredded
2 (10-ounce) cans cream of celery or cream of mushroom soup
4 eggs
Paprika to taste

Brown all the sausage with the onions in a skillet, stirring until the sausage is crumbly; drain well. Layer the cooked rice, 3½ cups rice cereal, sausage mixture and 1½ cups cheese in a greased 9x13-inch baking dish. Beat the eggs in a small bowl. Add the soup gradually, mixing until well blended. Pour the egg mixture evenly over the layers in the baking dish. Top with the remaining ½ cup cereal and ½ cup cheese. Sprinkle with paprika. Bake at 325 degrees for 30 to 40 minutes or until bubbly. Serve with baked curried fruit and croissants. Yield: 8 to 12 servings

Pat Harmon (Mrs. Bob Harmon)

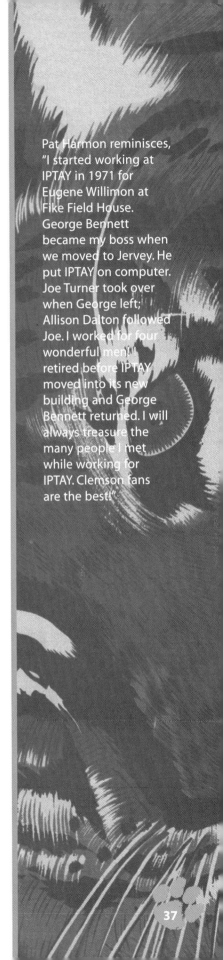

Pat Harmon reminisces, "I started working at IPTAY in 1971 for Eugene Willimon at Fike Field House. George Bennett became my boss when we moved to Jervey. He put IPTAY on computer. Joe Turner took over when George left; Allison Dalton followed Joe. I worked for four wonderful men! I retired before IPTAY moved into its new building and George Bennett returned. I will always treasure the many people I met while working for IPTAY. Clemson fans are the best!"

Overnight Sausage and Egg Casserole

1 (12-ounce) package pork sausage
3 cups cholesterol-free egg substitute
½ cup nonfat sour cream
1½ teaspoons dry mustard
1 teaspoon minced onion
3 cups French bread cubes
1 cup shredded Cheddar cheese
Paprika to taste

Brown the sausage in a medium skillet, stirring until crumbly; drain well and set aside. Combine the egg substitute, sour cream, dry mustard and onion in a large bowl, mixing well. Stir in the bread cubes, cheese and sausage. Pour into a greased 9x13-inch baking dish. Sprinkle with paprika. Refrigerate, covered, for at least 4 hours or overnight. Bake at 350 degrees for 45 to 55 minutes or until the center is slightly puffed and a knife inserted into the center comes out clean. Yield: 12 servings

Gail Jameson

Chiles Rellenos Casserole

3 (7-ounce) cans whole green chiles, drained
1 pound medium Cheddar cheese, cut into thick slices
1 pound Monterey Jack cheese, cut into thick slices
4 eggs
1 (12-ounce) can evaporated milk
3 tablespoons flour
2 (8-ounce) cans tomato sauce

Remove and discard the seeds from the chiles. Rinse the chiles and drain well. Place the Cheddar cheese on the bottom of a greased 7x11-inch baking dish. Arrange the chiles over the Cheddar cheese. Top with the Monterey Jack cheese slices. Beat the eggs in a bowl. Add the evaporated milk and flour and beat until smooth. Pour evenly over the layers in the baking dish. Bake, covered, at 325 degrees for 45 minutes. Remove from the oven. Top with the tomato sauce. Bake, uncovered, for 30 minutes or until bubbly.
Yield: 10 servings

Jimmy and Barbara Kinney

Christmas Morning Strata

1 pound pork sausage
6 eggs
2 cups milk
1 teaspoon dry mustard
Salt and pepper to taste
6 slices bread, cut into cubes
1½ cups shredded Cheddar or Swiss cheese
1 (4-ounce) can sliced mushrooms, drained (optional)

Brown the sausage in a skillet, stirring until crumbly; drain well. Beat the eggs in a small bowl. Add the milk, dry mustard, salt and pepper, mixing until well blended. Add the bread cubes and stir until softened. Stir in the cheese, sausage and mushrooms. Pour into a greased 9x13-inch baking dish. Refrigerate, covered, overnight. Bake at 350 degrees for 40 to 45 minutes or until a knife inserted into the center comes out clean. Yield: 6 to 8 servings

Diane Mahaffey (Mrs. Randy Mahaffey)

Orange French Toast

1 cup cholesterol-free egg substitute
1 egg white
Grated peel and juice of ½ orange
⅓ cup sugar
¼ cup skim milk
2 to 3 tablespoons orange-flavored liqueur
¼ teaspoon salt
3 drops of vanilla extract
5 thick slices white bread

Beat the egg substitute and egg white in a bowl. Add the orange peel, orange juice, sugar, milk, liqueur, salt and vanilla to the egg mixture. Soak the bread slices in the egg mixture. Remove the bread slices with a spatula and transfer to a generously buttered griddle or skillet. Cook over low heat for 5 to 10 minutes or until puffed and golden brown on both sides. Serve with a light sprinkle of confectioners' sugar and maple syrup if desired. For Banana French Toast, substitute 1 mashed ripe banana for the ½ orange and 3 tablespoons banana-flavored liqueur for the 2 to 3 tablespoons orange-flavored liqueur. Yield: 2 to 3 servings

Sandra McTeer (Mrs. Tom McTeer)

Tom McTeer

Brunch, Breads and Beverages

French Toast Casserole

2 cups skim milk
3 eggs, lightly beaten
12 slices whole wheat bread, halved
2 tablespoons melted margarine
½ cup confectioners' sugar
2 cups fresh raspberries or other fruit
1 teaspoon cinnamon

Beat the milk and eggs in a bowl until blended. Dip the bread halves in the egg mixture until coated. Arrange ⅓ of the bread in the bottom of a 9x9-inch baking dish sprayed with nonstick cooking spray. Drizzle ⅓ of the margarine over the bread. Sprinkle with 2½ tablespoons of the confectioners' sugar and top with half the raspberries. Repeat layers of bread, margarine, confectioners' sugar and raspberries once. Top with the remaining bread, margarine and sugar. Sprinkle with the cinnamon. Bake, covered, at 400 degrees for 25 minutes. Bake, uncovered, for 10 to 15 minutes or until a knife inserted into the center comes out clean. Yield: 6 to 8 servings

Alberta Bobo

Spicy Sausage Bread

1 pound hot or spicy pork sausage
1 loaf frozen bread dough, thawed
½ cup grated Parmesan cheese
1 egg
Paprika to taste

Brown the sausage in a skillet, stirring until crumbly; drain, reserving the drippings. Press the bread dough into a rectangle on a greased baking sheet. Combine the Parmesan cheese, egg and sausage in a bowl. Spread over the dough. Roll up, starting at a short side, as for a jelly roll. Place, seam side down, on the baking sheet. Brush the surface of the loaf with the reserved sausage drippings or melted butter. Bake at 375 degrees for 30 to 40 minutes or until golden brown. Sprinkle with paprika before serving. Yield: 8 to 10 servings

Carolyn Mathias

Betty's Beer Bread

3 cups self-rising flour
¼ cup sugar
1 (12-ounce) can beer, room temperature
Softened butter

Sift the flour and sugar into a bowl. Add the beer and mix well. Pour into a well-greased 5x9-inch loaf pan. Bake at 300 degrees for 1 hour or until golden brown. Remove from the pan. Generously butter the top and sides of the hot loaf. Serve with butter or honey butter. Yield: 1 loaf

Anne Addy

No-Knead Beer Bread

3 cups self-rising flour
2 to 3 tablespoons sugar
1 (12-ounce) can beer, at room temperature
1 egg (optional)

Combine the flour, sugar, beer and egg in a bowl, mixing well. Pour into a greased and floured 5x9-inch loaf pan. Bake at 350 degrees for 1 hour or until a wooden pick inserted into the center comes out clean. Note: Adding the egg makes a higher, lighter-textured loaf, but the bread is fine without it. Yield: 1 loaf

Devon Beaty

Yellow Bread

1 (2-layer) package yellow cake mix
1 (3-ounce) package vanilla instant pudding mix
4 eggs
3/4 cup vegetable oil
3/4 cup water
1 teaspoon vanilla extract
1 teaspoon imitation butter flavor
1/2 cup granulated sugar
1/2 cup packed brown sugar
1/2 cup chopped pecans
2 tablespoons cinnamon
1 cup confectioners' sugar
3 tablespoons milk
1 teaspoon vanilla extract
1 teaspoon imitation butter flavor

Combine the cake mix, pudding mix, eggs, oil, water, 1 teaspoon vanilla and 1 teaspoon butter flavor in a large mixer bowl. Beat for 8 minutes. Combine the granulated sugar, brown sugar, pecans and cinnamon in a bowl and mix well. Sprinkle 1/3 of the pecan mixture in the bottom of a greased and floured bundt pan. Top with half the cake batter, spreading evenly. Sprinkle half the remaining pecan mixture over the batter in the pan. Top with the remaining cake batter and pecan mixture. Swirl the layers with a knife for a marbleized effect. Bake at 325 degrees for 50 to 60 minutes or until a wooden pick inserted into the center comes out clean. Cool the cake in the pan for 10 minutes. Remove from the pan and cool slightly. Beat the confectioners' sugar, milk, 1 teaspoon vanilla and 1 teaspoon butter flavor in a bowl until creamy. Drizzle over the warm cake. Yield: 12 to 15 servings

Ruth Mahony (Mrs. Jim Mahony)

Raisin-Oat Muffins

1½ cups flour
1 cup quick-cooking oats
½ cup plus 2 tablespoons raisins
1 tablespoon baking powder
⅛ teaspoon salt
⅔ cup skim milk
¼ cup packed dark brown sugar
2 tablespoons frozen apple juice concentrate, thawed
2 tablespoons melted margarine, cooled
1 egg
1 teaspoon vanilla extract

Combine the flour, oats, raisins, baking powder and salt in a large bowl. Beat the milk, brown sugar, apple juice concentrate, margarine, egg and vanilla in a medium bowl. Add the milk mixture to the dry ingredients. Stir just until blended. Spoon the batter evenly into greased or paper-lined muffin pan cups. Bake at 400 degrees for 18 to 20 minutes or until the muffins spring back when lightly touched and are golden brown. Remove from the pan and cool on a wire rack. Yield: 12 muffins

Jodi Bennett (Mrs. Jeff Bennett)

Jodie, Jeff, Megan and Austin Bennett

Brunch, Breads and Beverages

Applesauce Muffins

1 cup margarine, softened
1 cup granulated sugar
1 cup packed brown sugar
2 eggs
1 teaspoon vanilla extract
4 cups flour
1 tablespoon cinnamon
2 teaspoons allspice
1 teaspoon ground cloves
1 cup chopped pecans
2 cups applesauce (purchased or homemade)
2 teaspoons baking soda

Cream the margarine, granulated sugar, brown sugar, eggs and vanilla in a mixer bowl until light and fluffy. Sift the flour, cinnamon, allspice and cloves together. Add to the creamed mixture, blending well. Stir in the pecans. Combine the applesauce and baking soda in a bowl. Add to the batter, mixing well. Spoon the batter evenly into greased muffin pan cups. Bake at 400 degrees for 12 to 15 minutes or until a wooden pick inserted into the centers comes out clean.
Yield: 48 muffins

Debbie DuBose (Mrs. Bob DuBose)
Chief Alumni and Development Officer

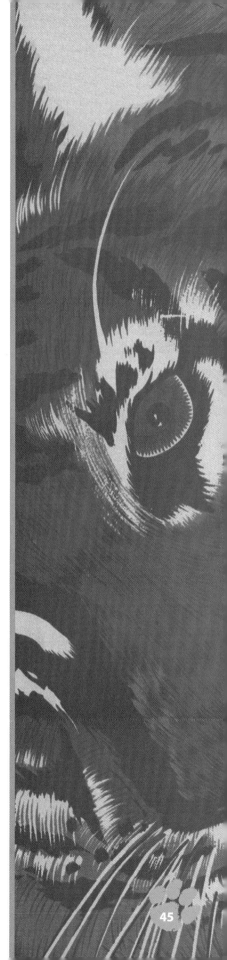

Brunch, Breads and Beverages

Smith Family Homemade Yeast Rolls

2 (¼-ounce) packages active dry yeast
¾ cup warm (105 to 115 degrees) water
1 cup shortening
1 cup boiling water
½ cup sugar
2 teaspoons salt
2 eggs, beaten
6 cups flour
½ cup melted butter

Dissolve the yeast in the warm water; set aside. Beat the shortening, boiling water, sugar and salt in a large mixer bowl until well mixed. Beat in the eggs. Add the yeast mixture and mix well. Add 1 cup flour, beating on low speed until blended. Add the remaining flour, 1 cup at a time, beating on medium speed. Place the dough in a large greased bowl. Refrigerate, covered, for 2 hours. Roll out the dough on a floured board. Cut out with a round cutter. Brush with melted butter. Fold in half or leave flat and place on buttered baking sheets. Cover and let rise for 2 hours. Bake at 425 degrees for 10 minutes or until golden brown. Yield: 40 rolls

Bill Smith

Bill Smith

Refrigerator Rolls

1 cup shortening or lard
²/₃ cup sugar
1 teaspoon salt
1 cup boiling water
2 (¹/₄-ounce) packages active dry yeast
1 cup warm (105 to 115 degrees) water
2 eggs, beaten
6 cups flour

Cream the shortening, sugar and salt in a large mixer bowl. Stir in the boiling water. Set aside to cool. Dissolve the yeast in the warm water in a small bowl. Stir the eggs and yeast mixture into the cooled shortening mixture. Add the flour gradually, mixing well after each addition. Refrigerate, covered, for at least 2 hours. Roll out the dough on a floured surface. Cut out with a round cutter. Fold over 1 side of each round ³/₄ of the way to form rolls. Place on greased baking sheets. Cover and let rise for 2 hours. Bake at 400 degrees for 10 to 12 minutes or until browned. Note: Rolls can instead be partially baked for 8 to 10 minutes or until set but not browned. Cool completely, wrap and freeze. When ready to serve, thaw the rolls. Bake at 400 degrees for about 5 minutes or until browned. Yield: 30 to 36 rolls

Ann L. Winfield (Mrs. Bob Winfield)

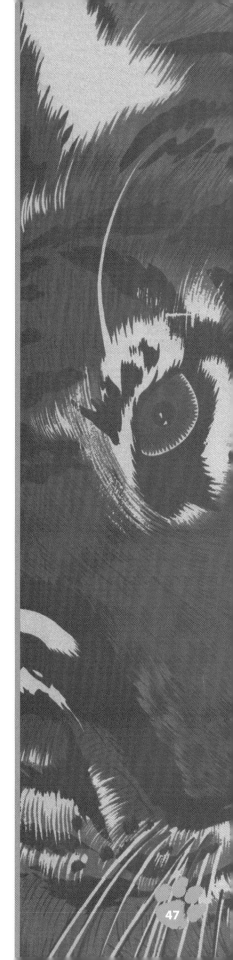

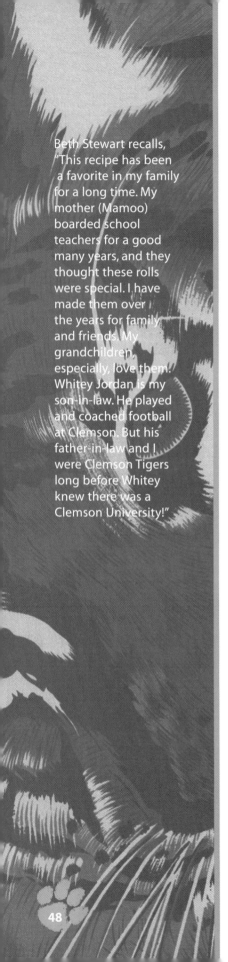

Mamoo's Refrigerator Rolls

1 cup shortening
½ cup sugar
1 cup boiling water
2 (½-ounce) packages active dry yeast
1 cup warm (105 to 115 degrees) water
2 eggs, beaten
6 cups flour
1 teaspoon salt

Cream the shortening and sugar in a large mixer bowl. Stir in the boiling water. Set aside to cool. Dissolve the yeast in the warm water in a small bowl. Stir the eggs and yeast mixture into the cooled shortening mixture. Sift in the flour and salt, stirring until thoroughly mixed. Refrigerate, covered, overnight. Roll out the dough on a floured surface. Cut out and shape into Parker House rolls. Cover and let rise for 2 hours. Bake at 350 degrees for 15 to 20 minutes or until browned. Yield: 48 rolls

Beth Stewart

Whitey Jordan with Coach Tommy West's father

Steve Gatlin's Mexican Corn Bread

1 cup cornmeal
1 cup chopped green chiles
1 cup milk
1 cup shredded longhorn cheese
1 (8-ounce) can cream-style corn
½ cup vegetable oil
2 eggs, beaten
1 small onion, chopped
1 to 2 jalapeño peppers, chopped
½ teaspoon baking powder
½ teaspoon salt

Combine the cornmeal, chiles, milk, cheese, cream-style corn, oil, eggs, onion, peppers, baking powder and salt in a bowl, mixing well. Pour into a greased 9-inch-square baking pan. Bake at 350 degrees for 1 hour or until a wooden pick inserted into the center comes out clean. Yield: 10 servings

Steve Gatlin

Steve Gatlin with Endowment Donors Mary and Ray Clanton of Darlington, South Carolina

Charlie Waters' Mexican Corn Bread

1 cup yellow cornmeal
½ teaspoon salt
½ teaspoon baking soda
⅓ cup melted shortening or bacon drippings
2 eggs, beaten
1 (8-ounce) cream-style corn
⅔ cup buttermilk
1 cup shredded sharp Cheddar cheese
1 cup finely chopped green chiles

Combine the cornmeal, salt and baking soda in a large bowl. Stir in the shortening. Add the eggs, cream-style corn and buttermilk, mixing well. Spoon half the batter into a greased 12-inch cast-iron or ovenproof skillet. Sprinkle with the cheese and chiles. Top with the remaining batter. Bake at 350 degrees for 30 to 45 minutes or until a wooden pick inserted into the center comes out clean.
Yield: 12 servings

Charlie and Rosie Waters

Charlie Waters

Brunch, Breads and Beverages

(Almost) Parklane Seafood Hush Puppies

2 pounds self-rising flour
1 cup dried minced onion
1 cup sugar
½ cup stone-ground cornmeal
¼ cup nonfat dry milk
Hot water
Peanut oil for frying

Combine the flour, onion, sugar, cornmeal and dry milk powder in a bowl. Stir in enough hot water to achieve the desired consistency. Let stand for 1 hour. Drop large spoonfuls of batter, a few at a time, into 2 to 3 inches of peanut oil heated to 350 degrees. Cook until golden brown. Remove from the oil and drain on paper towels.
Yield: 7 dozen

David Pressley

David Pressley, of Parklane Seafood, preparing hush puppies

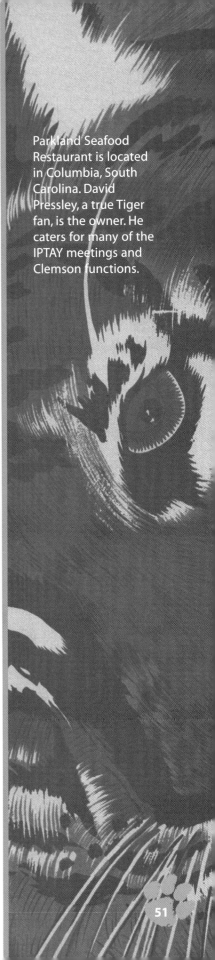

Parkland Seafood Restaurant is located in Columbia, South Carolina. David Pressley, a true Tiger fan, is the owner. He caters for many of the IPTAY meetings and Clemson functions.

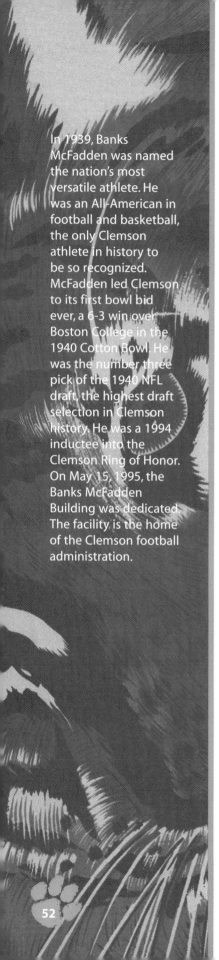

In 1939, Banks McFadden was named the nation's most versatile athlete. He was an All-American in football and basketball, the only Clemson athlete in history to be so recognized. McFadden led Clemson to its first bowl bid ever, a 6-3 win over Boston College in the 1940 Cotton Bowl. He was the number three pick of the 1940 NFL draft, the highest draft selection in Clemson history. He was a 1994 inductee into the Clemson Ring of Honor. On May 15, 1995, the Banks McFadden Building was dedicated. The facility is the home of the Clemson football administration.

52

McFadden's All-American Boiled Custard

2 (12-ounce) cans evaporated milk
2 evaporated milk cans water
¾ cup sugar
1 tablespoon flour
5 eggs, beaten
2 teaspoons vanilla extract

Pour evaporated milk into a saucepan. Add the water. Combine the sugar and flour in a small bowl. Stir in the eggs. Stir the egg mixture into the evaporated milk. Cook over medium heat for 20 minutes or until the custard just coats a metal spoon, stirring constantly. Strain the custard through cheesecloth into a bowl. Stir in the vanilla. Serve warm or cold with pound cake or fruit. Yield: 12 servings

Aggie McFadden (Mrs. Banks McFadden)

Banks McFadden

Athletic Department's Boiled Custard

1 quart milk
4 eggs
1 cup sugar
1 teaspoon vanilla extract

Heat the milk in the top of a double boiler over simmering water until hot but not boiling. Beat the eggs in a bowl until light. Add the sugar and mix well. Pour a small amount of the hot milk gradually into the egg mixture, stirring constantly. Pour the warmed egg mixture gradually into the remaining hot milk, stirring constantly. Cook until the custard coats a wooden spoon, stirring constantly. Remove from the heat. Stir in the vanilla. Cool slightly. Refrigerate, covered, until well chilled. Yield: 8 servings

Martha Garrison (Mrs. Glenn Garrison)

Martha Garrison

Martha Garrison says, "This custard recipe was one my grandmother made for us as children. For an added treat, she would freeze it in ice trays. Many have made this custard, and I believe all would agree 'it's in the stirring.'

"I worked at Jervey Athletic Center for 28 years as receptionist. This custard was the very favorite for many when they were a little under the weather. Special thoughts go to Captain Frank Jervey, Colonel Sam McDowell, 'Red' Ritchie, Coach Howard and Anna, Al Adams, and Joe Turner, who made me feel that it made a small difference. Also, to George Bennett, who thought it passed the taste test!"

Jerry's Bloody Mary Mix

1 (64-ounce) can Hunt's tomato juice
1 (10-ounce) can Campbell's beef broth
2 ounces fresh lime juice
2 ounces fresh lemon juice
2 ounces Lea & Perrins Worcestershire sauce
2 tablespoons celery salt
1 tablespoon Tabasco sauce
1½ teaspoons salt
1½ teaspoons pepper
Vodka

Combine the tomato juice, beef broth, lime juice, lemon juice, Worcestershire sauce, celery salt, Tabasco, salt and pepper, mixing well. To serve, add 1 part vodka to 3 or 4 parts Bloody Mary Mix for each cocktail. Note: This mix tastes better if prepared 1 or 2 days before using. Store in the refrigerator for up to several weeks.
Yield: 12 servings

Gerald Metts

Fruit Punch

2 quarts ginger ale
2 quarts strong brewed tea
3 cups sugar
1 (20-ounce) can crushed pineapple
1 (16-ounce) jar maraschino cherries
Juice of 6 oranges
Juice of 12 lemons
8 cups shaved ice

Combine the ginger ale, tea, sugar, undrained pineapple, undrained cherries, orange juice and lemon juice in a large punch bowl. Stir in the ice. Yield: 50 servings

Mary Katherine Littlejohn

Charleston Tea Plantation Wedding Punch

4 cups brewed American Classic Tea, chilled
4 cups apple juice, chilled
2 cups unsweetened pineapple juice, chilled
2 liters club soda
Orange slices, lemon slices and fresh mint

Combine the tea, apple juice and pineapple juice in a pitcher. Refrigerate until ready to serve. Pour the juice mixture into a punch bowl. Add the club soda, fruit slices and mint just before serving. Serve over ice. Yield: 24 servings

Charleston Tea Plantation

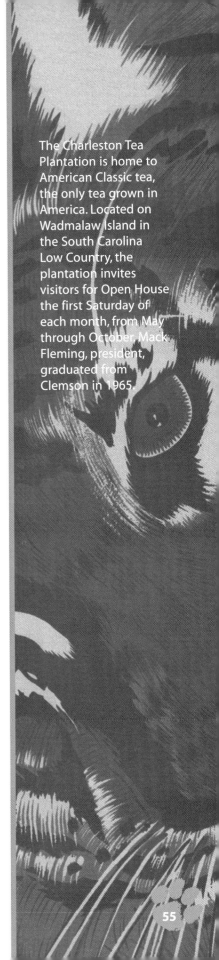

The Charleston Tea Plantation is home to American Classic tea, the only tea grown in America. Located on Wadmalaw Island in the South Carolina Low Country, the plantation invites visitors for Open House the first Saturday of each month, from May through October. Mack Fleming, president, graduated from Clemson in 1965.

Hot Spicy Cider

    1 gallon apple cider
    ½ cup packed brown sugar
    ½ teaspoon ground nutmeg
    20 whole cloves
    4 cinnamon sticks
    1 (6-ounce) container frozen orange juice concentrate
    ½ cup lemon juice

Combine the apple cider, brown sugar, nutmeg, cloves and cinnamon sticks in a saucepan. Bring to a boil; reduce the heat. Simmer for 10 minutes. Stir in the orange juice concentrate and lemon juice. Strain into a saucepan and keep warm. Yield: 20 servings

Joan S. Kennerty (Mrs. Bill Kennerty)

Wassail

    2 cinnamon sticks
    1 teaspoon whole cloves
    1 teaspoon whole allspice
    1 gallon apple juice or cider
    1 (46-ounce) can unsweetened pineapple juice
    1 cup orange juice

Tie up the cinnamon sticks, cloves and allspice in a small cheesecloth bag. Combine the apple juice, pineapple juice and orange juice in a saucepan. Bring to a boil; reduce the heat. Add the bag of spices. Simmer for 20 minutes. Remove and discard the spice bag before serving. Yield: 25 servings

Millicent Sease

Café Vienna

1 1/3 cups granulated sugar
1 1/3 cups nonfat dry milk
1 cup instant coffee
1 teaspoon cinnamon

Combine the sugar, dry milk powder, coffee powder and cinnamon in a bowl, blending to a powdery, lump-free consistency. Store in an airtight container. To serve, add 1 cup boiling water to 1 or 2 rounded teaspoons of the coffee mix for each cup of coffee. Stir briskly. For Toffee Coffee, mix 1 cup instant coffee powder with 1 cup packed brown sugar. For Swiss Mocha, mix 1 cup instant coffee powder, 1 cup sugar and 2 cups nonfat dry milk powder. Yield: 3 2/3 cups dry mix

Nancy M. Bennett (Mrs. George Bennett)

Sugar-Free Spiced Tea

2 tubs sugar-free Tang
1 (2-quart) package sugar-free lemonade mix
1 cup sugar-free lemon-flavored instant iced tea mix
1/2 teaspoon cinnamon
1/2 teaspoon ground cloves

Combine the Tang, lemonade mix, iced tea mix, cinnamon and cloves in a bowl and mix well. Store in an airtight container. To serve, add 1 cup boiling water to 1 rounded teaspoon of the tea mix for each cup of tea. Stir briskly. Yield: 60 servings

Nancy M. Bennett (Mrs. George Bennett)

Soup and Salads

The Clemson Tiger knows Howard's Rock brings good luck!

ROCK SOLID TASTES

Cream of Cauliflower and Leek Soup

3 large leeks, sliced
2 tablespoons olive oil
1 medium to large head cauliflower
1 to 2 cups milk
½ cup whipping cream
¼ cup chablis wine
3 tablespoons butter or margarine
1 teaspoon salt or to taste

Sauté the leeks in the oil in a large saucepan until tender, but not browned. Transfer the leeks to a blender or food processor. Separate the cauliflower into florets. Cook the florets in a pot of boiling water until tender; drain. Add the cauliflower and 1 cup milk to the leeks in the blender. Purée until smooth, adding more milk as necessary. Pour the cauliflower mixture into the large saucepan. Add the whipping cream, wine, butter and salt. Bring to a boil; reduce the heat. Simmer for 30 minutes. If the soup is too thick, add more milk or cream to achieve the desired consistency. Serve hot, spooning an additional tablespoon of chablis over each bowl, if desired. Notes: Two medium sweet onions can be substituted for the leeks. The leeks or onions can be cooked in the drippings of 4 cooked bacon slices. Crumble the bacon and sprinkle over the soup. Yield: 6 to 8 servings.

Jack Brunson

Jack Brunson

Cold Peach Soup

2 cups sliced peaches
1 (12-ounce) can peach or apricot nectar
16 ounces low-fat vanilla yogurt
½ cup fresh mint leaves, minced
2 tablespoons fruit liqueur
2 tablespoons rose water
1 tablespoon minced gingerroot
1 teaspoon orange or pineapple extract
2 to 3 tablespoons sugar

Purée the peaches in a blender or food processor until smooth.
Pour into a bowl. Add the nectar, yogurt, mint, liqueur, rose water,
gingerroot, orange extract and sugar to taste. Stir until smooth and
well blended. Garnish each serving with sprigs of fresh mint.
Yield: 8 servings

Martha Derrick (Mrs. Fletcher Derrick)

Catfish Stew

3½ pounds bacon
6 pounds onions, diced
7½ pounds potatoes, peeled and quartered
2 (8-ounce) cans tomato sauce
2 (14-ounce) bottles catsup
2 quarts tomato juice
7 pounds catfish fillets, cut into 2-inch pieces

Cut the bacon crosswise into ¼-inch strips. (This is easier to do
if the bacon is partially frozen.) Cook the bacon and onions in a
stockpot until the bacon is crisp and the onions are tender, stirring
frequently; drain. Add the potatoes to the stockpot with enough
cold water to cover. Stir in the tomato sauce, catsup and tomato
juice. Bring to a boil; reduce the heat. Simmer for 25 minutes,
stirring frequently. Add the catfish. Simmer for 10 minutes or until
potatoes are tender and catfish flakes easily with a fork.
Yield: 2½ gallons

Tom and Mildred Salisbury

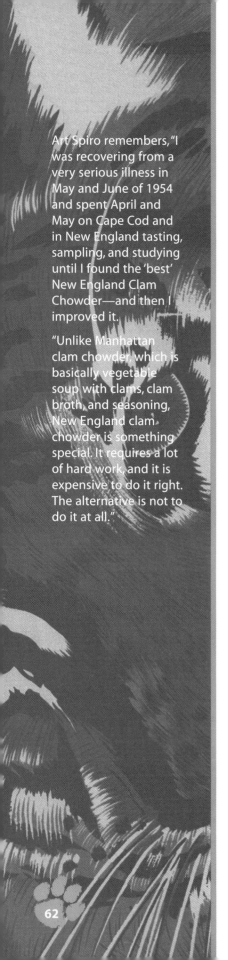

World's Best New England Clam Chowder

12 large hard-shell chowder clams
½ pound meaty salt pork, cut into cubes
2 large sweet onions, minced
3 cups cubed potatoes
2 (8-ounce) cans minced clams
1 quart clam juice or water
Salt and pepper to taste
¾ cup heavy cream
Paprika to taste
2 tablespoons butter or margarine, cut into 6 pieces

Shuck the chowder clams, reserving the juice. Strain the juice through cheesecloth. Cut the clams into bite-size pieces. Set aside. Sauté the salt pork and onions in a skillet until the onions are golden. Discard the pork and drippings, reserving the onions and any browned bits. Cook the potatoes in boiling water until tender, but firm; drain. Combine the chowder clams with their juice, the undrained minced clams and clam juice in a large saucepan. Simmer gently just until the clams are softened. Add the onion mixture, potatoes, salt, pepper and cream. Cook just until heated through. Pour into 6 serving bowls. Sprinkle each serving with paprika and top with a piece of butter. Yield: 6 servings

Arthur M. Spiro

Former Tiger Billy McMillian talks baseball with Art Spiro. Billy plays for the Philadelphia Phillies.

New England Clam Chowder

1 cup chopped onion
¼ cup butter or margarine
2⅔ cups milk
1 (12-ounce) can evaporated milk
2 (10-ounce) cans New England clam chowder
2 (10-ounce) cans cream of potato soup
1 (10-ounce) can clams
1 teaspoon salt
½ teaspoon pepper

Sauté the onion in the butter in a stockpot until tender. Stir in the milk, evaporated milk, clam chowder, potato soup, undrained clams, salt and pepper. Bring to a boil; reduce the heat to low. Simmer for 20 minutes. Yield: 10 servings

Katherine Black (Mrs. Doyle Black)

Spicy Seafood Chowder

1½ cups chopped onions
¾ cup chopped green bell pepper
1½ teaspoons minced garlic
1 to 2 tablespoons chili paste with garlic
½ cup olive oil
1½ cups coarsely chopped canned Italian plum tomatoes, drained
1½ cups dry red wine
2 cups bottled clam juice
1 tablespoon tomato paste
2 teaspoons oregano
1 teaspoon salt
½ teaspoon basil
½ teaspoon pepper
1 pound halibut or other white fish, cut into 1-inch pieces
1 pound shrimp, peeled and deveined
6 ounces crab meat
Minced fresh parsley

Sauté the onions, green pepper, garlic and chili paste in the oil in a Dutch oven until the vegetables are tender. Stir in the tomatoes, wine, clam juice, tomato paste, oregano, salt, basil and pepper. Bring to a boil; reduce the heat. Simmer for 10 minutes. Add the fish. Simmer, covered, for 10 minutes. Add the shrimp and crab meat. Simmer for 5 minutes. Sprinkle with the parsley and serve. Note: Chili paste with garlic is a spicy seasoning that can be found in the Asian section of most supermarkets. Adjust the amount to suit your taste. Yield: 6 servings

Jane Wehrenberg (Mrs. Bill Wehrenberg)

Primus Murphy's Seafood Chowder

1 quart whole milk
1 onion, finely chopped
4 tablespoons butter
2 to 3 baking potatoes, cut into 1/2-inch pieces
1 (7-ounce) can corn, drained
2 pounds flounder fillets, cut into 2-inch pieces
8 ounces popcorn shrimp
8 ounces crab meat
1 teaspoon pepper
1/2 teaspoon salt

Heat the milk in a Dutch oven until warm. Do not boil. Cover and keep warm. Sauté the onion in the butter in a skillet for 5 minutes. Add the onion mixture, potatoes, corn, flounder, shrimp, crab meat, pepper and salt to the milk. Bring to a simmer, stirring frequently. Do not boil. Simmer gently for 1 1/2 hours, stirring every 5 minutes. Season with additional pepper. Serve with Texas Pete, catsup and saltines. Yield: 8 servings

Leonard C. Butler

Clemson ran down the hill at Death Valley on a rug for the first time on September 20, 1958.

A new rug saw its first use on September 5, 1998, before the Clemson-Furman game. Milliken & Company made and gave the rug, spelling out CLEMSON. The Tigers won 33–0!

Terry's Chicken Stew

1 (3- to 4-pound) chicken
3 cups diced onions
2 cups diced potatoes
1 (16-ounce) can diced tomatoes
1 (16-ounce) can whole kernel corn
¼ cup butter
2 teaspoons salt
1 teaspoon pepper
1 (12-ounce) can evaporated milk (optional)
1 quart milk

Place the chicken in a stockpot. Add enough water to cover. Bring to a boil; reduce the heat. Simmer for 45 minutes or until the chicken is cooked through. Remove the chicken from the broth. Let chicken cool. Remove the meat and cut into ½-inch cubes. Refrigerate, covered, until ready to use. Strain the broth. Refrigerate, covered, until chilled. Remove any fat from the surface of the cold broth. Pour into a Dutch oven. Add the chicken, onions, potatoes, tomatoes, corn, butter, salt and pepper. Bring to a boil; reduce the heat. Simmer for 15 minutes or until heated through. Stir in the evaporated milk and milk. Return to a simmer. Do not boil. Season with salt and pepper. Serve with saltines, catsup and pickles. Note: Prepare 1 day in advance for the best flavor. Refrigerate until ready to reheat. Yield: 8 servings

Terry A. Kingsmore

Terry Kingsmore preparing to tailgate

Mario's Beef Stew

1 1/2 pounds beef stew meat, cut into cubes
1 1/2 cups dry red or white wine
2 large cloves of garlic, sliced
2 bay leaves
Salt and black pepper to taste
Minced fresh parsley to taste
2 medium onions, sliced
3 tablespoons olive oil
1 large carrot, sliced
1 1/2 pounds potatoes, peeled and cut into cubes
1 (15-ounce) can peas
2 medium tomatoes, peeled and chopped
Hot pepper sauce to taste

Place the stew meat in a shallow glass dish. Combine the wine, garlic, bay leaves, salt, black pepper and parsley in a bowl. Pour over the meat, stirring to coat evenly. Marinate, covered, in the refrigerator overnight. Sauté the onions in the oil in a Dutch oven until lightly browned. Remove the meat from the marinade, reserving the marinade. Add the meat to the Dutch oven. Cook until browned on all sides. Add the carrot. Cook and stir for 3 minutes. Reserve 2 tablespoons of the marinade; set aside. Discard the bay leaves. Add the remaining marinade to the stew. Cook, covered, until the meat is almost tender. Add the potatoes, peas and tomatoes. Season the 2 tablespoons reserved marinade with salt, pepper and pepper sauce. Stir into the stew, mixing gently. Simmer, covered, 20 to 30 minutes or until the meat and vegetables are tender. Serve immediately. Yield: 6 servings

Mario DeCarvalho and Jane Robelot-DeCarvalho

Jane Robelot and Mario De Carvalho

Jane Robelot graduated from Clemson in 1982 with a B.A. in economics. She has been a TV news anchor in Spartanburg, South Carolina, and in Philadelphia, and is now co-anchor of *CBS This Morning*. Her husband, Mario De Carvalho, proposed to Jane on Frank Howard Football Field, Clemson. They were married on January 10, 1998, in Greenville, South Carolina.

The original recipe for this stew called for boar meat.

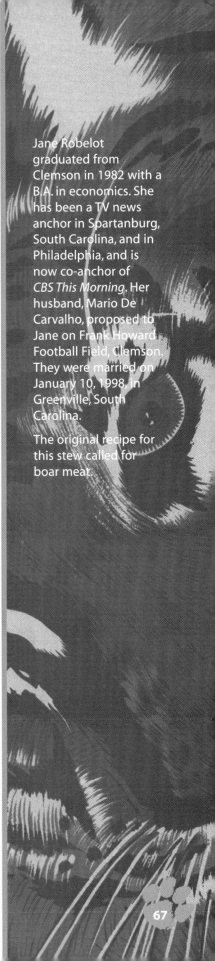

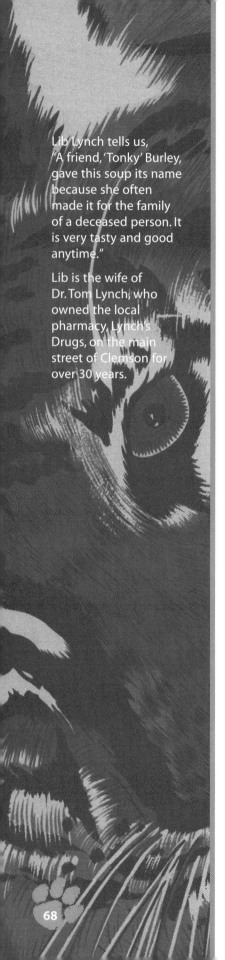

Funeral Soup

2 pounds ground round
4 (15-ounce) cans tomato sauce with onion, celery and green pepper
2 tomato sauce cans water
2 tablespoons dried minced onions
½ teaspoon salt
8 dashes Tabasco sauce

Brown the ground round in a skillet, stirring until crumbly; drain. Add the tomato sauce, water, onions, salt and Tabasco. Bring to a boil; reduce the heat. Simmer for 45 minutes. Yield: 8 to 10 servings

Lib Lynch (Mrs. Tom Lynch)

Tortilla Soup

1 medium onion, chopped
2 cloves of garlic, chopped
2 tablespoons vegetable or olive oil
3 cups beef broth
3 cups chicken broth
1 cup diced, peeled tomatoes, drained
6 ounces tomato juice or tomato sauce
2 tablespoons chopped green chiles
1 jalapeño pepper, chopped (optional)
1 teaspoon salt, or to taste
1 teaspoon cumin
1 teaspoon chili powder
1 teaspoon Worcestershire sauce
1 cup cubed cooked chicken breast
Shredded Monterey Jack cheese
Corn tortillas, cut into strips and fried

Sauté the onion and garlic in the oil in a Dutch oven until tender. Add the beef broth, chicken broth, tomatoes, tomato juice, chiles, jalapeño pepper, salt, cumin, chili powder and Worcestershire sauce. Bring to a boil; reduce the heat. Simmer, covered, for 1 hour. Add the chicken. Cook for 5 minutes. Place the cheese and a few tortilla strips in each soup bowl. Fill with the soup and top with additional tortilla strips and cheese. Yield: 8 to 10 servings

Diana B. Finlay

Soups and Salads

Chili con Carne

1 pound ground beef
1 medium green bell pepper, chopped
1 medium onion, chopped
2 (16-ounce) cans whole peeled tomatoes
1 (15-ounce) can kidney beans
2 teaspoons salt
1½ teaspoons chili powder
Dash of garlic powder

Brown the ground beef with the green pepper and onion in a skillet, stirring until the ground beef is crumbly; drain. Stir in the undrained tomatoes, undrained kidney beans, salt, chili powder and garlic powder. Bring to a boil; reduce the heat. Simmer for at least 1 hour. Yield: 4 to 6 servings

Ellen Dye (Mrs. Bob Dye)

Ellen and Bob Dye

The late Ellen Dye of Easley, South Carolina, was the wife of Bob Dye, Vice President of IPTAY, and a devoted Clemson supporter. She passed away March 18, 1998, after an extended battle with Lou Gehrig's disease. She was an inspiration to those around her and will not soon be forgotten by her friends and family. On a visit shortly before Ellen's passing, Nancy Bennett asked for Ellen's favorite recipe to include in this cookbook. Ellen's immediate response was this chili, which has always been a favorite of her family. It was especially popular for tailgating on chilly football afternoons in late fall. Ellen would be thrilled to share this recipe with everyone and would ask that you keep cheering loudly for her Tigers!

Bob Dye is an IPTAY Director.

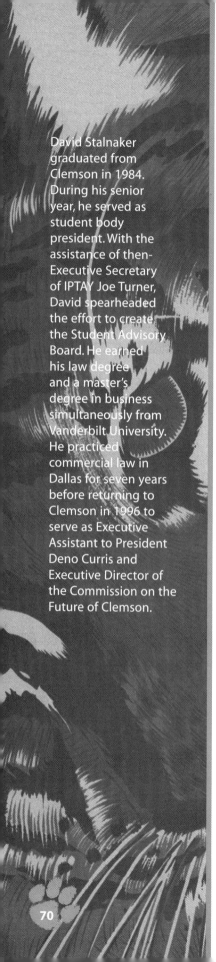

Texas-Style Chili

2 pounds lean ground beef
1 cup chopped onion
2 (14-ounce) cans stewed tomatoes
2 (15-ounce) cans kidney beans
1 tablespoon plus 1 teaspoon white vinegar
1 teaspoon chili powder
1 teaspoon cayenne
1 teaspoon salt
1 teaspoon Tabasco sauce
1 teaspoon Worcestershire sauce

Brown the ground beef with the onion in a skillet, stirring until the ground beef is crumbly; drain well on paper towels. Combine the undrained tomatoes, undrained kidney beans, vinegar, chili powder, cayenne, salt, Tabasco and Worcestershire sauce in a large saucepan. Bring to a simmer over low heat. Add the beef mixture. Simmer, covered, for 20 to 25 minutes, stirring occasionally.
Yield: 6 to 8 servings

W. David Stalnaker

Quick and Easy Chili

1 pound ground beef
1/2 cup chopped onion
3 (8-ounce) cans tomato sauce
2 (15-ounce) cans kidney beans
2 to 4 tablespoons chili powder
1 teaspoon salt
1/4 teaspoon pepper

Brown the ground beef with the onion in a skillet, stirring until the ground beef is crumbly; drain. Add the tomato sauce, undrained kidney beans, chili powder to taste, salt and pepper. Bring to a boil; reduce the heat. Simmer for 20 minutes, stirring occasionally.
Yield: 4 to 6 servings

Bebe Anderson (Mrs. Robert Anderson)

Southwestern Chicken Salad

6 chicken breast halves, skinned
1 teaspoon salt
¼ cup mayonnaise
¼ cup sour cream
¼ cup chopped onion
1 (4-ounce) can chopped green chiles, drained
1¼ teaspoons salt
1 teaspoon ground cumin
⅛ teaspoon pepper
3 cups shredded lettuce
4 (8-inch) flour tortillas
1 small tomato, diced
4 ounces shredded longhorn cheese
Picante sauce

Place the chicken in a Dutch oven. Add enough water to cover.
Add 1 teaspoon salt. Bring to a boil; reduce the heat. Simmer,
covered, 30 minutes or until the chicken is tender and cooked
through. Remove the chicken, reserving the broth for another use.
Let chicken cool. Remove the meat and shred into small pieces;
set aside. Combine the mayonnaise, sour cream, onion, chiles,
1¼ teaspoons salt, cumin and pepper in a large bowl. Stir in the
chicken. Divide the lettuce evenly among the tortillas. Top each
tortilla with one fourth of the chicken mixture, tomato and
cheese. Garnish with picante sauce. Yield: 4 servings

Rita Pruitt (Mrs. Mike Pruitt)

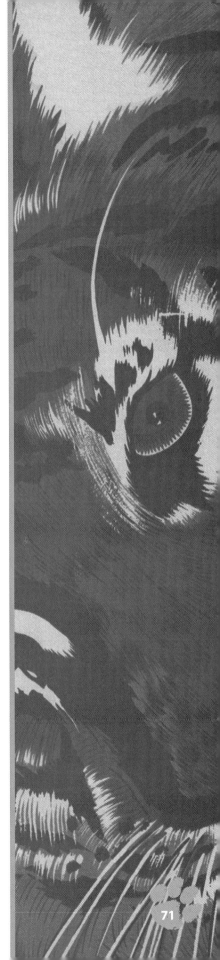

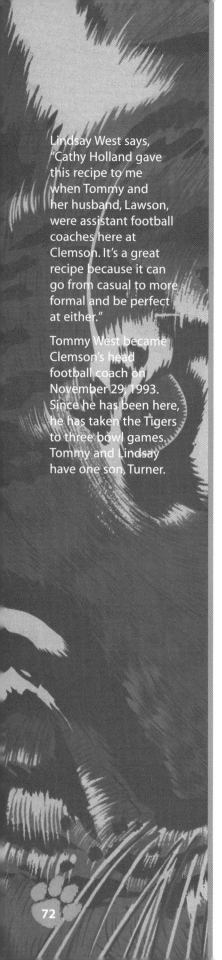

Lindsay West says, "Cathy Holland gave this recipe to me when Tommy and her husband, Lawson, were assistant football coaches here at Clemson. It's a great recipe because it can go from casual to more formal and be perfect at either."

Tommy West became Clemson's head football coach on November 29, 1993. Since he has been here, he has taken the Tigers to three bowl games. Tommy and Lindsay have one son, Turner.

Chicken Salad

1 cup mayonnaise
¼ cup pineapple juice
3 cups diced cooked chicken
2½ cups slivered almonds
1 cup diced celery
1 cup seedless grapes
1 avocado, diced
8 to 10 cantaloupe rings, cut ½ inch thick
Lettuce leaves

Combine the mayonnaise and pineapple juice in a large bowl. Add the chicken, almonds, celery, grapes and avocado. Stir to blend. Place the cantaloupe rings on beds of lettuce leaves. Serve the chicken salad on the cantaloupe rings. Yield: 8 to 10 servings

Coach Tommy and Lindsay West

Lindsay, Turner and Tommy West

Congealed Chicken Salad

1 (3-ounce) package lemon gelatin
1 cup boiling water
1 cup ginger ale
1 tablespoon lemon juice
1½ cups mayonnaise
2 cups cubed cooked chicken
⅔ cup seedless green grapes
½ cup chopped celery
½ cup chopped green bell pepper
3 ounces chopped almonds
3 tablespoons chopped pimento

Dissolve the gelatin in the boiling water in a large bowl. Stir in the ginger ale and lemon juice. Add the mayonnaise, stirring until blended. Refrigerate until slightly congealed. Stir in the chicken, grapes, celery, green pepper, almonds and pimento. Spoon into a 9x13-inch pan, spreading evenly. Refrigerate, covered, until firm.
Yield: 8 servings

Ava P. Campbell (Mrs. Lynn Campbell)

Lynn Campbell is an IPTAY Director.

Alvin's Chicken Salad

1 pound chicken breasts
Soy sauce
Lemon juice
1/2 cup toasted slivered almonds
1/2 cup sunflower seeds
1/2 cup chopped red onion
1/2 cup vegetable oil
3/4 cup red wine vinegar
1/4 cup sugar
1 (3-ounce) package chicken-flavored ramen noodles
1/2 head iceberg lettuce, shredded

Cook the chicken breasts in boiling water seasoned with soy sauce and lemon juice until tender and cooked through; drain. Cool the chicken and shred into pieces. Combine the chicken, almonds, sunflower seeds and onion in a large bowl. Combine the oil, vinegar, sugar and seasoning packet from the ramen noodles in a jar with a tight-fitting lid. Cover and shake until thoroughly blended. Pour over the chicken mixture. Crumble the uncooked ramen noodles into the bowl. Add the lettuce and toss well. Refrigerate, covered, overnight.
Makes 6 servings

Lisa Herring, wife of football Coach Reggie Herring

Beasley Chicken Salad

8 cooked chicken breast halves, cut into bite-size pieces
4 hard-cooked eggs, chopped
1 cup chopped sweet pickles
1 cup finely chopped pecans
1 cup finely chopped celery
1 cup mayonnaise
¼ cup sandwich spread
Salt and pepper to taste
2 tablespoons pickle juice
1½ cups butter
6 tablespoons cider vinegar
¼ cup sugar
3 eggs

Combine the chicken, hard-cooked eggs, sweet pickles, pecans and celery in a large bowl. Add the mayonnaise, sandwich spread, salt and pepper and toss. Add the pickle juice and toss again. Melt the butter in a small heavy saucepan. Whisk in the vinegar and sugar. Bring to a boil, stirring constantly. Remove from the heat. Whisk in the eggs, 1 at a time, stirring constantly to blend thoroughly. Return to medium heat. Cook and stir until the dressing mixture thickens slightly. Do not boil. Pour the hot dressing over the chicken salad and toss well. Refrigerate, covered, until ready to serve.
Yield: 12 servings

Mary Wood Beasley (Mrs. David Beasley)

David and Mary Wood Beasley with South Carolina Speaker of the House David Wilkins and his wife, Susan

David Muldrow Beasley played baseball at Clemson in 1975-76. He is now Governor David M. Beasley of the great state of South Carolina and is married to Mary Wood Payne Beasley. They have three children, Mary Hunter, 7, Sarah Catherine, 6, and David, Jr., 4.

Soups and Salads

Artichoke Rice Salad

2 cups chicken broth
1 cup long grain rice
½ cup mayonnaise
1 (6-ounce) jar marinated artichoke hearts, drained and halved
¼ cup chopped green bell pepper
¼ cup chopped green onions
¼ cup sliced pimento-stuffed olives
¼ to ½ teaspoon dillweed
½ teaspoon salt
⅛ teaspoon pepper
Lettuce leaves

Bring the broth to a boil in a medium saucepan. Stir in the rice. Return to a boil; reduce the heat. Simmer, covered, for 20 minutes or until all the broth is absorbed. Place rice in a large bowl. Stir in the mayonnaise, artichokes, green pepper, green onions, olives, dillweed, salt and pepper; mix well. Refrigerate, covered, until chilled. Spoon into a lettuce-lined bowl to serve. Garnish with additional olives.
Yield: 6 to 8 servings

Rosemary McGee (Mrs. Edgar McGee)

Edgar and Rosemary McGee and children, with Carol and Freddie Riley and children

Soups and Salads

Slaw Salad

1 cup raisins
Boiling water
3 cups shredded cabbage
2 red-skinned apples, chopped
1 cup mayonnaise
1 cup sugar
½ cup shredded carrots

Place raisins in a bowl. Pour enough boiling water over the raisins to cover. Let stand for 10 minutes to plump; drain well. Combine the raisins, cabbage, apples, mayonnaise, sugar and carrots in a bowl. Refrigerate, covered, for 1 hour before serving. Yield: 4 to 6 servings

Jake Meeks (Jake's Restaurant of Belton)

Jake Meeks

Jake Meeks tells us, "This recipe has been passed down through my family for years. It is very popular with the staff of IPTAY and the ticket office."

Jake owns Jake's Restaurant in Belton, South Carolina. He brings food and feeds the Athletic Department and IPTAY staffs about four times a year.

Tiger Crunch Slaw

1 (3-ounce) package pork-flavored ramen noodles
1 bunch green onions, sliced
½ cup salted sunflower seeds
½ cup toasted slivered almonds
½ medium head cabbage, shredded
½ cup olive oil
¼ cup sugar
2½ tablespoons white vinegar

Crumble the uncooked ramen noodles into a serving bowl. Add the green onions, sunflower seeds, almonds and cabbage; toss well. Combine the oil, sugar, vinegar and seasoning packet from the ramen noodles in a jar with a tight-fitting lid. Cover and shake until thoroughly blended. Pour the dressing over the cabbage mixture just before serving, tossing well. Yield: 6 servings

Marcia Barker (Mrs. Jim Barker)

Macaroni Salad

1 pound macaroni
1 large cucumber, diced
1 medium to large green bell pepper, chopped
2 medium tomatoes, diced
Salt and pepper to taste
1 cup ranch salad dressing
¾ to 1 cup salsa
Salt and pepper to taste

Cook the macaroni according to the package directions. Drain and rinse under cold water until cool. Place the cucumber, green pepper and tomatoes in a large bowl. Season with salt and pepper. Stir in the cooked macaroni. Combine the ranch dressing and salsa to taste in a bowl. Season with salt and pepper. Pour the dressing mixture over the macaroni and vegetables. Stir until blended. Refrigerate, covered, overnight. Stir before serving. Yield: 15 servings

Dora Bigbee

Best-Ever Broccoli Salad

1 bunch broccoli florets, cut into bite-size pieces
10 slices bacon, cooked and crumbled
1 cup chopped pecans
1 cup shredded cheese
½ cup raisins
1 cup mayonnaise
¼ cup sugar
2 teaspoons vinegar

Toss the broccoli, bacon, pecans, cheese and raisins in a bowl. Combine the mayonnaise, sugar and vinegar in a bowl. Stir until the sugar is dissolved. Pour the dressing mixture over the broccoli mixture and toss well. Refrigerate, covered, until chilled.
Yield: 6 servings

Glenda Russell

Erin Kathleen Russell and James Marion Russell IV

Glenda Russell tells us, "Over the years, we have kept our tailgating menus simple since we have to leave so early. This is a good quick salad that can be made in advance and that will enhance any Tiger meal! It is especially good with our normal menu of fried chicken, pimento cheese sandwiches, ham sandwiches, deviled eggs, and brownies."

Glenda graduated from Clemson in 1978.

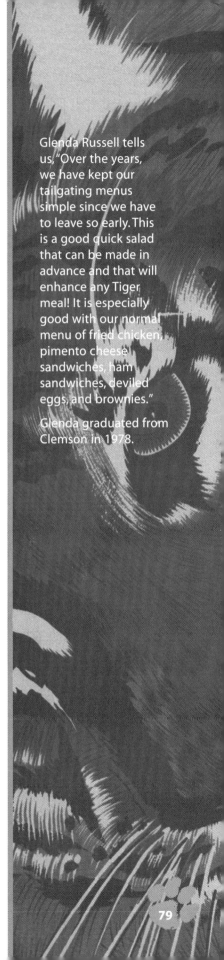

Harriet's father-in-law, Dr. Robert Poole, Sr., was Clemson's seventh president, from 1940 to 1958.

Bean Salad

2 (11-ounce) cans white shoepeg corn, drained
2 (14-ounce) cans French-style green beans, drained
2 (15-ounce) cans green peas, drained
1 cup finely chopped celery
1 (4-ounce) jar chopped pimentos, drained
4 green onions, chopped
2 cups sugar
1¼ cups vinegar
6 tablespoons vegetable oil
2 tablespoons water
2 teaspoons pepper

Combine the corn, beans, peas, celery, pimentos and green onions in a large bowl. Combine the sugar, vinegar, oil, water and pepper in a saucepan. Bring to a boil. Cook until the sugar dissolves. Pour the hot dressing mixture over the vegetables. Marinate until the vegetables have absorbed the flavor of the dressing. Store in a jar in the refrigerator. Drain before serving or serve with a slotted spoon.
Yield: 16 servings

Harriet M. Poole (Mrs. Frank Poole)

Soups and Salads

Chinese Almond Salad

Leaves of 1½ heads lettuce (iceberg and leaf)
1 red onion, sliced
5 slices bacon, cooked and crumbled
½ cup vegetable oil
¼ cup sugar
2 tablespoons white vinegar
1 teaspoon salt
¼ teaspoon pepper
3 ounces sliced almonds
¼ cup sesame seeds

Combine the lettuce, onion and bacon in a salad bowl. Combine the oil, sugar, vinegar, salt and pepper in a bowl and mix well. Pour over the lettuce mixture and toss. Top with the almonds and sesame seeds. Serve immediately. Yield: 8 servings

Susie McDaris (Mrs. Mac McDaris)

Clemson won the last Big Thursday game, defeating USC 27-0.

Easy Caesar Salad and Oil

3/4 cup canola oil
1/3 cup grated Parmesan cheese
3 tablespoons lemon juice
2 tablespoons chopped green onions
1 teaspoon salt
3/4 teaspoon dry mustard
1/2 teaspoon garlic salt
1/2 teaspoon Worcestershire sauce
1/4 teaspoon freshly ground black pepper
1 head romaine lettuce, torn into bite-size pieces
2 avocados, diced
1 cup croutons
2 ounces anchovies, cut up (optional)

Combine the oil, Parmesan cheese, lemon juice, green onions, salt, dry mustard, garlic salt, Worcestershire and pepper. Refrigerate, covered, for several hours. Combine the lettuce, avocados, croutons and anchovies in a salad bowl. Pour the chilled dressing over and toss well. Serve immediately. Yield: 6 to 8 servings

Vicki Kingsmore (Mrs. Doug Kingsmore)

Doug and Vicki Kingsmore

Soups and Salads

Vegetable Salad

2 cups diced carrots
2 cups sliced celery
1 cup diced cucumber
1/2 cup chopped green bell pepper
1/2 cup sliced radishes
1/4 cup chopped onion
1 1/2 cups cottage cheese
1/2 cup mayonnaise
1 1/2 teaspoons salt

Combine the carrots, celery, cucumber, green pepper, radishes and onion in a salad bowl. Combine the cottage cheese, mayonnaise and salt in a bowl. Pour over the vegetables and toss well. Yield: 8 servings

Mary Earle McCraw (Mrs. Les McCraw)

Molded Asparagus Salad

2 envelopes unflavored gelatin
1/2 cup cold water
3/4 cup sugar
1 cup water
1/2 cup vinegar
1 teaspoon salt
1 tablespoon minced onion
1 (14-ounce) can cut asparagus spears, drained
1 (8-ounce) can sliced water chestnuts, drained
1 cup chopped celery
1 (4-ounce) jar diced pimentos, drained

Combine the gelatin and 1/2 cup cold water. Let stand until the gelatin is softened. Combine the sugar, 1 cup water, vinegar and salt in a saucepan. Bring to a boil. Remove from the heat. Stir in the softened gelatin and onion; cool. Combine the asparagus, water chestnuts, celery and pimentos in a bowl. Add the gelatin mixture and mix well. Pour into a greased 7x11-inch dish or 2-quart mold. Refrigerate, covered, until firm. Yield: 8 servings

Jeanette H. Carter

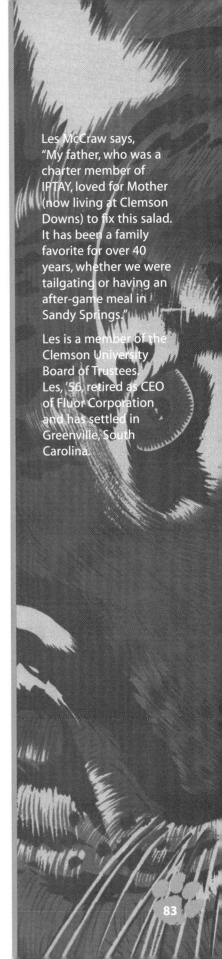

Les McCraw says, "My father, who was a charter member of IPTAY, loved for Mother (now living at Clemson Downs) to fix this salad. It has been a family favorite for over 40 years, whether we were tailgating or having an after-game meal in Sandy Springs."

Les is a member of the Clemson University Board of Trustees. Les, '56, retired as CEO of Fluor Corporation and has settled in Greenville, South Carolina.

Granny's Fruit Salad

1 (20-ounce) can pineapple chunks
1 (3-ounce) package instant vanilla pudding mix
3 tablespoons orange-flavored drink mix
1 (29-ounce) can sliced peaches, drained and cut into chunks
1 (10-ounce) package frozen sliced strawberries, thawed and drained
2 to 3 bananas, sliced

Drain the pineapple, reserving the juice. Combine the reserved pineapple juice, pudding mix and drink mix in a large bowl and blend well. Stir in the peaches, strawberries, bananas and pineapple. Refrigerate, covered, for several hours or until chilled. Serve over pound cake or with whipped topping. Yield: 4 to 6 servings

Mary Sease

Fruited Cream Salad

1 (3-ounce) package orange gelatin
1 cup boiling water
1 pint vanilla ice cream
1 (20-ounce) can crushed pineapple, drained
1 (6-ounce) jar maraschino cherries, drained and halved
1 cup chopped pecans

Dissolve the gelatin in the boiling water in a large bowl. Add the ice cream and stir until melted. Stir in the pineapple, cherries and pecans. Pour into a 2-quart mold. Refrigerate, covered, until firm. Makes 8 to 10 servings

Nancy Holmes

Blackberry Salad

2 (3-ounce) packages blackberry gelatin
1½ cups boiling water
1 (8-ounce) can crushed pineapple
1 (16-ounce) can blueberries
2 cups sour cream
8 ounces cream cheese, softened
½ cup sugar
1 teaspoon vanilla extract
½ cup finely chopped pecans

Dissolve the gelatin in the boiling water in a large bowl. Stir in the undrained pineapple and undrained blueberries and mix well. Pour into a 9x13-inch dish. Refrigerate, covered, until set. Cream the sour cream, cream cheese and sugar until light and fluffy. Stir in the vanilla and mix well. Spread over the set gelatin. Sprinkle the pecans over the top. Refrigerate, covered, until firm. Yield: 10 servings.

Betty MacIntyre (Mrs. George MacIntyre)

Cranberry Gelatin Salad

1 (16-ounce) can whole berry cranberry sauce
1 cup boiling water
1 (3-ounce) package strawberry gelatin
1 tablespoon lemon juice
¼ teaspoon salt
½ cup mayonnaise
1 apple, unpeeled and diced
⅓ cup chopped pecans

Combine the cranberry sauce and boiling water in a saucepan. Heat over low heat until the cranberry sauce is melted. Strain the mixture into a large bowl, reserving the cranberries. Add the gelatin to the cranberry liquid and stir until dissolved. Stir in the lemon juice and salt. Refrigerate until slightly thickened. Beat in the mayonnaise until fluffy. Fold in the reserved cranberries, apple and pecans. Pour into a lightly greased 4- to 6-cup mold. Refrigerate, covered, overnight or until firm. Unmold onto a lettuce-lined platter and garnish with apple slices that have been dipped in a mixture of lemon juice and water. Yield: 8 to 10 servings

Jean Kopczyk

Women became part of the Clemson student body on September 7, 1955, as the university became coeducational.

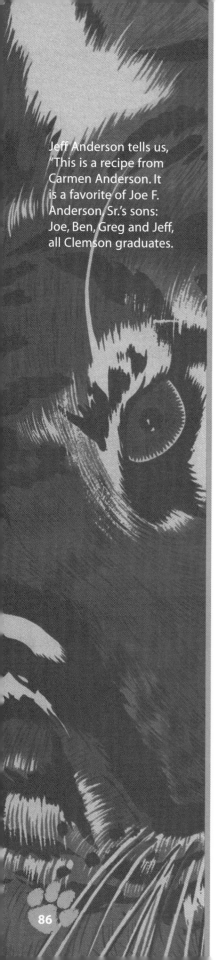

Lime Salad

8 ounces cream cheese, softened
1 (3-ounce) package lime gelatin
1 cup boiling water
1 (20-ounce) can crushed pineapple
1 cup whipping cream
1 tablespoon sugar
1 cup chopped pecans (optional)

Beat the cream cheese and gelatin in a large bowl. Stir in the boiling water. Drain the pineapple, reserving the juice. Add scant cup of pineapple juice to the cheese mixture and mix well. Refrigerate, covered, until the mixture has the consistency of thick custard. Whip the cream with the sugar in a mixer bowl. Fold the pineapple and pecans into the cheese mixture. Fold in the whipped cream. Pour into a 2-quart mold. Refrigerate, covered, until firm. Yield: 8 to 10 servings

Jeff M. Anderson

Sawdust Salad

1 (3-ounce) package lemon gelatin
1 (3-ounce) package orange gelatin
2 cups boiling water
1¼ cups cold water
1 (20-ounce) can crushed pineapple, drained
3 bananas, sliced
2 cups pineapple juice
1 cup sugar
5 tablespoons flour
2 eggs
2 cups miniature marshmallows
2 envelopes whipped topping mix
1 cup cold milk
8 ounces cream cheese, softened
Pecan meal

Dissolve the gelatins in the boiling water in a large bowl. Stir in the cold water, pineapple and bananas. Pour into a 9x13-inch dish. Chill, covered, until firm. Combine the pineapple juice, sugar, flour and eggs in a saucepan. Cook until thickened, stirring constantly. Cool completely. Sprinkle the marshmallows evenly over the firm gelatin mixture. Spread cooled juice mixture over the marshmallows. Beat the whipped topping mix and milk. Add the cream cheese and beat until blended. Spread over the top. Sprinkle with the pecan meal. Refrigerate, covered, overnight or until firm. Yield: 20 servings

Belva H. Bennett

Soups and Salads

Orange Bowl Salad

1 (6-ounce) package orange gelatin
12 ounces cottage cheese
2 (8-ounce) cans crushed pineapple, drained
2 (7-ounce) cans mandarin oranges, drained
12 ounces frozen nondairy whipped topping, thawed

Sprinkle the gelatin over the cottage cheese in a large bowl. Stir in the pineapple and oranges. Fold in the whipped topping. Refrigerate, covered, until chilled. Serve as a salad or dessert.
Yield: 8 to 10 servings

Blanche K. Caughman

Frozen Salad

1 (6-ounce) jar maraschino cherries
1 (8-ounce) can crushed pineapple
¾ cup whipped cream or whipped topping
½ cup mayonnaise
3 ounces cream cheese, softened
2 tablespoons toasted pecans
2 drops red food coloring
½ cup mayonnaise
¼ cup whipped cream or whipped topping

Drain the cherries, reserving 3 tablespoons juice. Finely chop the cherries. Drain the pineapple, reserving 1 tablespoon juice and 1 tablespoon pineapple. Combine the chopped cherries, 2 tablespoons cherry juice, ¾ cup whipped cream, ½ cup mayonnaise, remaining pineapple, cream cheese, pecans and food coloring in a bowl. Pour into an ice cube tray that has the insert removed. Freeze until firm. Combine ½ cup mayonnaise, ¼ cup whipped cream, reserved 1 tablespoon pineapple and 1 tablespoon pineapple juice and remaining 1 tablespoon cherry juice. Cut the frozen salad into squares. Arrange on lettuce leaves and top with dressing.
Yield: 8 servings

Evelyn L. Vickery (Mrs. Kenneth N. Vickery)

Main Dishes

Phil Prince, former University President and football player; Banks McFadden, former player and coach; Bobby Robinson, Athletic Director

Clemson Welcomes You To Death Valley

TIGER TRADITIONS

Tenderloins with Pepper Sauce (Medallions au Poivre)

4 (4-ounce) beef tenderloin steaks
1 teaspoon salt and white pepper blend
1 teaspoon cracked black pepper
1 tablespoon vegetable oil
1 tablespoon unsalted butter
1 tablespoon chopped shallots
1 tablespoon chopped parsley
¼ cup brandy
1 cup heavy cream
½ cup demi-glace
Salt and white pepper blend to taste

Season both sides of the steaks with salt and white pepper blend. Press cracked black pepper into 1 side of each steak. Heat the oil in an 8-inch skillet. Add the steaks, pepper side down, to the skillet. Cook for 6 to 7 minutes on each side for medium doneness. Drain off the drippings, leaving the steaks in the skillet. Add the butter and heat until melted. Add the shallots and cracked black pepper to taste. Cook for 30 seconds. Stir in the parsley. Add the brandy and heat until it flames. Remove the meat and keep warm. Stir in the cream, demi-glace and salt and white pepper blend to taste. Bring to a boil; reduce the heat. Simmer until the sauce is thickened and smooth. Serve over the steaks. Yield: 2 servings

Nancy Cathcart (Mrs. Foster Cathcart)

Jack Daniel's Tenderloin

5 to 8 pounds beef tenderloin
1½ cups soy sauce
½ cup Jack Daniel's bourbon
2 cloves of garlic, minced
Coarsely ground pepper to taste
2 to 3 slices bacon
1 onion, sliced

Place the tenderloins in large plastic food storage bags. Combine the soy sauce, bourbon, garlic and pepper in a bowl. Pour over the tenderloins. Seal the bags tightly. Refrigerate for 2 hours or overnight, turning occasionally. Allow the meat to come to room temperature before roasting. Remove the tenderloins from the marinade; discard the marinade. Arrange in a roasting pan. Top with the bacon and onion slices. Place in a 450 degree oven. Reduce the oven temperature immediately to 400 degrees. Bake for 35 to 40 minutes or until the internal temperature reaches 160 degrees for medium. Let stand for 10 minutes before carving into thin slices.
Yield: 15 to 25 servings

Nancy Matthews, for Lawrence Starkey

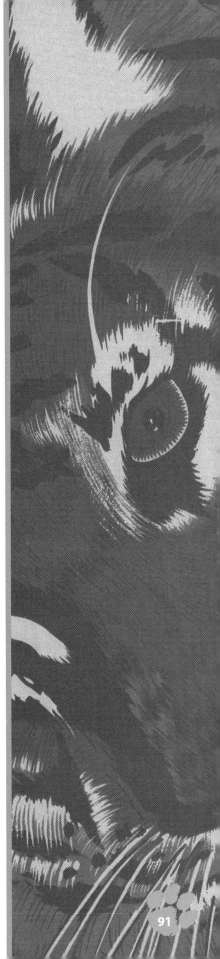

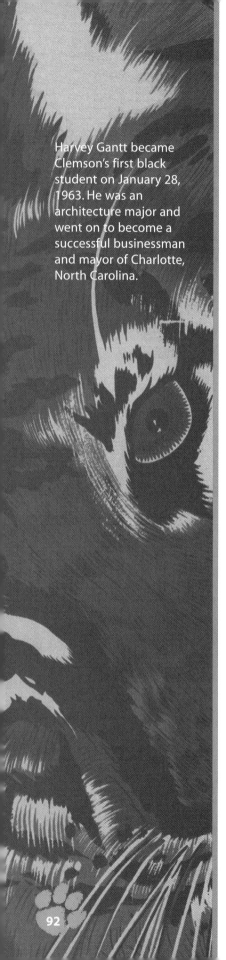

Sesame Seed Beef

⅔ pound flank steak
1½ tablespoons soy sauce
1½ tablespoons sesame oil
1 tablespoon rice wine or dry sherry
2 teaspoons cornstarch
1 teaspoon minced gingerroot
½ teaspoon baking soda
½ teaspoon sugar
1 cup vegetable oil
2 tablespoons chicken broth
1 tablespoon sesame seeds
1½ teaspoons hot bean sauce
1½ teaspoons hoisin sauce
1½ teaspoons oyster sauce
1 teaspoon sugar
1 teaspoon cornstarch
2 cloves of garlic, chopped
1 tablespoon sesame oil

Cut the flank steak across the grain into thin slices. Cut the slices into 2-inch squares. Combine the soy sauce, 1½ tablespoons sesame oil, rice wine, 2 teaspoons cornstarch, gingerroot, baking soda and ½ teaspoon sugar in a bowl. Add the steak squares and stir to coat. Refrigerate, covered, for 30 minutes. Drain the beef, discarding the marinade. Heat the vegetable oil in a deep skillet until hot. Add the beef. Stir-fry until the beef is lightly browned and cooked through. Remove the beef from the skillet. Drain off all but 2 tablespoons oil from the skillet. Combine the chicken broth, sesame seeds, bean sauce, hoisin sauce, oyster sauce, 1 teaspoon sugar and 1 teaspoon cornstarch in a bowl; set aside. Heat the oil in the skillet over high heat. Add the garlic. Stir-fry for 30 seconds. Add the broth mixture. Cook until it simmers and thickens, stirring constantly. Stir in the meat and 1 tablespoon sesame oil. Serve immediately.
Yield: 2 to 3 servings

Daisy Jean Cathcart

Shopping Day Beef

1½ pounds stew meat or chuck roast, cut into 1-inch cubes
1 (10-ounce) can French onion soup
1 (10-ounce) can cream of mushroom soup

Place the meat in a well-greased 8-inch baking dish. Combine the onion soup and mushroom soup in a bowl. Pour over the meat. Bake, uncovered, at 250 degrees for 6 to 8 hours or until done to taste. Serve over rice or wide noodles. Yield: 4 to 6 servings

Eva Holmes (Mrs. Lewis F. Holmes)

Barbecue Meat Loaf

1½ pounds lean ground beef
1 onion, chopped
½ (8-ounce) can tomato sauce
½ cup fresh bread crumbs
1 egg
1½ teaspoons salt
½ teaspoon pepper
1½ (8-ounce) cans tomato sauce
½ cup water
3 tablespoons brown sugar
3 tablespoons vinegar
1 tablespoon Worcestershire sauce
2 tablespoons prepared mustard

Combine the ground beef, onion, ½ can tomato sauce, bread crumbs, egg, salt and pepper in a bowl and mix lightly. Shape the meat mixture into a loaf. Place in a 9x13-inch baking pan. Combine the 1½ cans tomato sauce, water, brown sugar, vinegar, Worcestershire sauce and mustard in a bowl. Pour over the meat loaf. Bake at 350 degrees for 1 hour and 15 minutes or until cooked through. Yield: 6 servings

Betty S. Monroe (Mrs. Bill Monroe)

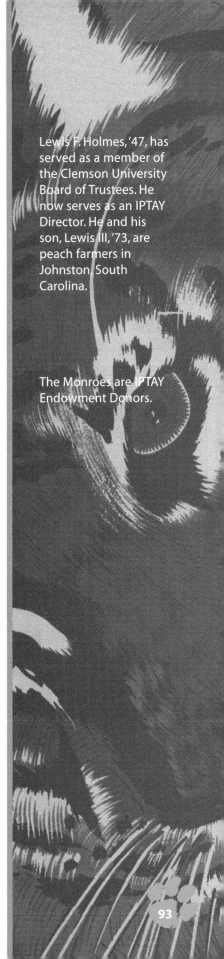

The Provost's Welsh Pasties

2 recipes pastry for double-crust pie
3/4 pound beef sirloin steak, cut into 1/2-inch cubes
3/4 pound round steak, cut into 1/2-inch cubes
1 cup thinly sliced potatoes
1/2 cup finely chopped onion
Salt and pepper to taste
Butter
Suet chunk
1/2 cup half-and-half

Divide the pastry into 4 equal portions. Roll out each portion on a lightly floured surface. Cut out two 6-inch circles for a total of 8 circles. Layer the steak, potatoes and onion on 1 side of each pastry circle. Season with salt and pepper. Dot with butter. Scrape off a little piece of suet and place over the butter. Moisten the edges of the pastry with water. Fold the pastry over the filling to make a half circle. Pinch the edges of the pastry to seal. Place the pasties on a baking sheet. Bake at 375 degrees for 10 minutes. Reduce the oven temperature to 350 degrees. Bake for 50 minutes or until golden brown. Remove from the oven. Turn off the oven. Cut a slit in the top of each pasty. Pour 1 tablespoon half-and-half into each slit. Return to the oven for 5 minutes. Serve hot. Yield: 8 servings

Athena Rogers (Mrs. Steffen Rogers)

Main Dishes

Guy's Favorite Casserole

1½ pounds ground beef
1 large onion, finely chopped
1 (10-ounce) can cream of mushroom soup
1 soup can milk
1 (10-ounce) package frozen butter beans
8 ounces thin noodles, cooked and drained
Salt and pepper to taste

Brown the ground beef with the onion in a skillet, stirring until the ground beef is crumbly; drain. Add the soup, milk, butter beans and noodles. Season with salt and pepper and mix thoroughly. Pour into a greased 9x13-inch baking dish. Bake at 325 degrees for 1 hour.
Yield: 10 servings

Carolyn O. Hendrix (Mrs. L.J. Hendrix)

Carolyn Hendrix tells us, "This dish went to Clemson many times to tailgates when my son Guy, '77, was there. It travels well in a Styrofoam™ chest."

Carolyn was the 1997 Tiger Brotherhood Mother of the Year. Her son Bill is a Clemson Trustee. Bill's son, Jim, was the 1997-98 President of the Student Body. The new Student Union will be named for the Hendrix family.

Swedish Tiger Meatballs

1 1/4 pounds ground beef or turkey
2 1/2 cups bread crumbs
1 egg, slightly beaten
1 tablespoon sugar
1/2 teaspoon salt
1/4 teaspoon pepper
2 tablespoons shortening
1/2 cup Naturally Fresh Jackaroo Meat Sauce
1/2 cup heavy cream

Combine the ground beef, bread crumbs, egg, sugar, salt and pepper in a bowl. Shape into 1 1/2-inch balls. Melt the shortening in a skillet. Add the meatballs. Cook until browned on all sides. Place the meatballs in a shallow 1-quart baking dish. Pour the meat sauce over the meatballs. Bake, covered, at 325 degrees for 25 minutes. Add the cream. Bake, uncovered, for 15 minutes or until the meatballs are cooked through. Yield: 3 servings

Jean Greene (Mrs. Jerry Greene)

Busy Day Beef and Noodles

1 pound ground beef
1 cup chopped onion
2 tablespoons margarine or butter
3 cups tomato juice
3 cups uncooked macaroni
2 teaspoons Worcestershire sauce
1 teaspoon salt
1 to 2 teaspoons celery salt
Dash of pepper
1 cup sour cream

Brown the ground beef with the onion in the margarine in a large skillet, stirring until the ground beef is crumbly; drain. Stir in the tomato juice, macaroni, Worcestershire sauce, salt, celery salt and pepper. Bring to a boil; reduce the heat. Simmer until the macaroni is tender. Remove from the heat. Stir in the sour cream. Serve immediately. Yield: 6 servings

Edythe Lambert (Mrs. Robert F. Lambert)

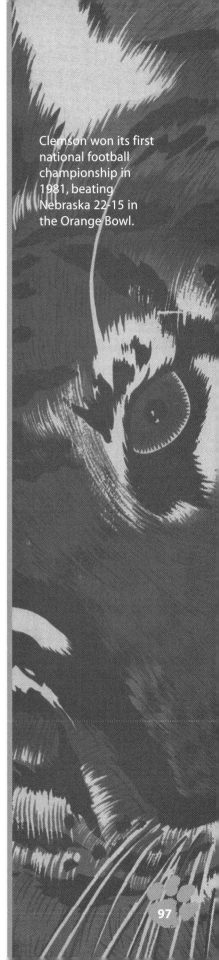

Clemson won its first national football championship in 1981, beating Nebraska 22-15 in the Orange Bowl.

Foster Cathcart, president of the Class of '51, spent 36 years with the DuPont Company. His last assignment with DuPont was as President of DuPont Mexico, where he developed his taste for all things Mexican. He then spent 18 months as Economic Officer for the State Department at the Embassy in Jamaica.

Cathcart has come full circle after 24 career transfers that also included assignments in Switzerland. He has returned to the Clemson area to retire in the shadow of the Blue Ridge Mountains. He and Nancy have purchased a home on beautiful Lake Keowee. An avid sports fan, Foster rarely misses an athletic event when Clemson is competing.

Cathcart's Mexican Goulash

1 shaker salt
1 quart Sauza Conmemorativo Tequila
2 limes, quartered
2 pounds ground chuck or ground round
1 large onion, chopped
4 teaspoons margarine or butter
2 cloves of garlic, minced
¼ cup chili powder
1 teaspoon pepper
½ teaspoon salt
1 (15-ounce) can tomato sauce
2 (15-ounce) cans kidney beans

Lick the top of left hand (at base of thumb) and sprinkle salt on top of hand. Lick off salt, drink 1 jigger of tequila slowly (savoring the flavor) and bite into 1 piece of lime, squeezing slightly to release juice. Brown the ground beef with the onion in the margarine in a large skillet until the ground beef is crumbly; drain. Repeat salt, tequila and lime routine. Stir in the garlic, chili powder, pepper and salt. Cook for 5 minutes over medium heat, stirring frequently. Repeat salt, tequila and lime routine. Add the tomato sauce and kidney beans (drain the liquid from 1 can of beans and feed to your pet dog or goat). Cook, covered, over low heat for 20 to 25 minutes, stirring frequently. Repeat salt, tequila and lime routine 2 more times during this period. Dish up a good-size helping of goulash onto each plate. Serve with a salad, corn on the cob and garlic toast or warm flour tortillas. Serves 2 to 8 people, depending on how hungry they are. Ideal for "after football game" parties or sorority slumber parties. (I would be able to attend either of these parties to assure that the above preparation is done correctly.) Note: If you do not like tequila, omit the shaker of salt and lime. Substitute two 6-packs of Mexican beer. Chill before drinking for best results. Yield: 8 servings

Foster Cathcart

Main Dishes

Corned Beef and Cabbage Casserole

4 to 5 cups stemmed cabbage leaves
1 (12-ounce) can corned beef, shredded
2 tablespoons margarine
2 tablespoons flour
¼ teaspoon salt
⅓ teaspoon pepper
1 cup milk
2 to 3 pieces toasted bread
1 cup shredded Cheddar cheese

Steam the cabbage until tender. Place in the bottom of a greased 9x13-inch baking dish. Spread the shredded corned beef over the cabbage. Melt the margarine in a saucepan over low heat. Blend in the flour, salt and pepper. Cook until smooth and bubbly. Remove from the heat. Stir in the milk. Return to the heat. Bring to a boil, stirring constantly. Cook for 1 minute. Pour the white sauce over the corned beef. Crumble the toasted bread into crumbs. Sprinkle the crumbs and cheese over the sauce. Bake, uncovered, at 350 degrees for 30 minutes or until bubbly. Yield: 10 servings

Pam Watkins Powell (Mrs. Tommy Powell)

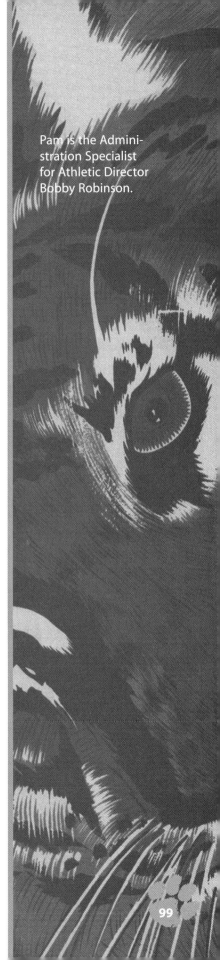

Pam is the Administration Specialist for Athletic Director Bobby Robinson.

Bean Pot

2½ pounds lean ground beef
1 (8-ounce) can tomato sauce
½ cup packed brown sugar
1 tablespoon Worcestershire sauce
1 (28-ounce) can pork and beans
1 large sweet onion, thinly sliced
Pepper to taste

Brown the ground beef in a skillet, stirring until crumbly; drain. Combine the tomato sauce, brown sugar and Worcestershire sauce in a bowl. Layer half the browned ground beef, pork and beans, onion and tomato sauce mixture in a greased 2-quart baking dish. Season with pepper. Repeat the layers. Bake, uncovered, at 300 degrees for 1 hour or until bubbly. Yield: 6 to 8 servings

Weezie Willimon Gibson (Mrs. Jim Gibson)

Spring Chicken

3 large onions
3 large green bell peppers
3 lemons
1 quart prepared mustard
1 quart tomato juice
1 quart vinegar
1 quart mayonnaise
1 quart catsup
2 cups white wine
2 cups butter
1 (2-ounce) bottle hot sauce
1/2 to 3/4 cup packed brown sugar
Salt and pepper to taste
20 (3- to 4-pound) broiler-fryer chickens, halved

Cut the onions, green peppers and unpeeled lemons into chunks. Purée in a blender or food processor until liquefied. Strain into an 8-quart stockpot. Stir in the mustard, tomato juice, vinegar, mayonnaise, catsup, wine, butter and hot sauce. Bring to a boil; reduce the heat. Simmer for 10 minutes. Add the brown sugar and salt and pepper to taste. Simmer for 5 minutes; set aside. Grill the chickens slowly, skin sides down, over low coals until three fourths cooked. Turn and grill until the chickens are cooked through, basting thoroughly with the sauce mixture 2 to 3 times.
Yield: 40 servings

Jim and Barbara McCabe

Jim McCabe relates the origin of this recipe's title. "Years ago at our summer home in Saluda, North Carolina, my cousin Tennent Hane and I decided to cook chickens for 120 people (60 chickens, 1/2 per person). We didn't have a cooker big enough, so we dragged out an old bedspring from under the house, cleaned it up, put it up on concrete blocks, and laid the chickens on the springs with the charcoal underneath. Pieces of roofing tin were put on top and leaned on their sides to hold in the heat. Needless to say, it was a hit. From then on it was known as Spring Chicken."

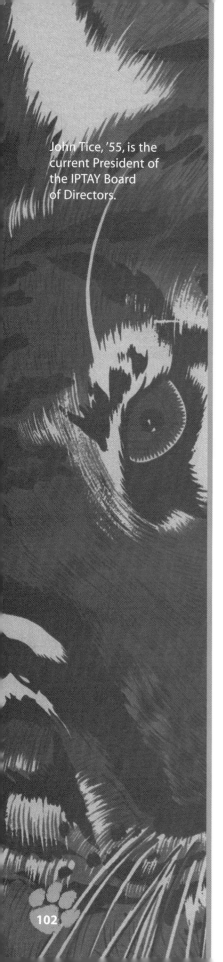

Anne's Chicken

8 chicken breast halves
1 cup vegetable oil
½ cup lemon juice
1 clove of garlic
1 tablespoon salt
2 teaspoons basil, crushed
½ teaspoon thyme, crushed
2 teaspoons onion powder
1 teaspoon paprika

Place the chicken in a large shallow baking dish. Combine the oil, lemon juice, garlic, salt, basil, thyme, onion powder and paprika in a bowl. Pour over the chicken. Refrigerate, covered, for 2½ hours. Remove the chicken from the marinade. Pour the marinade into a saucepan. Bring to a boil. Boil for 2 to 3 minutes; set aside. Grill the chicken, skin sides down, for 25 minutes. Turn and brush with the boiled marinade. Grill for 20 to 25 minutes or until the chicken is cooked through. Yield: 8 servings

Ila Jo Tice (Mrs. John Tice)

Main Dishes

Chicken Parmesan

4 boneless skinless chicken breast halves
1 egg
2 to 3 cups Italian-style bread crumbs
2 tablespoons grated Parmesan cheese
1 to 2 tablespoons vegetable oil
1 (26-ounce) jar spaghetti sauce
1 cup shredded mozzarella cheese

Cut the chicken breasts lengthwise in half. Pound each half between 2 pieces of plastic wrap until flattened. Beat the egg in a small bowl. Combine the bread crumbs and Parmesan cheese in another bowl. Dip each chicken piece into the egg and then into the crumb mixture to coat. Heat the oil in a skillet. Add the chicken pieces. Cook for 4 minutes per side or until golden brown, turning once. Place the chicken in a single layer in a greased 9x13-inch baking dish. Pour the spaghetti sauce over the chicken. Top with the mozzarella cheese. Bake at 350 degrees for 30 minutes or until the mixture is bubbly and the chicken is cooked through. Serve over spaghetti or angel hair pasta with additional spaghetti sauce.
Yield: 6 to 8 servings

Beth Gilreath Jansto

Phil Prince was named interim president of Clemson in 1993 and served until the current president, Dr. Deno Curris, was named on May 22, 1995.

Fiesta Chicken

6 skinless chicken breast halves (bone-in or boneless)
1 (16-ounce) jar salsa (mild or medium)
1 (15-ounce) can black beans, drained
1 (11-ounce) can Shoe Peg corn, drained

Place chicken in greased 9x13-inch baking pan. Pour the salsa, black beans and corn over the chicken. Bake, covered, at 350 degrees for 45 minutes to 1 hour or until the chicken is cooked through. Uncover the pan during the last 10 minutes of baking. Serve over rice. Yield: 6 servings

Elaine Henderson

Julie's Chicken Casserole

½ cup melted butter or margarine
35 butter crackers, crushed
4 large chicken breast halves, cooked and chopped
1 (10-ounce) can cream of chicken soup
1 (10-ounce) can cream of mushroom soup
8 ounces sour cream
1 (5-ounce) can sliced water chestnuts, drained

Mix the butter and crackers in a bowl. Pat into a greased 2-quart shallow baking dish. Combine the chicken, chicken soup, mushroom soup, sour cream and water chestnuts in a bowl. Spread evenly over the cracker mixture. Bake at 350 degrees for 30 to 45 minutes or until bubbly. Note: Do not use fat-free sour cream. Yield: 8 servings

Jeanne G. Fowler

Main Dishes

Hawaiian Chicken

2 pounds chicken breast halves
Garlic salt to taste
2 eggs
1 cup flour
2 to 3 tablespoons vegetable oil
1½ cups catsup
¾ cup sugar
½ cup vinegar
¼ cup crushed pineapple or pineapple juice
1 teaspoon salt
1 teaspoon soy sauce

Sprinkle the chicken with garlic salt. Refrigerate, covered, for 15 to 30 minutes. Beat the eggs in a bowl. Pour the flour into another bowl. Dip the chicken in the eggs, then in the flour to coat. Heat the oil in a skillet. Add the chicken. Cook until browned on both sides. Place in a greased 9x13-inch baking pan. Combine the catsup, sugar, vinegar, pineapple, salt and soy sauce in a saucepan. Bring to a boil. Pour over the chicken. Bake at 350 degrees for 1 to 1½ hours or until the chicken is cooked through. Serve over rice. Yield: 6 servings

Sharon Irvin

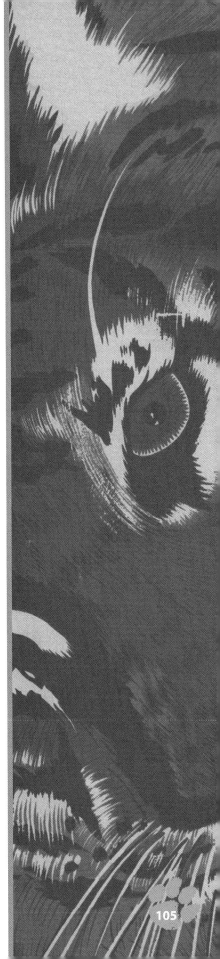

Phoenix Chicken

12 boneless skinless chicken breast halves
Orange juice
Hot pepper sauce to taste
1 to 2 (15-ounce) cans black beans
2 cups ranch salad dressing
¾ cup chopped roasted red bell pepper
¾ cup chopped tomato
¾ cup chopped green bell pepper
¼ cup chopped green onions
½ cup sliced black olives (optional)

Place the chicken in a large shallow baking dish. Add enough orange juice to cover. Season with pepper sauce. Refrigerate, covered, overnight. Remove the chicken from the marinade; discard the marinade. Grill the chicken until cooked through. Heat the black beans in a saucepan. Combine the ranch dressing with the pepper sauce in a bowl. Place the chicken on serving plates. Top each with black beans, roasted red pepper, tomato, green pepper, green onions, olives and dressing mixture. Yield: 12 servings

Laurie Haughey

Chattanooga Chicken Breasts

2 (2-ounce) jars sliced dried beef
6 boneless skinless chicken breast halves
Flour
1 pint sour cream
1 (10-ounce) can cream of mushroom soup
½ to 1 cup cooking sherry
Dash of dried minced onions

Shred the beef over the bottom of a lightly greased 11x13-inch baking dish. Dredge the chicken breasts in flour to coat. Place the chicken over the beef. Combine the sour cream, mushroom soup, sherry and onions in a bowl until blended. Pour over the chicken. Bake at 350 degrees for 1½ hours or until the chicken is cooked through. Yield: 6 servings

Judy Cone (Mrs. Fred Cone)

Fred Cone

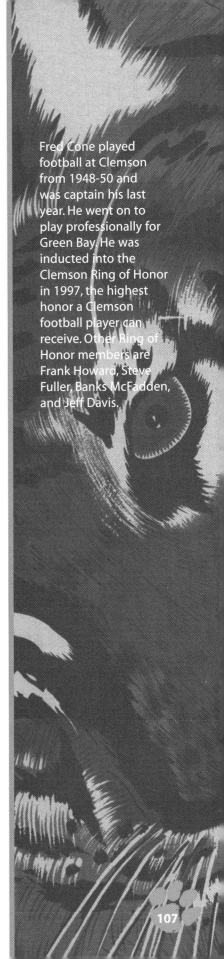

Fred Cone played football at Clemson from 1948-50 and was captain his last year. He went on to play professionally for Green Bay. He was inducted into the Clemson Ring of Honor in 1997, the highest honor a Clemson football player can receive. Other Ring of Honor members are Frank Howard, Steve Fuller, Banks McFadden, and Jeff Davis.

Chicken Breasts Wellington

1 (6-ounce) package long grain and wild rice mix
Grated peel of 1 orange
6 boneless chicken breast halves
Seasoned salt and pepper to taste
1 egg white
1 (10-ounce) package frozen patty shells, thawed
1 (12-ounce) jar red currant jelly
1 tablespoon orange juice
1 tablespoon white wine
1/2 teaspoon Dijon mustard

Cook the rice mix according to the package directions. Stir in the orange peel. Cool completely. Pound the chicken breasts between 2 pieces of plastic wrap until slightly flattened. Sprinkle with seasoned salt and pepper. Beat the egg white in a bowl until soft peaks form. Fold into the cooled rice mixture. Roll out each patty shell on a floured surface to an 8-inch circle. Place a chicken breast in the center of each circle. Top each chicken breast with 1/4 to 1/3 cup of the rice mixture. Roll up the pastry jelly roll style, bringing the edges up to enclose the filling. Place seam sides down in a 9x13-inch baking pan. Refrigerate, covered, overnight. Do not remove the chicken from the refrigerator until ready to bake. Bake, uncovered, at 375 degrees for 35 to 45 minutes or until the chicken is cooked through. (If the pastry becomes too brown, cover the pan loosely with foil.) Heat the jelly in a saucepan until melted. Stir in the orange juice, wine and mustard gradually. Serve warm with the chicken. Yield: 6 servings

Ann Gilreath (Mrs. John Gilreath)

Chicken Sauce Piquant

1 (2- to 3-pound) chicken
5 tablespoons vegetable oil
5 tablespoons flour
2 medium onions, diced
2 ribs celery, diced
1 medium green bell pepper, chopped
1 clove of garlic, chopped
1 (28-ounce) can crushed tomatoes
3 to 5 dashes Worcestershire sauce
½ teaspoon oregano
½ teaspoon thyme
2 bay leaves
Salt and pepper to taste
Tabasco sauce to taste
1 (16-ounce) can small green peas, drained
1 (4-ounce) can mushrooms, drained
6 cups cooked rice

Place the chicken in a stockpot. Add enough water to cover. Bring to a boil; reduce the heat. Simmer for 45 minutes or until the chicken is cooked through. Remove the chicken from the stock. Remove the meat when the chicken is cool enough to handle and cut into chunks. Strain the stock and reserve 2 cups. Heat the oil in a deep skillet. Add the flour gradually, stirring until it turns a light brown. Add the onions, celery, green pepper and garlic gradually. Cook until the onions are tender. Stir in the 2 cups reserved stock, tomatoes, Worcestershire sauce, oregano, thyme, bay leaves, salt, pepper and Tabasco. Bring to a boil; reduce the heat. Simmer until bubbly and slightly thickened. Stir in the chicken, peas and mushrooms. Cook for 3 minutes or until heated through. Remove and discard the bay leaves. Season to taste. Serve over rice. Yield: 6 servings

Edmée Reel (Mrs. Jerry Reel)

Vice Provost Jerry Reel, speaking at the 1986 Founder's Day Banquet, said, "If you seek the real monument of Mr. Clemson, it is the steady and increasing stream of young people who have learned lessons of scholarship, education, and service in Mr. Clemson's homeplace, Clemson University."

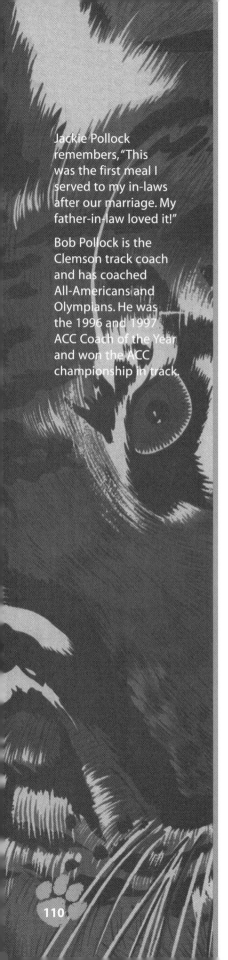

Chicken and Dried Beef Casserole

1 (2-ounce) jar sliced dried beef
4 boneless chicken breast halves
2 (10-ounce) cans cream of chicken soup
8 ounces sour cream

Arrange the dried beef on the bottom of a 9x13-inch baking dish. Place the chicken on top of the beef. Combine the chicken soup and sour cream. Pour over the chicken, spreading to cover evenly. Bake, covered, at 350 degrees for 1 hour or until the chicken is cooked through. Serve over rice or mashed potatoes.
Yield: 4 to 6 servings

Jackie Pollock, wife of Coach Bob Pollock

Jackie and Bob Pollock and children

Main Dishes

Chicken, Sausage and Rice Casserole

4 chicken breast halves, or 1 (3½- to 4-pound) chicken
1 to 2 ribs celery
2 bay leaves
2½ cups water
1 (6-ounce) package wild rice mix
1 pound mild sausage
2 medium onions, chopped
2 (4-ounce) cans mushrooms, drained
2 (10-ounce) cans cream of mushroom soup
1 cup buttered bread crumbs

Place the chicken, celery, bay leaves and water in a Dutch oven. Bring to a boil; reduce the heat. Simmer for 40 minutes or until the chicken is cooked through. Remove the chicken from the stock. Remove the meat when the chicken is cool enough to handle and cut into chunks. Strain the stock and reserve. Cook the wild rice according to the package directions using the reserved chicken stock in place of water. Sauté the sausage, onions and mushrooms in a skillet until the sausage is browned and onions are tender. Stir in the mushroom soup and chicken. Pour into a greased 9x13-inch baking dish. Sprinkle the bread crumbs over the top. Bake at 350 degrees for 30 to 35 minutes or until bubbly. Yield: 10 to 12 servings

Margaret Reaves (Mrs. Bill Reaves), sister of Jack Lunn

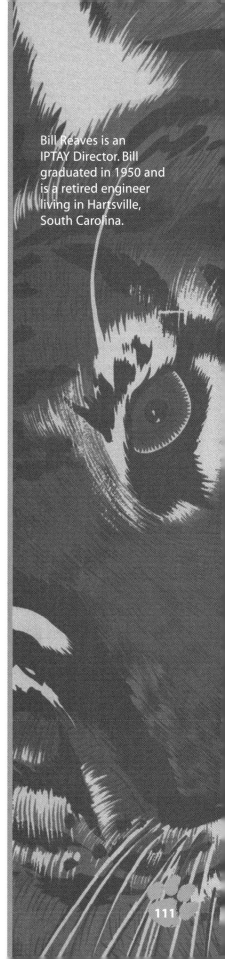

Bill Reaves is an IPTAY Director. Bill graduated in 1950 and is a retired engineer living in Hartsville, South Carolina.

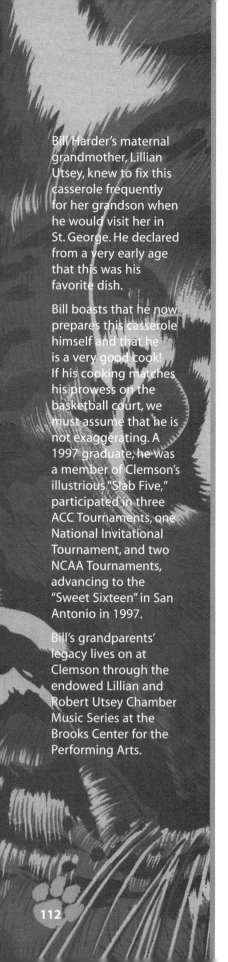

Bill Harder's maternal grandmother, Lillian Utsey, knew to fix this casserole frequently for her grandson when he would visit her in St. George. He declared from a very early age that this was his favorite dish.

Bill boasts that he now prepares this casserole himself and that he is a very good cook! If his cooking matches his prowess on the basketball court, we must assume that he is not exaggerating. A 1997 graduate, he was a member of Clemson's illustrious "Slab Five," participated in three ACC Tournaments, one National Invitational Tournament, and two NCAA Tournaments, advancing to the "Sweet Sixteen" in San Antonio in 1997.

Bill's grandparents' legacy lives on at Clemson through the endowed Lillian and Robert Utsey Chamber Music Series at the Brooks Center for the Performing Arts.

Bill Harder's Favorite Chicken Rice Casserole

1½ cups long grain rice
3 cups boiling water
1 envelope onion soup mix
4 boneless skinless chicken breast halves, cut into strips
½ cup margarine, cut into small pieces

Place the rice in a 9-inch square baking dish. Pour the boiling water over the rice. Sprinkle with the onion soup mix. Top with the chicken strips and margarine. Bake, covered, at 350 degrees for 1 hour. Yield: 4 servings

Bill Harder

Bill Harder as a ball boy

Main Dishes

Chicken Pilaf

1 (3- to 4-pound) chicken, cut up
4 chicken breasts
4 chicken legs
1 onion, cut up
8 ounces fatback, cut up
Salt and pepper to taste
3 pounds long grain rice

Place the cut-up chicken, chicken breasts and legs, onion, fatback, salt and pepper in a stockpot. Add enough water to cover. Bring to a boil; reduce the heat. Simmer until the chicken is tender and cooked through. Remove the chicken from the stock. Remove and discard the skin and bones when the chicken is cool enough to handle. Strain the stock and return to the stockpot. Add the rice and chicken meat to the stock. Bring to a boil. Boil for 5 to 10 minutes; reduce the heat to low. Simmer until the rice is tender and has absorbed all the liquid. Yield: 20 servings

Samual M. Harper

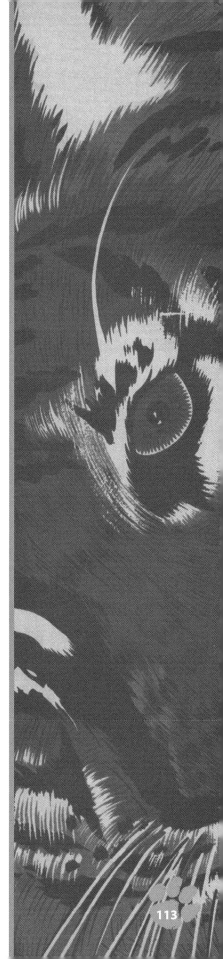

Coronation Chicken

1 onion, chopped
1 cooking apple, chopped
1 cup dry white wine
1/2 cup water
1 tablespoon honey
1 teaspoon each curry powder
1 teaspoon tomato paste
1 tablespoon apricot jam
1 1/4 cups mayonnaise
3/4 cup whipping cream, whipped
1 broiler-fryer, roasted, sliced
1/2 cup sliced almonds, toasted

Cook the onion and apple in a large nonstick skillet until tender. Stir in the wine, water, honey, curry powder and tomato paste. Simmer gently for 30 minutes. Stir in the jam. Cool completely. Combine the mayonnaise and whipped cream in a bowl. Fold in the cooled curry mixture. Carve the roasted chicken and arrange on a serving platter. Top with the curry sauce. Sprinkle with the almonds. Serve with rice. Yield: 4 to 6 servings

Bess Cecil (Mrs. Bill Cecil)

Texas Chicken

1 (3- to 4-pound) chicken
2 cups torn bread
2 cups cooked rice
1½ cups milk
4 eggs, beaten
6 tablespoons chicken fat
Salt and pepper to taste
Paprika
¼ cup butter
¼ cup flour
1 (10-ounce) can cream of mushroom soup
2 tablespoons lemon juice
Cholesterol-free egg substitute equivalent to 2 egg yolks, beaten

Combine the chicken with water to cover in a stockpot. Simmer until the chicken is cooked through. Remove the chicken from the stock; let cool. Cut the chicken into small pieces. Strain the stock and reserve. Combine the chicken, bread, rice, milk, ½ cup reserved chicken stock, eggs, chicken fat, salt and pepper in a bowl. Spoon into a greased 9x13-inch baking dish. Sprinkle with paprika. Bake at 350 degrees for 1 hour. Melt the butter in a saucepan. Stir in the flour until smooth. Stir in 1 cup reserved chicken stock and mushroom soup. Cook until thickened. Remove from the heat; stir in the lemon juice and egg substitute. Sprinkle with paprika. Cut the chicken mixture into squares. Serve with the sauce. Yield: 10 servings

Claudia Ware (Mrs. Billy Ware)

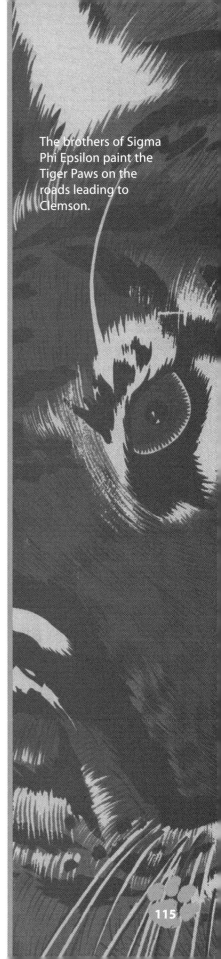

The brothers of Sigma Phi Epsilon paint the Tiger Paws on the roads leading to Clemson.

Chicken Tetrazzini

6 to 8 large mushrooms
2 tablespoons butter or margarine
½ cup dry sherry
2 tablespoons butter or margarine, softened
2 tablespoons flour
2 cups hot milk
Salt, pepper and nutmeg to taste
2 egg yolks
1 cup heavy cream
5 cups diced cooked chicken
9 ounces thin spaghetti
1 cup grated Parmesan cheese

Sauté the mushrooms in 2 tablespoons butter in a skillet until tender. Add the sherry. Cook for 3 minutes; set aside. Combine 2 tablespoons softened butter and flour in a double boiler. Stir in the hot milk gradually. Cook over simmering water for 20 minutes or until smooth and thickened, stirring constantly. Season with salt, pepper and nutmeg. Blend the egg yolks and cream in a bowl. Stir the egg yolk mixture into the thickened sauce. Cook and stir for 5 minutes. Add the chicken. Season with salt and pepper. Add the mushrooms. Cook the spaghetti according to the package directions; drain. Place the spaghetti in a greased 9x13-inch baking dish. Pour the creamed chicken mixture over the spaghetti. Sprinkle with the cheese. Broil until golden brown and bubbly. Yield: 6 to 8 servings

Jo Byrd (Mrs. James E. Byrd)

Main Dishes

Santa Fe Chicken

4 boneless skinless chicken breast halves
1 onion, chopped
Dash of Worcestershire sauce
Dash of lime juice
1 teaspoon minced garlic
1 (14-ounce) can Mexican or regular stewed tomatoes
1 (15-ounce) can black beans, drained
1 (5-ounce) package saffron or yellow rice
1/2 cup water
1 cup shredded low-fat Cheddar cheese

Place the chicken and onion in a greased 2-quart baking dish. Sprinkle with the Worcestershire sauce, lime juice and garlic. Bake at 350 degrees for 30 minutes or until the chicken is cooked through. Cut up the stewed tomatoes. Add to the baking dish with the black beans, rice and water and mix well. Cover the dish tightly. Bake for 45 to 60 minutes or until the rice is tender. Sprinkle with the cheese. Cover and let stand until the cheese is melted. Garnish with chopped fresh cilantro. Yield: 4 servings

Ginny Skelton (Mrs. Tom Skelton)

Ginny Skelton, '58, was the first female Clemson University Alumni President and the second to receive the Clemson University Distinguished Service Award. Carolyn Creel was the first female recipient in 1996.

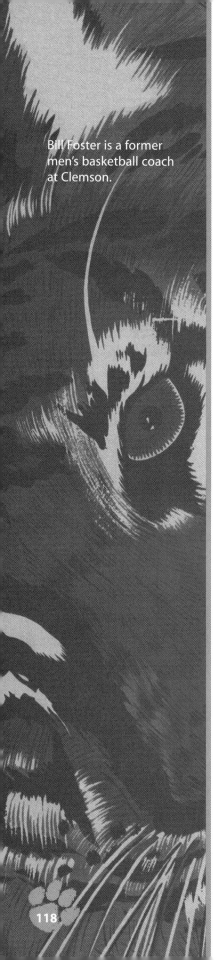

Sausalito Scampi

⅓ cup butter
⅓ cup olive or vegetable oil
2 cloves of garlic, minced
6 boneless skinless chicken breast halves, cut into 1-inch pieces
1 pound shrimp, peeled and deveined
1 teaspoon salt
Freshly ground pepper to taste
Juice of 1 lemon
Chopped fresh parsley

Heat the butter and oil in a large skillet. Add the garlic. Sauté for 2 minutes. Add the chicken. Cook until browned, stirring constantly. Push the chicken to 1 side of the skillet. Add the shrimp. Cook until the shrimp turn pink, stirring constantly. Season with salt and pepper. Sprinkle with lemon juice and top with parsley. Cook for 1 minute. Serve with rice and a green salad. Yield: 6 to 8 servings

Linda Foster (Mrs. Bill Foster)

Main Dishes

Texas Pile Up

1 (10-ounce) package saffron rice, cooked
16 to 20 skinless chicken strips, cooked
3 (15-ounce) cans black beans, drained
2 large tomatoes, diced
1 green onion, diced
1 (6-ounce) can sliced black olives
1 pound shredded Cheddar cheese
16 ounces sour cream
1 (16-ounce) jar mild or medium salsa
Tortilla chips

Layer the cooked rice, cooked chicken strips, black beans, tomatoes, green onion, olives, cheese, sour cream and salsa in a greased 9x13-inch baking dish. Bake at 350 degrees for 45 minutes or until heated through. Serve with tortilla chips. Note: For more zesty flavor, cook the chicken in additional salsa. Yield: 12 servings

Jimmy Carol Avent (Mrs. Mark Avent)

Jimmy Carol, Kirkham, Slade and Hammond Avent

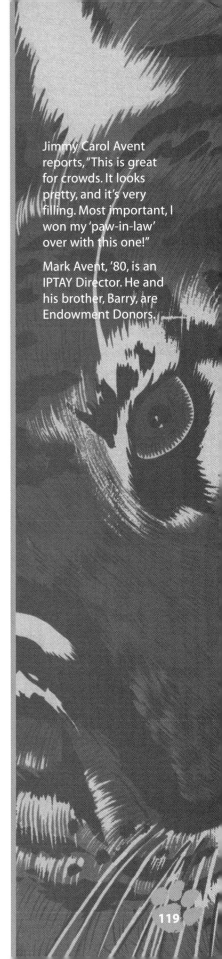

Jimmy Carol Avent reports, "This is great for crowds. It looks pretty, and it's very filling. Most important, I won my 'paw-in-law' over with this one!"

Mark Avent, '80, is an IPTAY Director. He and his brother, Barry, are Endowment Donors.

Easy Chicken Potpie

3 cups cooked vegetables
4 boneless skinless chicken breast halves, cooked and chopped
2 hard-cooked eggs, chopped
2 cups chicken broth
1 (10-ounce) can cream of chicken soup
½ cup melted butter
1 cup buttermilk
1 cup self-rising flour
Salt and pepper to taste

Place the vegetables on the bottom of a greased 9x13-inch baking dish. Top with the cooked chicken and eggs. Combine the chicken broth and chicken soup in a bowl. Pour the soup mixture over the eggs, spreading evenly. Combine the butter, buttermilk, flour, salt and pepper in a bowl. Pour over the soup mixture. Bake, uncovered, at 350 degrees for 45 minutes or until browned and bubbly.
Yield: 4 servings

Candy Barnes (Mrs. Rick Barnes)

Gamecock Potpie

2 refrigerated piecrusts
2 to 3 boneless skinless chicken breasts, cooked, chopped
1 (10-ounce) can cream of chicken soup
1 (10-ounce) can cream of potato soup
¼ cup milk

Line a 9-inch pie plate with 1 piecrust. Combine the cooked chicken, chicken soup, potato soup and milk in a bowl; mix well. Pour into the pie plate. Place the remaining piecrust over the filling. Trim the top crust even with the bottom crust. Crimp the edges together to seal. Cut 3 to 4 slits in the top crust to let the steam escape. Bake at 350 degrees for 45 minutes or until browned and bubbly. Yield: 4 to 6 servings

Penni Hawley

Main Dishes

Tom Stewart's Barbecue Sauce

    1 quart vinegar
    2 cups corn oil
    1 cup sugar
    ½ small bottle catsup
    ½ cup prepared mustard
    ½ cup salt, or to taste
    ¼ cup Worcestershire sauce
    ¼ bottle onion salt
    2 teaspoons (heaping) black pepper

Combine the vinegar, oil, sugar, catsup, mustard, salt, Worcestershire sauce, onion salt and pepper in a large bowl. Brush on chicken, beef or pork during grilling, broiling or baking. Yield: 2 quarts (enough for 100 chicken halves).

Ruby Thompson

Deep-Fried Turkey

    1 (10- to 12-pound) fresh or thawed frozen turkey
    Cajun spice blend to taste
    Peanut oil for deep-frying

Wash the turkey thoroughly. Season inside and out with Cajun spices. Heat enough peanut oil to 325 degrees in a large stockpot to completely cover the turkey. Immerse the turkey carefully into the hot oil. Cook for 3 to 3½ minutes per pound (30 to 35 minutes for a 10-pound turkey) or until the internal temperature reaches 180 degrees and the turkey floats freely in the oil. Remove the turkey carefully from the hot oil. Drain thoroughly. Cover and let stand for 15 minutes before carving. Yield: 12 to 14 servings

George Les Jones
Associate Athletic Director

"Clemson's former students have gone out from their institution with, I think, the finest education in the United States. I watch all the schools, and I don't believe there is a finer institution than Clemson."

—Charles L. Horn, President of the Olin Foundation

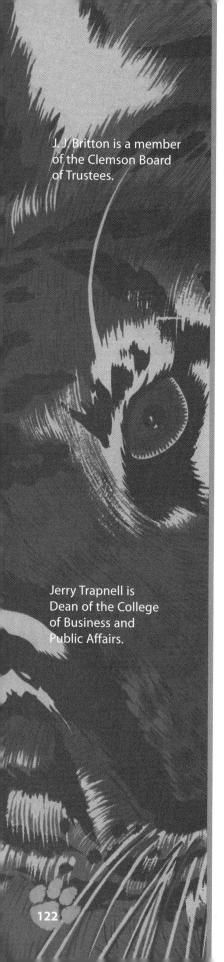

No-Fat Barbecue Turkey

2 cups vinegar
2 large onions, chopped
½ cup butter (optional)
3 tablespoons catsup
3 tablespoons Worcestershire sauce
3 tablespoons hot pepper sauce
2 tablespoons pepper
1 tablespoon salt
1 clove of garlic, minced (optional)
1 (5- to 6-pound) bone-in whole turkey breast

Combine the vinegar, onions, butter, catsup, Worcestershire sauce, pepper sauce, pepper, salt and garlic in a Dutch oven or stockpot. Simmer for 15 minutes. Remove the skin from the turkey breast. Add the turkey breast side up. Cook slowly, covered, for 2 to 3 hours or until the internal temperature reaches 170 degrees, basting occasionally. When the turkey is cool enough to handle, remove the meat from the bones. Shred the turkey meat into the sauce. Add a little water to thin the sauce, if necessary. Cook until heated through. Note: The barbecued turkey can be frozen for later use. Yield: 10 servings

Connie Britton (Mrs. J.J. Britton)

Marinated Turkey Tenderloins

1 cup white wine
½ cup vegetable oil
½ cup soy sauce
3 to 4 cloves of garlic, minced
6 turkey tenderloins

Combine the wine, oil, soy sauce and garlic in a bowl and mix well. Place the turkey in plastic food storage bags. Pour the marinade over the turkey. Seal the bags tightly and turn to coat the turkey evenly with the marinade. Refrigerate for at least 24 hours or for up to 2 days. Remove the turkey from the marinade; discard the marinade. Grill the turkey over medium coals for 8 to 10 minutes per side or until cooked through. Serve immediately or cool and refrigerate for later use. Yield: 6 to 8 servings

Sally D. Trapnell (Mrs. Jerry Trapnell)

Main Dishes

Slow-Cooker Ribs

6 pounds beef or pork ribs
1 (12-ounce) bottle chili sauce
1/2 cup water
1/2 cup chopped onion
1/4 cup packed light brown sugar
2 tablespoons wine vinegar
1 tablespoon mustard
1 clove of garlic, minced
2 teaspoons salt

Place the ribs in a single layer on a foil-lined baking pan. Bake at 350 degrees for 30 minutes, turning once. Combine the chili sauce, water, onion, brown sugar, vinegar, mustard, garlic and salt in a bowl. Dip the baked ribs, 1 at a time, into the sauce mixture. Place in a slow cooker. Pour the remaining sauce over the ribs. Cook for 8 to 12 hours on low heat or until the ribs are tender. Yield: 8 to 10 servings

Faith Reeves

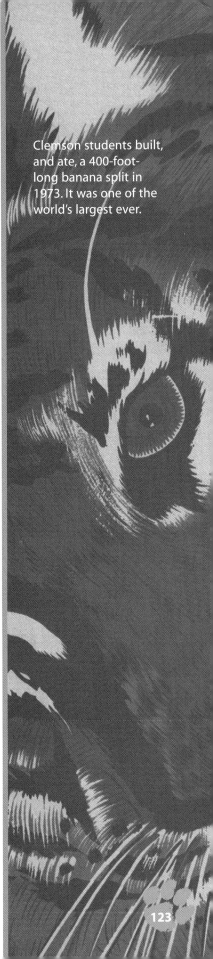

Clemson students built, and ate, a 400-foot-long banana split in 1973. It was one of the world's largest ever.

"Tiger" Ribs

40 pounds pork ribs, cut into 2- to 4-rib portions
1 gallon apple cider
2 (12-ounce) cans beer
2 cups lemon juice, or mixed lemon juice and lime juice
8 ounces salt
2 cups black pepper
1 (64-ounce) bottle Naturally Fresh Catsup
2 cups Naturally Fresh Mustard

Trim any excess fat from the ribs before soaking and cleaning them. Place the ribs in a large stockpot and add enough water to cover. Bring to a boil; reduce the heat. Simmer for 1½ hours. Combine the cider, beer, lemon juice, salt and pepper in a large container. Add the boiled ribs. Refrigerate, covered, for 4 to 6 hours. Remove the ribs from the sauce, reserving the sauce. Grill, bone sides down, over low coals for 30 minutes. Stir the catsup and mustard into the reserved sauce and mix well. Brush the sauce mixture on the ribs. Cook for 30 to 45 minutes or until lightly browned, basting occasionally.
Yield: 60 servings

Robert (Bird Dog) Hughes

"Paws" for Ribs

1 whole rack spareribs
Salt and pepper to taste
½ onion, chopped
1 (18-ounce) jar Naturally Fresh Jackaroo Barbecue Sauce

Season the spareribs with salt and pepper. Place on a broiler pan. Broil for 15 minutes. Split the ribs into individual portions. Place the onion in a slow cooker. Add the ribs. Pour the barbecue sauce over to cover. Cook for 8 to 10 hours on low heat or 4 to 5 hours on high heat or until the ribs are tender and cooked through.
Yield: 2 to 4 servings

Coach Jolene Hoover

Jolene Hoover and her family

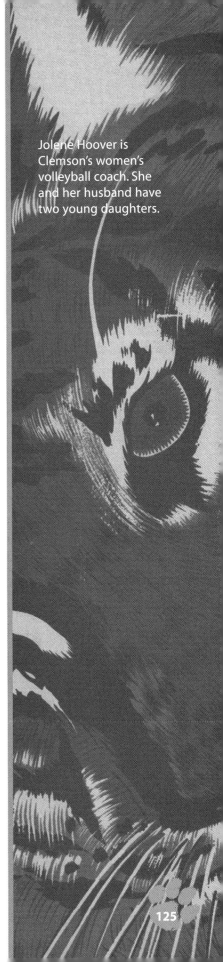

Jolene Hoover is Clemson's women's volleyball coach. She and her husband have two young daughters.

San Francisco Pork Chops

4 pork chops, cut ½ to ¾ inch thick
1 tablespoon vegetable oil
1 clove of garlic, minced
¼ cup dry sherry
¼ cup soy sauce
2 tablespoons brown sugar
2 teaspoons vegetable oil
¼ teaspoon crushed red pepper
2 teaspoons cornstarch
2 tablespoons water

Brown the pork chops in the 1 tablespoon oil in a skillet. Remove from the skillet. Add the garlic. Sauté for 1 minute; do not brown. Combine the sherry, soy sauce, brown sugar, 2 teaspoons oil and red pepper in a bowl. Return the pork chops to the skillet. Pour the sherry mixture over the pork chops. Simmer, tightly covered, over low heat for 20 minutes or until the pork chops are tender and cooked through. Add 1 to 2 tablespoons water to the skillet if the sauce cooks down too much. Remove the pork chops to a serving platter. Dissolve the cornstarch in the water. Stir into the sauce in the skillet. Cook until the sauce thickens. Pour over the pork chops. Serve over linguine. Note: The crushed red pepper intensifies during cooking. Reduce the amount if you prefer less heat. Yield: 4 servings

Emily Gilreath Leviner

John's No-Mess Pork Marinade

1 (16-ounce) bottle zesty Italian salad dressing
1 tablespoon dried minced onions
1 tablespoon paprika
1 teaspoon thyme
1 teaspoon oregano
½ teaspoon garlic powder

Combine the salad dressing, onions, paprika, thyme, oregano and garlic powder in a bowl. Refrigerate, in a sealed container, until ready to use. Place pork chops or other meats in a plastic food storage bag. Pour over enough marinade to coat the meat well. Seal the bag tightly. Refrigerate for 8 hours, turning occasionally. Remove the meat from the marinade, reserving the marinade. Pour the reserved marinade into a saucepan. Bring to a boil. Boil for 2 to 3 minutes. Reserve half the boiled marinade for a sauce. Grill the meat, basting occasionally with the remaining boiled marinade. Serve with the reserved sauce. Yield: 2 cups

John and Diane Walker

Diane and John Walker

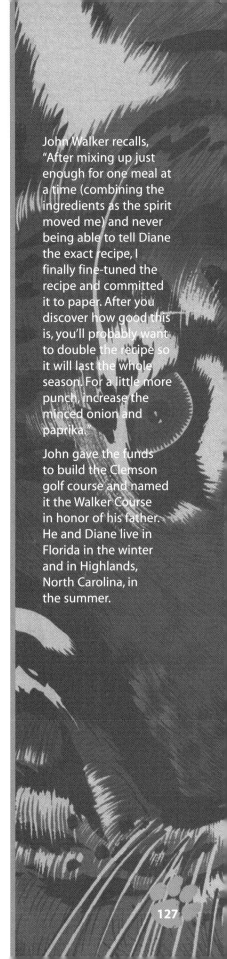

John Walker recalls, "After mixing up just enough for one meal at a time (combining the ingredients as the spirit moved me) and never being able to tell Diane the exact recipe, I finally fine-tuned the recipe and committed it to paper. After you discover how good this is, you'll probably want to double the recipe so it will last the whole season. For a little more punch, increase the minced onion and paprika."

John gave the funds to build the Clemson golf course and named it the Walker Course in honor of his father. He and Diane live in Florida in the winter and in Highlands, North Carolina, in the summer.

Roast Pork Loin with Red Plum Sauce

1 (5- to 8-pound) boneless pork loin, trimmed
Garlic salt to taste
Onion salt to taste
2 tablespoons butter
¾ cup chopped onion
1 cup red plum preserves
¾ cup water
½ cup packed brown sugar
⅓ cup chili sauce
¼ cup soy sauce
2 tablespoons lemon juice
2 teaspoons prepared mustard
3 drops Tabasco sauce (or to taste)

Season the pork with garlic salt and onion salt. Place the pork, fat side up, on a rack in a roasting pan. Pour a little water into the bottom of the pan. Bake at 325 degrees for 25 minutes per pound. Melt the butter in a saucepan. Add the onion. Sauté until tender. Add the plum preserves, water, brown sugar, chili sauce, soy sauce, lemon juice, mustard and Tabasco. Bring to a boil; reduce the heat. Simmer for 15 minutes. Pour off the drippings from the pork. Remove the rack. Pour half the plum sauce over the pork in the pan. Bake for 20 minutes or until the internal temperature reaches 160 degrees, basting often. Serve with the remaining plum sauce. Yield: 10 to 12 servings

Florence G. Geiger (Mrs. Martin Geiger)

Florence G. Geiger

Main Dishes

Buck Breazeale's Garden City Frogmore Stew

2 tablespoons Italian seasoning
1 cup pasta sauce
½ cup corn oil
1 large onion, chopped
1 large green bell pepper, chopped
3 ribs celery, chopped
Salt and pepper to taste
1 pound hot Polish sausage, cut into 1½-inch pieces
4 ears corn, husked and broken in half
1 pound shrimp, unpeeled

Tie up the Italian seasoning in a small piece of cheesecloth.
Combine the Italian seasoning, pasta sauce, oil, onion, green
pepper, celery, salt and pepper in a Dutch oven. Add enough
water to cover. Bring to a boil; reduce the heat. Simmer for
10 to 15 minutes. Add the sausage. Simmer for 10 minutes.
Add the corn. Simmer for 5 to 10 minutes. Add the shrimp.
Simmer for 2 to 3 minutes or just until pink. Remove from
the heat. Let stand, covered, for 2 minutes. Drain.
Yield: 4 to 6 servings

Buck and Ann Breazeale

Sausage Casserole

1½ pounds lean pork sausage
1 medium bunch celery with leaves, chopped
1 large green bell pepper, chopped
4 to 5 green onions with tops, chopped
Salt and pepper to taste
2 envelopes chicken noodle soup mix
4½ cups boiling water
1 cup brown rice
1 (8-ounce) can sliced water chestnuts, drained
¼ cup slivered almonds

Brown the sausage in a skillet, stirring until crumbly. Remove the sausage from the skillet; set aside. Drain off all but 2 to 3 tablespoons drippings from the skillet. Add the celery, green pepper and green onions. Sauté until tender. Season with salt and pepper. Cook the chicken noodle soup mix in the boiling water in a large saucepan for about 7 minutes. Stir in the brown rice and water chestnuts. Add the cooked sausage and vegetables. Pour into a greased 2-quart baking dish. Sprinkle with the almonds. Bake, covered, at 350 degrees for 1½ to 2 hours or until the rice is tender. Remove the cover during the 30 minutes of baking.
Yield: 8 to 10 servings

Mary M. Clanton (Mrs. Ray Clanton)

Main Dishes

Ruth's Casserole

8 ounces elbow macaroni
2 (15-ounce) cans tomatoes, drained
1 (6-ounce) can tomato paste
1/2 teaspoon sugar
1/4 teaspoon salt
Italian seasoning to taste
8 ounces smoked sausage or kielbasa, cut into thin rounds
12 ounces shredded Cheddar cheese

Cook the macaroni according to the package directions; drain. Purée the tomatoes, tomato paste, sugar, salt and Italian seasoning in a blender or food processor until smooth. Layer half the macaroni, kielbasa, tomato mixture and cheese in a greased 2-quart baking dish. Repeat the layers. Bake at 350 degrees for 45 minutes or until bubbly. Yield: 6 servings

Holley Hewitt Ulbrich (Mrs. Carl Ulbrich)

Kielbasa Casserole

8 ounces macaroni
1 1/2 cups milk
2 eggs
1 onion, chopped
1 green bell pepper, chopped
1 pound kielbasa, cut into small chunks
1 cup shredded sharp Cheddar cheese
Salt and pepper to taste

Cook the macaroni according to the package directions; drain. Combine the milk and eggs in a bowl. Layer half the macaroni, onion, green pepper, kielbasa, milk mixture, cheese, salt and pepper in a greased 1 1/2-quart baking dish. Repeat the layers. Bake at 350 degrees for 30 to 40 minutes or until light brown. Yield: 6 servings

Shirley P. Byers

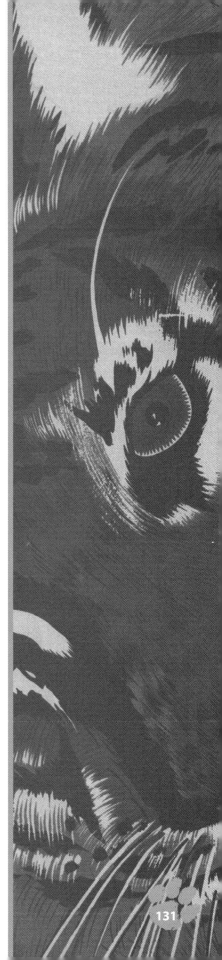

Main Dishes

Crab Cakes

1 egg
1½ teaspoons chopped parsley
1½ teaspoons mayonnaise
½ teaspoon each Worcestershire sauce and crab seasoning
¼ teaspoon dry mustard
⅛ teaspoon hot pepper sauce
¼ cup diced onion
¼ cup each diced green and yellow bell pepper
1 pound lump crab meat, flaked
2 cups fresh unseasoned bread crumbs
2 tablespoons olive oil

Mix the egg, parsley, mayonnaise, Worcestershire sauce, crab seasoning, dry mustard and pepper sauce in a bowl. Stir in the onion, green pepper, yellow pepper and crab meat. Shape ⅓ cup at a time into cakes. Coat the crab cakes with bread crumbs. Heat the oil in a 12-inch skillet. Add the crab cakes. Fry until golden brown on both sides. (If the crab cakes are too moist, add more bread crumbs.) Garnish with lemon wedges. Serve with dirty rice and a green salad. Yield: 4 to 6 servings

Dwight Rainey
Senior Associate Athletic Director

Crab Spaghetti

1 cup half-and-half
1 pound Velveeta cheese
1 cup butter
8 ounces fresh mushrooms, sliced
12 ounces vermicelli, cooked, drained
1 bunch green onions, chopped
1 (2-ounce) jar pimentos, drained
White pepper to taste
1 pound fresh or thawed frozen crab meat

Cook the half-and-half, Velveeta and ½ cup butter in a saucepan over low heat until the cheese and butter are melted, stirring occasionally. Melt the remaining ½ cup butter in a skillet. Add the mushrooms. Cook, covered, over low heat for 10 minutes or until tender. Mix the vermicelli, cheese sauce, mushrooms, green onions, pimentos and white pepper in a bowl. Fold in the crab meat. Pour into a greased 2½-quart baking dish. Bake at 350 degrees for 30 minutes or until bubbly. Yield: 8 to 10 servings

Grady Brasington

Main Dishes

Shrimp Creole

2 medium onions, chopped
1 green bell pepper, chopped
½ cup minced celery
¼ cup bacon drippings
1 (28-ounce) can tomatoes
3 tablespoon catsup
1 tablespoon Worcestershire sauce
1 teaspoon sugar
2 tablespoons flour
2 tablespoons water
3 cups shrimp, peeled and deveined
1 teaspoon salt
½ teaspoon pepper

Sauté the onions, green pepper and celery in the bacon drippings in a skillet until tender. Add the undrained tomatoes, catsup, Worcestershire sauce and sugar. Combine the flour and water in a bowl. Stir into the skillet. Bring to a boil; reduce the heat. Simmer for 20 minutes or until smooth and slightly thickened, stirring frequently. Add the shrimp, salt and pepper. Cook for 10 minutes. Serve over hot rice. Yield: 6 servings

Mrs. Frank Barnes

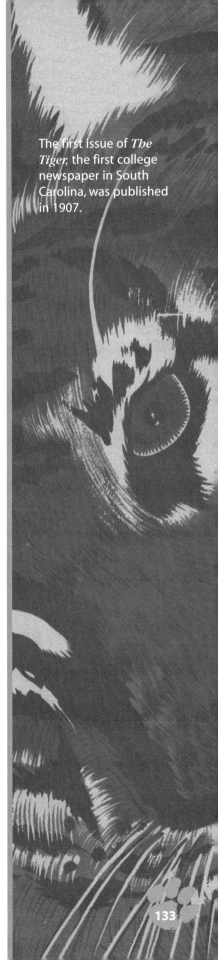

The first issue of *The Tiger*, the first college newspaper in South Carolina, was published in 1907.

Celeste Prince relates, "The Japanese Consul-General was visiting Clemson, and Phil wanted to entertain him for lunch in the President's Home. Mot Dalton and I planned a typical Southern menu—fried chicken, biscuits, potato salad, etc. Phil said, 'No, I want to have fried shrimp and grits.' With raised eyebrows we replanned according to his wishes. The lunch was a huge success. I ate in the kitchen, as it was an all-male group, and when James Greer cleared the table and brought the dishes into the kitchen, they were all wiped clean. Phil said the Consul-General's remark was, 'My compliments to the chef!'"

Pawley's Island Fried Shrimp

1½ pounds shrimp, unpeeled
8 slices bacon
1 cup chopped onion
Salt and pepper to taste

Boil the shrimp for 3 minutes or until pink; drain. Peel and devein the shrimp when they are cool enough to handle. Cook the bacon in a skillet until crisp. Remove the bacon leaving the drippings in the skillet; drain. Add the shrimp, onion, salt and pepper to the bacon drippings. Cook for 15 minutes, stirring frequently. Crumble the bacon over the shrimp. Serve with hot grits and butter.
Yield: 2 generous servings

Celeste O. Prince (Mrs. Phil H. Prince)

Phil Prince

Main Dishes

Dockside Spicy Shrimp and Grits

1/2 cup butter
1/4 cup crumbled blue cheese
1 tablespoon chopped shallot
1/2 tablespoon chopped garlic
Pepper to taste
8 slices French bread
10 cups water
1/2 cup butter
1 tablespoon chopped garlic
Salt and pepper to taste
2 cups stone-ground white grits
2 cups milk
1/2 cup butter
1/2 cup sliced tasso, cut into 1-inch strips
1/2 cup sliced smoked sausage
2 pounds shrimp, peeled and deveined
1/4 cup flour
4 cups chicken broth
1 bunch green onions, chopped
1 tomato, chopped
1/4 cup chopped fresh parsley

Place 1/2 cup butter, blue cheese, shallot, 1/2 tablespoon garlic and pepper in a saucepan. Cook over low heat until the butter and cheese are melted, stirring occasionally. Cool completely. Spread the cheese mixture on the bread slices. Place on a baking sheet. Bake at 375 degrees for 10 minutes or until lightly browned; set aside. Combine the water, 1/2 cup butter, 1 tablespoon garlic, salt and pepper in a saucepan. Bring to a boil. Stir in the grits. Cook over medium-high heat until thick, stirring occasionally. Stir in the milk. Reduce the heat to medium low. Cook for 10 minutes; set aside. (If using stone-ground yellow grits, cook for 45 minutes, adding more water if the grits become too thick.) Melt 1/2 cup butter in a large sauté pan. Add the tasso and smoked sausage. Sauté until browned. Add the shrimp. Sauté until the shrimp turn light pink. Stir in the flour. Cook until the flour is absorbed. Add the chicken broth, green onions, tomato and parsley. Stir until well blended. Season with salt and pepper. Serve the shrimp mixture over the grits. Place 1 blue cheese crouton on each plate. Yield: 8 servings

David and Deborah Owens
Dockside Restaurant, Murrell's Inlet, South Carolina

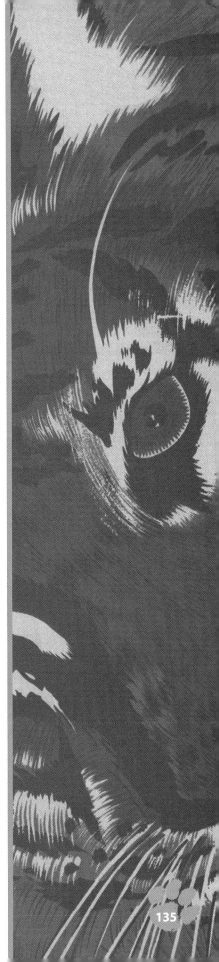

Shrimp in Sour Cream and Wine Sauce

    ½ cup margarine or butter
    2 pounds shrimp, peeled and deveined
    2 (4-ounce) cans mushrooms
    1 pint sour cream
    1 cup self-rising flour
    6 to 8 tablespoons sherry
    Salt and pepper to taste
    Toast points

Melt the margarine in a large skillet. Add the shrimp. Cook and stir until the shrimp turn pink. Add the undrained mushrooms. Bring to a boil. Remove from the heat. Stir in the sour cream. Add enough water to the flour to make a thin paste. Stir into the shrimp mixture. Simmer until thickened. Stir in the sherry, salt and pepper. Serve over toast points. Yield: 8 servings

Doris Belser

Cajun Shrimp and Peppers Pasta

    1 tablespoon vegetable oil
    2 small green or yellow bell peppers, cut into strips
    1 cup sliced mushrooms
    1 teaspoon basil, crushed
    ¼ teaspoon garlic powder or 2 cloves of garlic, minced
    3 Roma tomatoes, seeded and diced
    1 pound medium shrimp, peeled and deveined
    Hot pepper sauce to taste
    3¼ cups cooked penne or mostaccioli
    2 tablespoons grated Parmesan cheese

Heat the oil in a skillet over medium heat. Add the bell peppers, mushrooms, basil and garlic powder. Cook until the peppers are tender-crisp. Stir in the tomatoes, shrimp and pepper sauce. Bring to a boil; reduce the heat to low. Cook for 5 minutes or until the shrimp turn pink. Serve over the pasta. Sprinkle with Parmesan cheese. Yield: 4 servings

Tottie Marchbanks (Mrs. Claude Marchbanks)

Main Dishes

Captain Jervey's Southern Shrimp Pie

2 pounds shrimp, unpeeled
4 slices white bread
1 1/2 cups white wine
1/8 teaspoon salt
1/8 teaspoon mace
1/8 teaspoon nutmeg
1/8 teaspoon cayenne (or to taste)

Place the shrimp in boiling salted water for no more than 3 minutes; drain. Process the bread in a blender or food processor to form coarse crumbs. Place the crumbs in a bowl. Pour the wine over to soak the crumbs. Peel and devein the shrimp. Add to the bread crumb mixture. Stir in the salt, mace, nutmeg and cayenne. Spoon the shrimp mixture into a buttered 9-inch pie plate or baking dish. Bake at 400 degrees for 50 minutes. Yield: 6 servings

Mary Jervey Kilby (Mrs. Ed Kilby)

Captain Jervey's Red Sauce

5 large cans tomatoes
2 pounds onions, chopped
30 cayenne peppers
1 tablespoon salt
2 quarts cider vinegar

Combine the tomatoes, onions, peppers and salt in a large stockpot. Simmer for 2 hours. Add the vinegar. Bring to a boil. Let cool. Purée the mixture in a blender or food processor. Store in jars. Sauce does not have to be refrigerated. Yield: 6 to 8 quarts

Mary Jervey Kilby
(Mrs. Ed Kilby)

Captain Frank Jervey

According to his daughter, Mary Jervey Kilby, Captain Jervey ate grits for breakfast every day of his life. Being raised in Charleston, he preferred adding shrimp and red sauce to his grits and continued to enjoy this combination during his Clemson years anytime shrimp was available!

Jervey Athletic Center is named for him.

This family recipe from Greece's "Low Country" has been prepared in the Curris household for at least four generations. It was adapted to American cuisine by the mother of Clemson University President Constantine W. Curris.

Mary Curris' Shrimp Pilaf

1½ pounds medium shrimp, unpeeled
3 cups water
2 teaspoons Old Bay seasoning (optional)
⅔ cup finely chopped onion
4 to 6 tablespoons olive oil
1½ cups long grain rice
3 tablespoons chopped dill
3 tablespoons chopped fresh parsley
1 (14-ounce) can diced tomatoes
Salt and pepper to taste

Peel and devein the shrimp, reserving the shells; set the shrimp aside. Bring the water to a boil in a saucepan. Add the shrimp shells and Old Bay seasoning. Reduce the heat. Simmer for 10 minutes. Strain the broth, discarding the shells. Return the broth to the saucepan and keep hot. Sauté the onion in the oil in a skillet until tender. Add the rice. Sauté until golden. Combine the dill and parsley in a bowl. Add half the herb mixture, the undrained tomatoes and shrimp broth to the skillet. Stir once. Simmer, covered, for 13 minutes. Add the shrimp and remaining herb mixture. Simmer, covered, for 7 minutes. Season with salt and pepper. Serve hot or warm. Yield: 4 to 6 servings

Mary Curris, mother of President Constantine Curris

Dr. Curris at the "Welcome Back" social, downtown Clemson, fall 1997

Main Dishes

Low Country Shrimp, Corn and Sausage

2 (12-ounce) cans beer
5 pounds shrimp, unpeeled
20 ears corn, husked
3 pounds Polish sausage, cut into 1½-inch pieces

Fill a Dutch oven or stockpot three quarters full of water. Stir in the beer. Add the unpeeled shrimp, corn and sausage. Bring to a boil. Do not stir. Cook until the shrimp rise to the surface and turn pink. Drain off the liquid and empty the pan onto a newspaper-covered table. Let everyone serve themselves. Provide containers to discard the shrimp shells. Serve with your favorite shrimp sauce for dipping. After eating, simply fold up the newspaper and discard. Yield: 10 servings

Tom (Sarge) and Jane Burton

Saucy Seafood Casserole

1 onion, chopped
1 green bell pepper, chopped
1 (8-ounce) can mushrooms, drained
6 to 8 tablespoons butter or margarine
½ cup butter or margarine
6 to 8 tablespoons flour
2 cups milk
2 teaspoons lemon juice (or to taste)
1 teaspoon Worcestershire sauce (or to taste)
1 teaspoon Tabasco sauce (or to taste)
¼ teaspoon garlic powder (or to taste)
Salt to taste
1 pound crab meat
2 pounds cooked peeled shrimp, deveined
½ cup bread crumbs, toasted

Sauté the onion, green pepper and mushrooms in 6 to 8 tablespoons butter in a skillet until tender. Melt ½ cup butter in a large saucepan over medium heat. Stir in the flour until smooth. Cook and stir for 1 minute. Stir in the milk gradually. Cook until the mixture simmers and thickens, stirring constantly. Season with lemon juice, Worcestershire sauce, Tabasco, garlic powder and salt. Stir in the crab meat, shrimp and onion mixture. Pour into a greased 2-quart baking dish. Bake, covered, at 350 degrees for 45 minutes. Top with the bread crumbs. Bake, uncovered, for 2 to 3 minutes or until golden. Yield: 6 to 8 servings

Joan S. Kennerty (Mrs. Bill Kennerty)

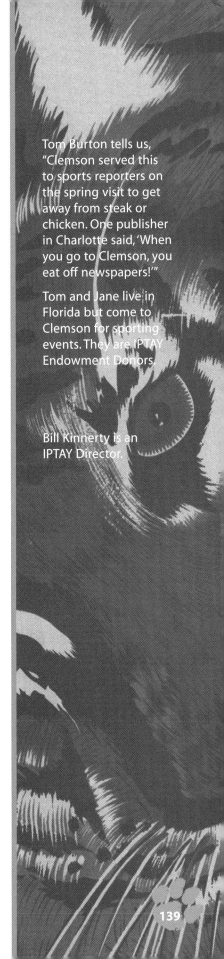

Tom Burton tells us, "Clemson served this to sports reporters on the spring visit to get away from steak or chicken. One publisher in Charlotte said, 'When you go to Clemson, you eat off newspapers!'"

Tom and Jane live in Florida but come to Clemson for sporting events. They are IPTAY Endowment Donors.

Bill Kinnerty is an IPTAY Director.

Tracey Leone is head coach of Clemson's women's soccer team, and Ray is assistant head coach. This recipe came from Ray's mom, Linda Leone.

Heavenly Fillet

Lemon juice
1/2 cup grated Parmesan cheese
1/4 cup margarine, softened
3 tablespoons mayonnaise
3 tablespoons chopped green onions
2 tablespoons lemon juice
1/4 teaspoon salt
Dash of hot pepper sauce
2 pounds fresh fish fillets

Brush a greased broiler-proof baking dish with a small amount of lemon juice. Let stand for 10 minutes. Combine the Parmesan cheese, margarine, mayonnaise, green onions, 2 tablespoons lemon juice, salt and pepper sauce in a bowl; set aside. Arrange the fish fillets in the prepared baking dish. Broil 4 inches from the heat source for 6 to 8 minutes. Remove from the oven. Spread the cheese mixture evenly over the fillets. Broil for 2 to 3 minutes or until lightly browned and the fish is cooked through. Yield: 8 servings

Coaches Ray and Tracey Leone

Chuck Kriese's Salmon-Arama

1 pound salmon fillets
1 small Vidalia onion, sliced
1 cup sliced mushrooms
2 cloves of garlic, chopped
2 tablespoons butter or olive oil
Salt and pepper to taste
½ cup red wine

Arrange the salmon fillets on a large piece of heavy-duty foil. Top with the onion, mushrooms and garlic. Place a pat of butter on each fillet. Season with salt and pepper. Pour the wine over the top. Wrap the foil tightly around the fish to seal. Bake at 350 degrees (or grill over medium-hot coals) for 25 minutes or until the fish is cooked through. Note: Adjust the amounts of onion, mushrooms and garlic to taste. Yield: 4 servings

Coach Chuck Kriese

Chuck Kriese

Chuck Kriese says, "This is the only meal I can cook that's not out of a can!"

Chuck is the Clemson men's tennis coach.

Baked Flounder

2 fresh flounder fillets
Salt to taste
1 teaspoon lemon juice
1 tablespoon dry vermouth
½ cup sour cream
1 teaspoon drained capers
2 tablespoons grated Parmesan cheese
Paprika
Minced fresh parsley

Place the flounder fillets in a greased 9x13-inch baking dish. Season with salt. Top the fillets with the lemon juice, vermouth, sour cream, capers and Parmesan cheese. Bake at 350 degrees for 20 to 25 minutes or until the fish is cooked through. Sprinkle with paprika and parsley. Serve immediately. Yield: 2 servings

Julia Holcombe (Mrs. John Holcombe)

IPTAY Directors' wives working on the cookbook

Main Dishes

Crab and Shrimp Casserole

½ medium onion, chopped
1 cup diced celery
¼ cup margarine
3 tablespoons flour
1 cup milk
¼ cup sherry
1 cup shredded American cheese
1 pound shrimp, cooked and peeled
1 pound crab meat
2 tablespoons chopped fresh parsley
½ cup bread crumbs
¼ cup shredded American cheese

Sauté the onion and celery in the margarine in a skillet until tender.
Stir in the flour. Add the milk and sherry gradually, stirring constantly.
Cook and stir until thickened. Stir in the 1 cup cheese, shrimp, crab
meat and parsley. Pour into a greased 2-quart baking dish. Sprinkle
with the bread crumbs and ¼ cup cheese. Bake at 450 degrees for
20 to 30 minutes or until bubbly. Yield: 6 to 8 servings

Joan S. Kennerty (Mrs. Bill Kennerty)

Bill and Joan Kennerty

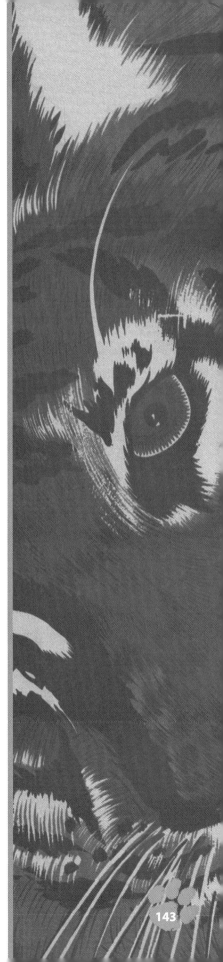

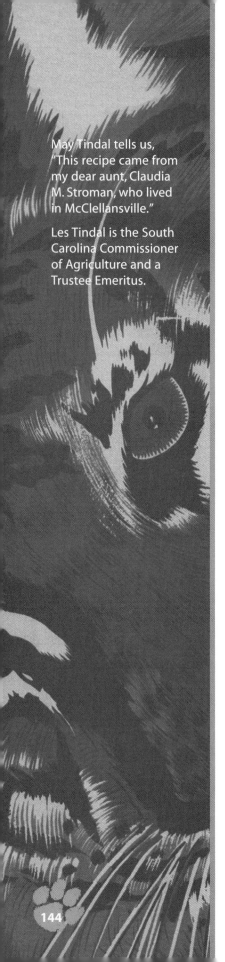

Seafood Casserole

1½ pounds shrimp, peeled and deveined
1 pound crab meat or 2 (6-ounce) cans crab meat, drained
1 cup mayonnaise
1 cup half-and-half
1 cup cooked rice
1 cup chopped celery
½ cup chopped onion
½ cup chopped green bell pepper
1 (4-ounce) can mushrooms, drained
1 tablespoon margarine
Salt and pepper to taste
½ cup bread crumbs

Combine the shrimp, crab meat, mayonnaise, half-and-half, rice, celery, onion, green pepper, mushrooms, margarine, salt and pepper in a bowl. Pour into a greased 7x11-inch baking dish. Sprinkle with the bread crumbs. Bake at 350 degrees for 30 minutes or until bubbly and seafood is cooked through. Yield: 8 servings

May Tindal (Mrs. Les Tindal)

May and Les Tindal

Special Seafood Casseroles

2 pounds shrimp, peeled and deveined
1 pound scallops
2 (1-ounce) packages lemon-dill sauce mix
¾ cup chopped onion
¾ cup chopped celery
2 (6-ounce) cans crab meat, drained
¾ cup grated Parmesan cheese
½ cup shredded Colby and Monterey Jack cheese blend
2 tablespoons mayonnaise
2 tablespoons sherry
1 teaspoon Mrs. Dash seasoning
½ teaspoon pepper

Sauté the shrimp and scallops in a nonstick skillet for 3 minutes or until partially cooked. Pour the juices from the pan into a measuring cup. Prepare the lemon-dill sauce mix according to the package directions using the reserved seafood juices as part of the liquid; set aside. Sauté the onion and celery in a skillet until tender. Combine the onion mixture, shrimp, scallops, crab meat, Parmesan cheese, Colby and Monterey Jack cheese blend, mayonnaise, sherry, Mrs. Dash seasoning and pepper in a bowl. Pour the lemon-dill sauce over and mix well. Divide the seafood mixture between 8 greased individual baking dishes. Bake at 350 degrees for 35 minutes or until bubbly. Note: Half-and-half can be substituted for the milk in the lemon-dill sauce mix. Yield: 8 servings

Kay Dimmock (Mrs. Charles Dimmock)

Easy Cheese Lasagna

1 (15-ounce) can tomato sauce
1 (14-ounce) jar spaghetti sauce
16 ounces cottage cheese
½ cup grated Parmesan cheese
9 uncooked lasagna noodles
8 ounces shredded reduced-fat mozzarella cheese

Combine the tomato sauce and spaghetti sauce in a small bowl; set aside. Combine the cottage cheese and Parmesan cheese in a bowl; set aside. Arrange 3 lasagna noodles in a buttered 9x13-inch baking pan. Top with one third the sauce mixture, cottage cheese mixture and mozzarella cheese. Repeat the layers of noodles, sauce, cottage cheese mixture and mozzarella 2 more times. Cover the pan tightly with foil. Bake at 350 degrees for 1 hour or until heated through and noodles are tender. Let stand for 15 minutes before serving. Yield: 6 servings

Cindy Grandy (Mrs. B.R. Grandy)

Hunter's Quail

8 (4- to 6-ounce) quail
Salt and pepper to taste
Flour
⅓ cup vegetable oil
¼ cup flour
Salt and pepper to taste
Butter to taste

Season the quail with salt and pepper and dredge in flour to coat. Heat the oil in a Dutch oven until hot. Brown the quail in the hot oil quickly, turning to brown all sides. Remove from the pan; drain. Pour off all but 3 tablespoons drippings. Stir in ¼ cup flour until smooth. Cook and stir until the flour browns. Add enough water to make a thick gravy. Season the gravy with salt, pepper and butter. Return the quail to the pan. Cook, covered, over low heat for 1 to 1½ hours or until tender and cooked through. Add water to the pan as needed to maintain about 1 inch of gravy. Baste frequently during cooking.
Yield: 4 servings

Margaret Reaves (Mrs. Bill Reaves), sister of Jack Lunn

Pictured in their Clemson barracks are John Napier, Bennettsville, and brothers Ed and Will Lunn, Florence. All are Class of '08. Ed is the father of Jack Lunn, '52, and the father-in-law of Bill Reaves, '50. For years it was a fall tradition for Will Lunn to bring co-workers from Washington, D.C., to Ed Lunn's Florence County farm for quail hunting and Clemson football games. The recipe on this page is the one they always used.

Main Dishes

Pheasant Pie

1 (2- to 3-pound) pheasant
1 medium onion, cut up
2 ribs celery with leaves, cut up
Salt and pepper to taste
1 medium onion, diced
2 ribs celery, diced
7 mushrooms, sliced
2 tablespoons butter
¼ cup butter
3 tablespoons flour
1 teaspoon Worcestershire sauce
2 drops yellow food coloring
1 refrigerated piecrust

Place the pheasant in a Dutch oven. Add the cut-up onion, cut-up celery, salt, pepper and enough water to cover. Bring to a boil; reduce the heat. Simmer until the pheasant is cooked through. Remove the pheasant from the broth; let cool. Remove the meat and dice. Strain the broth and reserve 3 cups. Sauté the diced onion, diced celery and mushrooms in 2 tablespoons butter in a skillet until tender. Do not brown; remove and set aside. Melt ¼ cup butter in the same skillet. Stir in the flour until smooth. Add the reserved pheasant broth gradually, stirring constantly. Cook and stir until thickened. Stir in the Worcestershire sauce and food coloring. Add the cooked onion mixture. Place the diced pheasant meat in a greased 1½-quart baking dish. Pour in the sauce mixture. Top with the piecrust, pinching to seal against the dish. Cut a few slits in the top of the crust. Bake at 450 degrees for 30 minutes or until the crust is golden brown. Yield: 4 servings

Libby McLeod (Mrs. Ben McLeod)

Former baseball coach Bill Wilhelm and Endowment Donor and Baltimore Oriole pitcher Jimmy Key enjoy an evening with IPTAY members Libby and Ben McLeod of Baltimore.

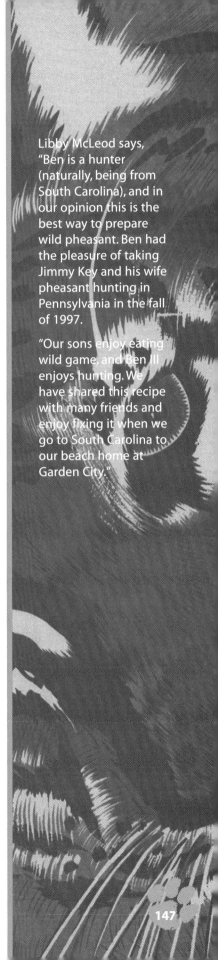

Libby McLeod says, "Ben is a hunter (naturally, being from South Carolina), and in our opinion this is the best way to prepare wild pheasant. Ben had the pleasure of taking Jimmy Key and his wife pheasant hunting in Pennsylvania in the fall of 1997.

"Our sons enjoy eating wild game, and Ben III enjoys hunting. We have shared this recipe with many friends and enjoy fixing it when we go to South Carolina to our beach home at Garden City."

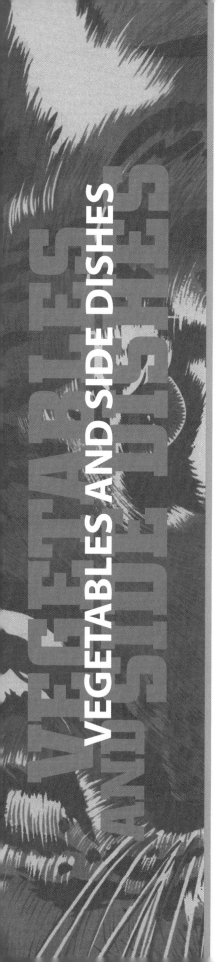

Vegetables and Side Dishes

The football stadium's lighted Tiger Paw is a beacon for Clemson fans.

SIDELINES

Asparagus Casserole

2 eggs, lightly beaten
½ cup mayonnaise
1 (10-ounce) can cream of mushroom soup
2 (10-ounce) cans cut asparagus, well drained
1 cup shredded mild Cheddar cheese

Combine the eggs and mayonnaise in a bowl. Stir in the mushroom soup. Add the asparagus and cheese; mix lightly. Spoon into a 1½-quart casserole. Bake at 350 degrees for 30 to 40 minutes or until set. Yield: 6 servings

Cindy Stallings

Asparagus Soufflé

4 eggs, well beaten
1 cup mayonnaise
1 (10-ounce) can cream of mushroom soup
1 (10-ounce) can cut asparagus spears, drained, mashed
1 cup shredded sharp Cheddar cheese

Combine the eggs and mayonnaise in a bowl. Stir in the mushroom soup. Add the asparagus spears and cheese; mix lightly. Spoon into a 1½-quart casserole; place the casserole in a larger pan filled with water. Bake at 325 degrees for 1 hour or until set. Yield: 8 servings

Ann Christenberry (Mrs. Robert Christenberry)

Broccoli and Clemson Bleu Cheese

2 (10-ounce) packages frozen chopped broccoli
1/8 teaspoon salt, or to taste
1/4 teaspoon lemon juice
8 ounces cream cheese
4 to 5 ounces Clemson bleu cheese
1 1/4 cups milk
1/2 cup fresh bread crumbs

Cook the broccoli according to the package directions; drain. Finely chop the broccoli. Place in a bowl. Add the salt and lemon juice; mix lightly. Combine the cream cheese, bleu cheese and milk in a saucepan. Cook until the bleu cheese is melted and the sauce is thickened, stirring constantly. Add the broccoli mixture; mix well. Spoon into a well-greased 1 1/2-quart casserole. Sprinkle with the bread crumbs. Bake at 350 degrees for 30 minutes. Note: Recipe can be assembled and refrigerated overnight. Yield: 6 to 8 servings

Vangie Holmes Rainsford

At Clemson College's first commencement, 14 students received agricultural degrees and 18 received mechanical degrees.

This is Cam's favorite food. He learned to cook it when he was a toddler and he still cooks it often.

Broccoli Casserole

1 (10-ounce) package frozen chopped broccoli
1 egg, beaten
½ (10-ounce) can cream of mushroom soup
½ cup mayonnaise
1 cup shredded sharp Cheddar cheese
1 teaspoon minced onion
Salt and pepper to taste
½ cup herb-seasoned stuffing mix
¼ cup melted butter

Cook the broccoli according to the package directions; drain. Combine the egg, mushroom soup, mayonnaise, cheese and onion in a bowl. Add the broccoli; mix well. Season with the salt and pepper to taste. Spoon into a 1½-quart casserole. Bake at 350 degrees for 30 minutes. Top with the stuffing mix. Drizzle with the butter. Bake for 10 minutes or until hot and bubbly.
Yield: 4 to 6 servings

Cam Golightly

Cam Golightly with South Carolina Governor David Beasley

Carrot Ring

2 tablespoons margarine
1/4 cup flour
3/4 cup milk
4 egg yolks
2 cups mashed cooked carrots
1 cup fresh bread crumbs
1 teaspoon salt
Pepper to taste
Onion juice to taste
4 egg whites

Melt the margarine in the top of a double boiler. Stir in the flour. Add the milk and egg yolks; cook until thickened. Add the carrots, bread crumbs and salt. Season with pepper and onion juice. Beat the egg whites in a mixer bowl until stiff peaks form. Fold into the carrot mixture. Spoon into a well-greased 6-cup ring mold. Bake at 350 degrees for 30 minutes. Note: Peeled squash can be substituted for the carrots. Yield: 6 to 8 servings

Retta C. Hughes (Mrs. Forest Hughes)

Copper Carrots

2 pounds carrots, sliced
1 (10-ounce) can tomato soup
1/2 cup vegetable oil
3/4 cup vinegar
1/2 cup sugar
1 teaspoon prepared mustard
1 teaspoon Worcestershire sauce
Salt to taste
Pepper to taste
1 green bell pepper, sliced
1 or 2 medium onions, sliced

Cook the carrots in water to cover in a saucepan until tender; drain. Combine the tomato soup, vegetable oil, vinegar, sugar, mustard and Worcestershire sauce in a bowl. Season with salt and pepper. Add the carrots, green pepper and onions; mix lightly. Refrigerate, covered, for several hours or overnight. Note: Two 14-ounce cans drained carrot slices can be substituted for the cooked fresh carrots. Yield: 8 servings

Frankie Meenaghan (Mrs. George Meenaghan)

Forest Hughes is an IPTAY Director.

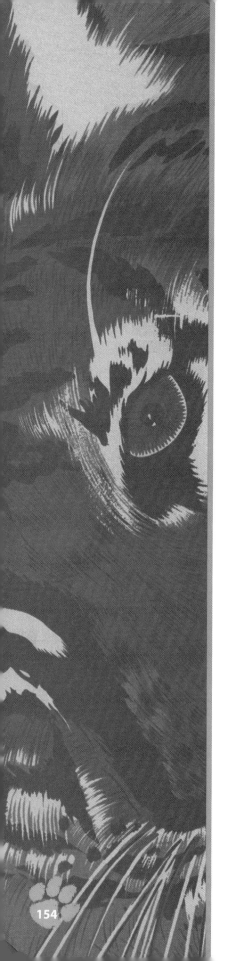

"Guess What" Carrots

    1 pound carrots, sliced
    1/2 cup margarine, melted
    3 eggs
    1 cup sugar
    1/4 cup flour
    1 teaspoon baking powder
    1 1/2 teaspoons vanilla extract

Cook the carrots in water to cover in a saucepan until tender; drain. Place the carrots and the margarine in a blender container; blend until smooth. Add the eggs, sugar, flour, baking powder and vanilla; blend well. Pour into a greased 1-quart casserole. Bake at 350 degrees for 45 minutes or until set. Yield: 8 servings

Eva Holmes (Mrs. Lewis F. Holmes)

Oregano Peas

    1 (10-ounce) package frozen peas
    1/4 cup butter
    1/4 pound fresh mushrooms, sliced
    1 tablespoon minced onion
    1/2 teaspoon salt
    1/2 teaspoon oregano
    1/4 teaspoon seasoned salt

Cook the peas in the butter in a saucepan until tender, stirring frequently. Add the mushrooms, onion, salt, oregano and seasoned salt. Cook until the mushrooms are tender and the mixture is heated through, stirring occasionally. Yield: 4 servings

Ava P. Campbell (Mrs. Lynn Campbell)

Vegetables and Side Dishes

Corn Pudding

1/2 cup margarine
3 cups whole-kernel corn (fresh, frozen or canned), drained
1 1/2 cups milk
3 eggs, lightly beaten
3/4 cup sugar

Melt the margarine in a saucepan. Add the corn, milk, eggs and sugar; mix well. Spoon into a 1 1/2-quart casserole. Bake at 425 degrees for 45 minutes or until the center is set; do not overbake.
Yield: 6 to 8 servings

Joyce M. Bussey (Mrs. Charlie Bussey)

Joyce and Charlie Bussey with their grandchildren

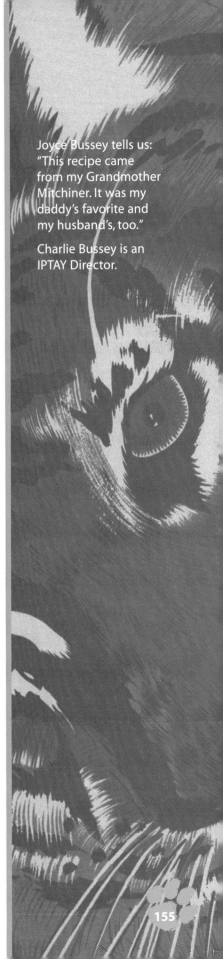

Joyce Bussey tells us: "This recipe came from my Grandmother Mitchiner. It was my daddy's favorite and my husband's, too."

Charlie Bussey is an IPTAY Director.

Vegetables and Side Dishes

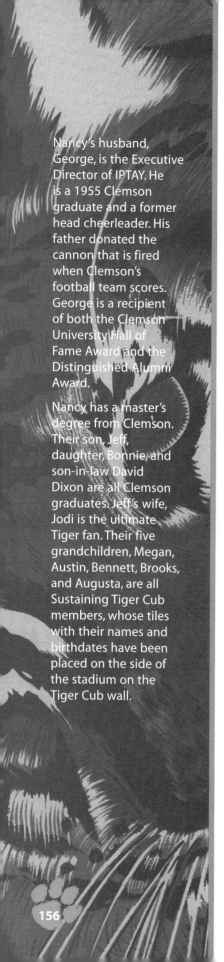

Nancy's husband, George, is the Executive Director of IPTAY. He is a 1955 Clemson graduate and a former head cheerleader. His father donated the cannon that is fired when Clemson's football team scores. George is a recipient of both the Clemson University Hall of Fame Award and the Distinguished Alumni Award.

Nancy has a master's degree from Clemson. Their son, Jeff, daughter, Bonnie, and son-in-law David Dixon are all Clemson graduates. Jeff's wife, Jodi is the ultimate Tiger fan. Their five grandchildren, Megan, Austin, Bennett, Brooks, and Augusta, are all Sustaining Tiger Cub members, whose tiles with their names and birthdates have been placed on the side of the stadium on the Tiger Cub wall.

Tiger Deluxe Hash Browns

1 (32-ounce) bag frozen hash brown potatoes, thawed
1 (10-ounce) can cream of celery soup
1 (10-ounce) can cream of potato soup
1 cup sour cream
3 tablespoons chopped green bell pepper
2 tablespoons chopped onions
1 teaspoon salt
¼ teaspoon pepper
Paprika to taste

Combine the potatoes, celery soup, potato soup, sour cream, green pepper, onion, salt and pepper in a bowl; mix well. Spoon into a greased 9x13-inch baking dish. Sprinkle with paprika. Bake at 300 degrees for 1½ hours. Yield: 10 servings

Nancy M. Bennett (Mrs. George Bennett)

Nancy and George Bennett rubbing Howard's Rock for good luck

Spinach Casserole

2 cups sour cream
1 (10-ounce) can cream of mushroom soup
3 tablespoons grated Parmesan cheese
$1/2$ teaspoon salt
$1/2$ teaspoon pepper
2 (10-ounce) packages frozen chopped spinach, thawed and well drained
1 (6-ounce) package medium egg noodles, cooked
8 ounces Swiss cheese
1 cup sour cream
$1/8$ teaspoon paprika

Combine 2 cups sour cream with the mushroom soup, Parmesan cheese, salt and pepper in a bowl. Squeeze the spinach dry. Add to the sour cream mixture; mix well. Add the noodles; toss lightly until well coated with the spinach mixture. Layer $1/2$ of the spinach mixture in a greased 9x12-inch baking dish; cover with $1/2$ of the Swiss cheese. Repeat the layers. Top with the remaining 1 cup sour cream. Sprinkle with the paprika. Bake at 350 degrees for 1 hour. Note: Recipe can be assembled and refrigerated overnight. Yield: 12 servings

Coach Nancy Ann Harris

Nancy Harris

Nancy Harris relates, "This recipe came from my great-aunt, Jake Durbin, who lives in Laurel, Maryland."

Nancy is the Clemson women's tennis coach.

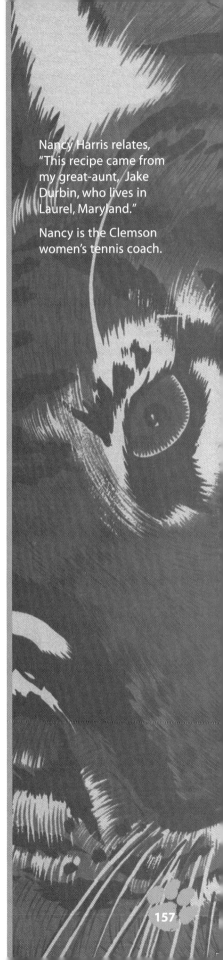

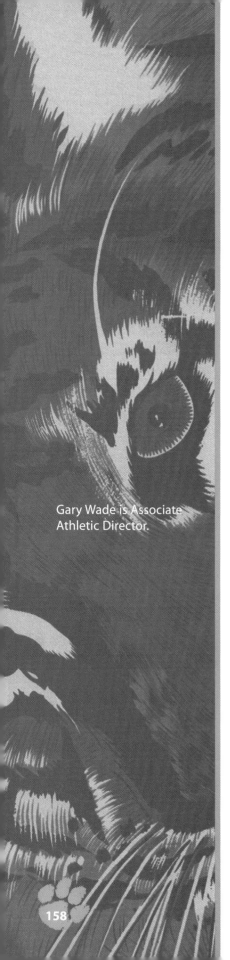

Gary Wade is Associate
Athletic Director.

Squash Soufflé

2 pounds yellow summer squash
2 large onions, sliced
¼ cup butter
1 teaspoon salt
¼ teaspoon pepper
2 eggs, lightly beaten
¾ cup whipping cream or evaporated milk
1 cup herb-seasoned stuffing mix
½ cup crushed potato chips

Scrub the squash; cut into 1-inch-thick slices. Cook the squash and onions in a small amount of water in a saucepan until tender; drain. Add the butter, salt and pepper. Add the eggs, whipping cream and stuffing mix; beat until smooth. Spoon into a 2-quart casserole; top with the potato chips. Bake at 350 degrees for 20 to 25 minutes or until set. Yield: 8 servings

Clyde M. Park (Mrs. Eugene Park)

Summer Squash Casserole

2 pounds yellow summer squash or zucchini, sliced (about 6 cups)
¼ cup chopped onion
Salt to taste
1 (10-ounce) can cream of chicken soup
1 cup sour cream
1 cup shredded carrots
2 cups seasoned stuffing mix
1 cup melted butter or margarine

Cook the squash and onion in boiling salted water in a saucepan for 5 minutes; drain. Combine the soup and sour cream in a bowl. Stir in the carrots, squash and onion. Combine the stuffing mix and butter in a bowl. Spread ½ of the stuffing mixture onto the bottom of a 9x13-inch baking dish; cover with the vegetable mixture. Top with the remaining stuffing mixture. Bake at 350 degrees for 25 to 30 minutes or until heated through. Yield: 6 servings

Andrée Wade (Mrs. Gary Wade)

Vegetables and Side Dishes

Squash Casserole

2 pounds squash, sliced 1-inch thick
1 medium onion, chopped
¼ cup butter
Salt and pepper to taste
1 egg, lightly beaten
½ cup milk
1 cup butter cracker crumbs
1 cup shredded Cheddar cheese

Cook the squash and onion in the butter in a saucepan until tender, stirring occasionally. Season with salt and pepper. Combine the egg and milk in a bowl. Add the cracker crumbs and cheese; mix well. Add the squash mixture; mix lightly. Spoon into an ungreased 1½-quart casserole. Bake at 350 degrees for 30 to 40 minutes or until set. Note: You may substitute eggplant for the squash.
Yield: 8 to 10 servings

Mary Frances Kerr

Zucchini Casserole

2 eggs, lightly beaten
1 (10-ounce) can cream of mushroom soup
½ cup mayonnaise
12 ounces shredded sharp Cheddar cheese
2 cups shredded zucchini or yellow summer squash
1 medium onion, chopped
1 cup (about) saltine cracker crumbs
⅓ to ½ cup margarine, cut into pieces
Salt and pepper to taste

Mix the eggs, mushroom soup, mayonnaise, cheese, zucchini, onion, cracker crumbs and margarine in a bowl. Season with salt and pepper. If the mixture is too thin, stir in additional cracker crumbs. Spoon into a 1½-quart casserole. Bake at 350 degrees for 30 to 40 minutes or until set. Yield: 8 to 10 servings

Louise Stone (Mrs. Herbert Stone)

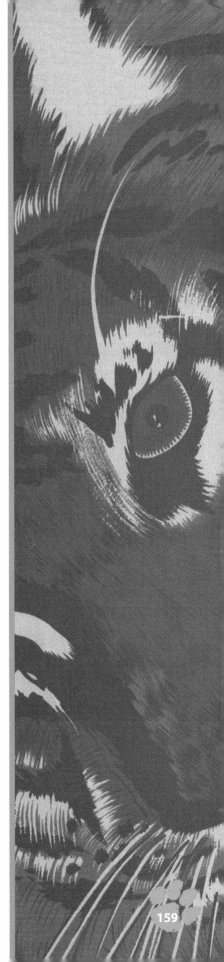

Vegetables and Side Dishes

Charley's Sweet Potato Casserole

2 eggs, lightly beaten
½ cup melted butter
⅓ cup evaporated milk
1 teaspoon vanilla extract
3 cups cooked sweet potatoes
¾ cup granulated sugar
1 (1-pound) box light brown sugar
½ cup melted butter
½ cup self-rising flour
1 cup chopped pecans

Combine the eggs, ½ cup melted butter, evaporated milk and vanilla in a bowl. Stir in the sweet potatoes and granulated sugar. Spread onto the bottom of a 9x13-inch baking dish. Combine the brown sugar, remaining ½ cup melted butter and flour in a bowl and mix until crumbly. Stir in the pecans. Sprinkle over the sweet potato mixture. Bake at 325 degrees for 25 to 30 minutes or until thoroughly heated. Note: Any remaining brown sugar mixture can be used as a topping for ice cream. Store refrigerated in a covered container until ready to use. Yield: 10 servings

Charley and Ward Pell

Ward and Charley Pell at the Gator Bowl

Vegetables and Side Dishes

Aunt Julie's Tomato Pie

1 (8-inch) pie shell
4 medium tomatoes, thinly sliced
3/4 cup mayonnaise
1/2 teaspoon salt
1/2 teaspoon pepper
1/2 cup finely chopped onion
1 cup shredded Cheddar cheese

Bake the pie shell at 350 degrees for 10 minutes. Remove from the oven; set aside. Place the tomatoes in a colander to drain. Combine the mayonnaise, salt and pepper in a bowl. Add the tomatoes and onion; mix lightly. Spoon into the pie crust; sprinkle with the cheese. Bake at 350 degrees for 30 minutes. Serve hot. Yield: 8 servings

Robin Mahony (Mrs. Bob Mahony)

Tomato Pie

1 (9-inch) pie shell
2 medium tomatoes, thinly sliced
1 cup mayonnaise
1 cup shredded Cheddar cheese
3/4 teaspoon basil

Bake the pie shell at 350 degrees for 10 minutes. Remove from the oven; set aside. Pat the tomatoes dry with paper towels. Layer the tomatoes in the pie shell. Combine the mayonnaise, cheese and basil in a bowl; spread evenly over the tomatoes. Bake at 350 degrees for 30 to 40 minutes or until lightly browned and bubbly. Yield: 6 servings

Pet Kinney Harper

Vegetables and Side Dishes

Vegetable Casserole

1 (10-ounce) can cream of celery soup
½ cup nonfat yogurt or sour cream
1 (15-ounce) can white Shoe Peg corn, drained
1 (14-ounce) can French-style green beans, drained
½ cup chopped celery
½ cup chopped onion
¼ cup chopped green bell pepper
Salt and pepper to taste
1 cup fresh bread crumbs or cracker crumbs
½ cup slivered almonds
¼ cup melted margarine or butter

Combine the soup and yogurt in a bowl. Add the corn, beans, celery, onion and green pepper; mix lightly. Season with salt and pepper. Spoon into a 9x13-inch baking dish. Combine the bread crumbs, almonds and margarine in a bowl; mix well. Sprinkle over the vegetable mixture. Bake at 350 degrees for 45 minutes.
Yield: 8 servings

Katie Spurlock (Mrs. Hooper Spurlock)

Veggie Casserole

1 medium onion, chopped
1 cup chopped celery
1 (15-ounce) can mixed vegetables, drained
1 (10-ounce) cream of chicken soup
½ cup mayonnaise
1 cup shredded Cheddar cheese
1 (5-ounce) can sliced water chestnuts
½ cup butter cracker crumbs

Combine the onion, celery, mixed vegetables, soup, mayonnaise, cheese and water chestnuts in a bowl; mix lightly. Spoon into a 1-quart casserole; sprinkle with the cracker crumbs. Bake at 350 degrees for 30 minutes or until a knife inserted into the center comes out clean. Yield: 6 to 8 servings

Patsy Rickenbaker

Vegetables and Side Dishes

Cheesy Rice Overnight Casserole

3 cups cooked long-grain white rice
8 ounces shredded sharp Cheddar cheese
1 (4-ounce) jar chopped pimentos
2½ cups milk
4 eggs, lightly beaten
½ teaspoon pepper
½ teaspoon dry mustard
¼ teaspoon hot pepper sauce
¼ teaspoon garlic powder
1 tablespoon dry sherry
⅛ teaspoon salt
⅛ teaspoon nutmeg

Place ½ of the rice in a lightly greased 9x13-inch baking dish; sprinkle with ½ of the cheese. Top with the pimentos. Repeat the layers. Combine the milk, eggs, pepper, dry mustard, hot pepper sauce, garlic powder, sherry, salt and nutmeg in a bowl; mix well. Pour over the rice mixture. Refrigerate, covered, overnight. Bake at 325 degrees for 45 minutes or until set. Yield: 10 to 12 servings

Marie Herbert (Mrs. Dick Herbert)

Dick and Marie Herbert

Marie and Dick Herbert are IPTAY Scholarship Endowment Donors from Anderson, South Carolina.

Artichoke Pickles

1 peck (8 quarts) Jerusalem artichokes
1 medium head white cabbage
Salt to taste
3 quarts vinegar
7½ cups sugar
2 cups ground onions
2 (7-ounce) jars chopped pimentos
2 tablespoons celery seeds
½ cup flour
1 tablespoon dry mustard
¼ cup turmeric

Clean the artichokes; grind in a coarse-grind food chopper. Grind the cabbage. Place a layer of the artichokes and cabbage in a 2-gallon pan; sprinkle with salt. Repeat the layers until the pan is full, sprinkling each layer with salt. Let stand for 30 minutes. Squeeze the vegetables to remove all of the liquid; discard the liquid. Place the vinegar, sugar, onions, pimentos and celery seeds in a large pan. Bring to a boil. Add the artichoke mixture; boil for 10 minutes. Combine the flour, mustard and turmeric. Add enough cold water gradually to make a smooth paste. Add to the hot artichoke mixture gradually, stirring until well mixed. Cook for 20 minutes, stirring constantly. Spoon the artichoke mixture into hot sterilized jars; seal with 2-piece lids. Process in a boiling water bath for 10 minutes. Yield: 15 pints.

Gatsie Paulling (Mrs. Gene Paulling)

Pineapple Casserole

2 cans crushed pineapple, partially drained
¾ cup sugar
⅓ cup flour
2 cups shredded sharp Cheddar cheese
1 sleeve butter crackers, crushed
¾ cup melted margarine

Mix pineapple, sugar and flour in a bowl. Spoon into a large casserole sprayed with nonstick cooking spray. Cover with the cheese. Sprinkle with the cracker crumbs; drizzle with the melted margarine. Bake at 350 degrees for 30 to 35 minutes or until browned and heated through. Serve with ham. Yield: 6 to 8 servings

Brannon Holmes

Pineapple Au Gratin Casserole

1 (20-ounce) can pineapple chunks, drained
1 cup shredded sharp Cheddar cheese
½ cup sugar, or to taste
3 tablespoons flour
¾ cup crushed butter crackers
¼ cup butter, melted

Combine the pineapple, cheese, sugar and flour in a bowl; mix well.
Spoon into a 1-quart baking dish. Sprinkle with the cracker crumbs;
drizzle with the melted butter. Bake at 350 degrees for 30 minutes.
Yield: 4 servings

Mary Katherine Littlejohn

Over the years, Littlejohn Coliseum has been the scene of countless Clemson victories over
top-ranked teams.

The Littlejohn Coliseum,
where the Tigers play
basketball, is named for
Mary Katherine's father.

Desserts

Celebrating Clemson University's most important asset, her students

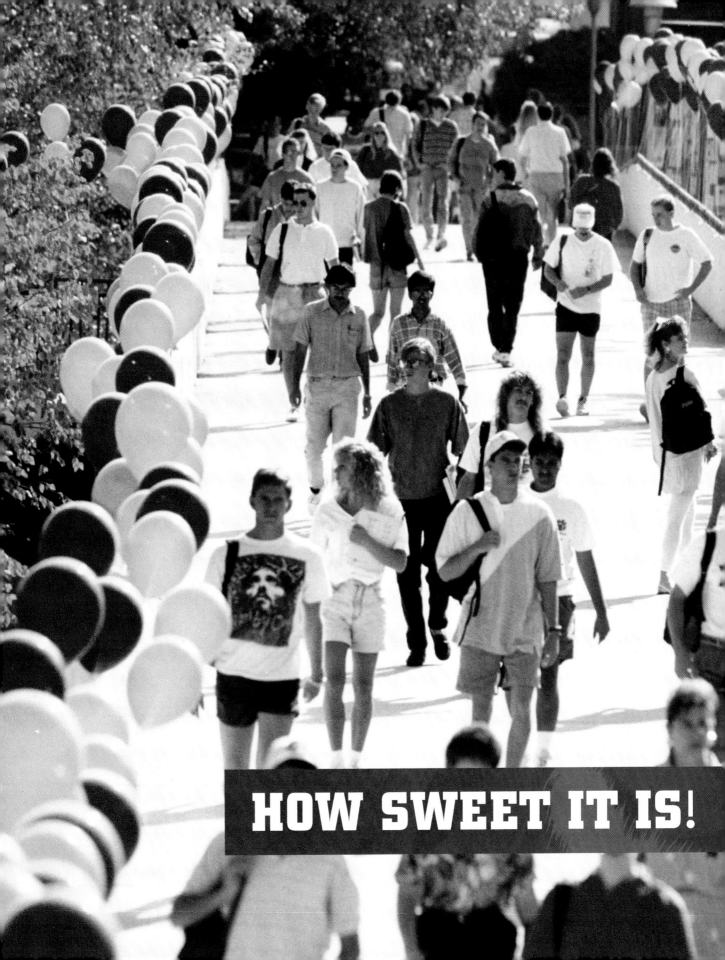

HOW SWEET IT IS!

Red Cake

1/2 cup shortening
11/2 cups sugar
2 eggs
1/4 cup (2 ounces) red food coloring
2 tablespoons baking cocoa
1 teaspoon vanilla extract
21/4 cups cake flour
1 teaspoon salt
1 cup buttermilk
1 teaspoon baking soda
1 teaspoon vinegar
3 tablespoons all-purpose flour
1 cup milk
1 cup butter, softened
1 cup sugar
1 teaspoon vanilla extract

Cream the shortening and 1 1/2 cups sugar in a large mixer bowl until light and fluffy. Add the eggs, 1 at a time, beating well after each addition. Combine the food coloring and cocoa in a small bowl. Add to the egg mixture along with the 1 teaspoon vanilla; beat until well blended. Combine the cake flour and salt in a small bowl. Add to the sugar mixture alternately with the buttermilk, mixing well after each addition. Add the baking soda and vinegar; mix well. Pour the batter evenly into two greased and floured 9-inch round cake pans. Bake at 350 degrees for 30 minutes or until a wooden pick inserted into the center comes out clean. Remove the pans to wire racks. Cool for 10 minutes. Remove from the pans; cool completely. Combine the all-purpose flour and milk in a saucepan. Cook until thickened, stirring constantly. Remove from the heat; cool. Cream 1 cup butter and 1 cup sugar in a small mixer bowl until light and fluffy. Blend in 1 teaspoon vanilla. Add the flour mixture; mix until well blended. Split both cake layers horizontally in half. Spread the frosting onto the tops of 3 of the cake layers; stack the layers. Frost the top and outside edge of the cake with the remaining frosting. Yield: 12 servings

Senator Strom Thurmond

Pumpkin Torte

24 graham cracker squares (12 whole crackers), finely crushed
1/3 cup sugar
1/2 cup melted butter
8 ounces cream cheese, softened
3/4 cup sugar
2 eggs
1 (15-ounce) can pumpkin (about 2 cups)
3 egg yolks
1/2 cup sugar
1 tablespoon cinnamon
1/2 teaspoon salt
1/2 cup milk
1 envelope unflavored gelatin
1/4 cup cold water
3 egg whites
1/4 cup sugar
1 cup whipping cream
1/4 cup sugar
1 teaspoon vanilla extract

Mix the graham cracker crumbs, 1/3 cup sugar and butter in a medium bowl. Press into a 9x13-inch baking pan. Beat the cream cheese and 3/4 cup sugar in a small mixer bowl until creamy. Beat in 2 eggs 1 at a time. Pour over the crust. Bake at 350 degrees for 20 minutes. Remove to a wire rack to cool. Combine the pumpkin, egg yolks, 1/2 cup sugar, cinnamon and salt in a medium saucepan. Stir in the milk gradually. Bring to a boil. Cook until thickened, stirring constantly. Remove from the heat. Dissolve the gelatin in 1/4 cup cold water. Add to the pumpkin mixture; mix well. Cool completely. Beat the egg whites with 1/4 cup sugar in a small mixer bowl until stiff peaks form. Fold into the pumpkin mixture. Pour over the cream cheese layer. Refrigerate, covered, until chilled. When ready to serve, beat the whipping cream with 1/4 cup sugar and vanilla in a small mixer bowl until stiff peaks form. Spoon over the torte. Yield: 15 servings

Patsy L. Gilliam (Mrs. Whit Gilliam)

IPTAY Representatives Sonny Dukes (left) and Whit Gilliam (right) congratulate Senator Thurmond on his long support of IPTAY and his lengthy service to our country.

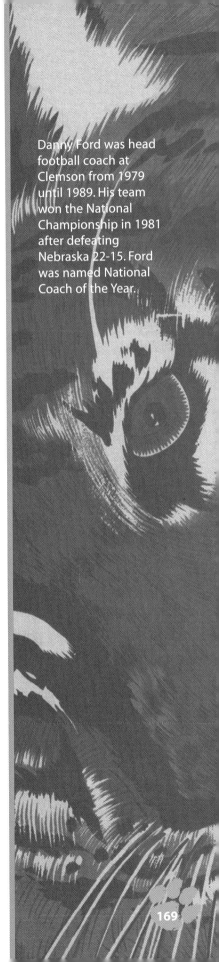

Danny Ford was head football coach at Clemson from 1979 until 1989. His team won the National Championship in 1981 after defeating Nebraska 22-15. Ford was named National Coach of the Year.

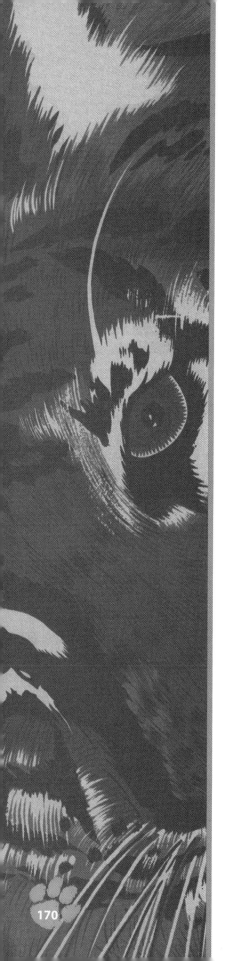

Fruit Dessert Pizza

1 (18-ounce) package refrigerated sugar cookie dough
1 cup granulated sugar
3 tablespoons cornstarch
1 cup orange juice
½ cup each lemon juice and hot water
8 ounces cream cheese, softened
1 cup confectioners' sugar
3 tablespoons fresh lemon juice
3 to 4 cups cut-up assorted fruits

Cut the cookie dough into ¼-inch-thick slices. Place in concentric circles on a lightly greased 12-inch pizza pan to form a crust. Bake at 450 degrees for 10 minutes or until lightly browned. Cool on a wire rack. Combine sugar and cornstarch in a medium saucepan. Add the orange juice, ½ cup lemon juice, and hot water. Bring to a boil. Cook until thickened, stirring occasionally. Remove from the heat; cool. Beat the cream cheese, confectioners' sugar and 3 tablespoons lemon juice in a mixing bowl. Spread over the crust. Arrange the fruit over the cream cheese mixture; top with the glaze. Refrigerate, covered, until well chilled. Cut into wedges to serve. Yield: 8 servings

E.O. (Sonny) and Ann Dukes

Chocolate Syrup Cake

4 eggs
1 (16-ounce) can chocolate syrup
½ cup melted butter
1 teaspoon vanilla extract
1 cup each sugar and self-rising flour
½ cup butter
1 cup sugar
½ cup semisweet chocolate chips
⅓ cup evaporated milk
½ cup chopped pecans

Combine the eggs, chocolate syrup, ½ cup butter and vanilla in a bowl. Add 1 cup sugar and flour; mix well. Pour into a greased 9x13-inch cake pan. Bake at 350 degrees for 30 minutes. Remove to a wire rack. Bring ½ cup butter, 1 cup sugar, chocolate chips and evaporated milk to a boil in a saucepan, stirring frequently. Cook until slightly thickened, stirring constantly. Stir in the pecans. Pour over the warm cake. Cool completely. Yield: 24 servings

Diane Mahaffey (Mrs. Randy Mahaffey)

Desserts

Crazy Chocolate Cake with Orange Icing

1 cup shortening
2 cups sugar
2 eggs
3 cups flour
1 cup baking cocoa
2 teaspoons baking soda
½ teaspoon salt
1 cup milk
1 cup boiling water
2 teaspoons vanilla extract
⅓ cup butter, softened
Grated rind of 1 orange
Juice of 1 orange (½ to ¾ cup)
1 (1-pound) box confectioners' sugar

Cream the shortening and sugar in a large mixer bowl until light and fluffy. Add the eggs, 1 at a time, beating well after each addition. Add the flour, cocoa, baking soda and salt. Blend in the milk, boiling water and vanilla. Beat for 3 minutes or until well blended. Pour into a greased 9x13-inch baking pan. Bake at 325 degrees for 1 hour or until a wooden pick inserted into the center comes out clean. Remove to a wire rack to cool completely. Beat the butter in a large mixing bowl until smooth and creamy. Add the orange rind and orange juice; mix well. Add the confectioners' sugar gradually, beating well after each addition. Spread over the cake. Note: If the icing is too thick, add a small amount of milk; if the icing is too thin, add additional confectioners' sugar. Yield: 18 servings

Jo Hern Curris (Mrs. Constantine Curris)

Dr. and Mrs. Deno Curris and family

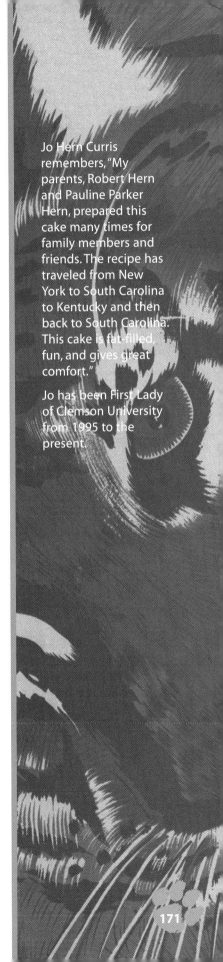

Jo Hern Curris remembers, "My parents, Robert Hern and Pauline Parker Hern, prepared this cake many times for family members and friends. The recipe has traveled from New York to South Carolina to Kentucky and then back to South Carolina. This cake is fat-filled, fun, and gives great comfort."

Jo has been First Lady of Clemson University from 1995 to the present.

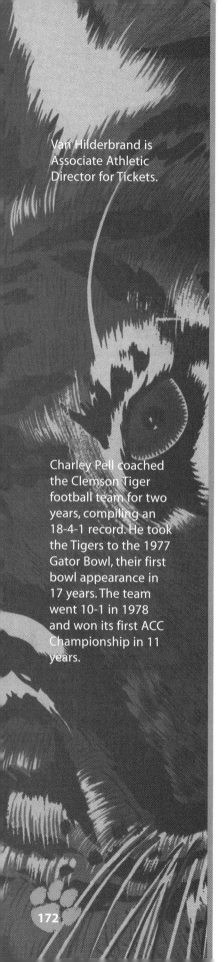

Chess Cake

1 (2-layer) package yellow cake mix
½ cup melted margarine
1 egg
8 ounces cream cheese, softened
2 eggs
1 (1-pound) box confectioners' sugar
1 cup chopped pecans

Blend the cake mix, margarine and 1 egg in a large bowl. Spread in a greased 9x13-inch baking pan. Beat the cream cheese and 2 eggs in a large mixer bowl. Add the confectioners' sugar gradually; beat well. Pour over the batter in the pan. Sprinkle with the pecans. Bake at 350 degrees for 40 minutes. Yield: 15 servings

Diane Hilderbrand (Mrs. Van Hilderbrand)

Charley's Favorite Coconut Cake

1 (2-layer) package yellow cake mix
1 (4-ounce) package vanilla instant pudding
1⅓ cups water
¼ cup vegetable oil
4 eggs
6 cups flaked coconut
1 cup chopped walnuts
½ cup butter, softened
16 ounces cream cheese, softened
7 cups sifted confectioners' sugar
4 teaspoons milk
1 teaspoon vanilla extract

Beat the first 5 ingredients in a mixer bowl at medium speed for 4 minutes. Stir in 2 cups of the coconut and walnuts. Pour into 3 greased and floured 9-inch cake pans. Bake at 350 degrees for 35 minutes. Cool on wire racks for 10 minutes. Remove from the pans; cool completely. Melt ¼ cup of the butter in a large skillet over low heat. Add the remaining 4 cups coconut. Cook, stirring constantly, until golden brown. Spread on paper towels to cool. Blend ¼ cup butter and cream cheese in a mixer bowl. Add the confectioners' sugar and milk alternately, beating well after each. Blend in the vanilla. Stir in 3 cups of the toasted coconut. Spread the frosting between the layers and over the top and side of the cake. Sprinkle with the remaining 1 cup toasted coconut. Yield: 12 servings

Charley and Ward Pell

Cool Breeze Strawberry Delight

1 (2-layer) package white cake mix
8 ounces cream cheese, softened
½ cup confectioners' sugar
½ cup granulated sugar
12 ounces whipped topping
1 (16-ounce) bag fresh or frozen sweetened strawberries

Prepare the cake mix according to the package directions. Pour the batter into 3 greased and floured round cake pans. Bake as directed. Remove to wire racks; cool for 10 minutes. Remove from the pans; cool completely. Beat the cream cheese, confectioners' sugar and granulated sugar in a small mixer bowl until well blended. Add the whipped topping; mix well. Frost 2 of the cake layers with the whipped topping mixture; cover with the strawberries and strawberry juice. Stack the layers. Cover with the top cake layer. Frost the top and side of the cake with the remaining whipped topping mixture. Spoon the remaining strawberries and juice over the top of the cake. Refrigerate, covered, until ready to serve.
Yield: **12 servings**

Bobbie Davis, wife of Coach Jim Davis

Jim Davis, hard at work

Jim Davis has been the women's basketball coach at Clemson University for 11 years. He is the winningest women's basketball coach in Clemson history. He guided Clemson to an ACC Championship in 1996 and has taken Clemson to the NCAA Tournament in 10 of his 11 years.

Crème de Menthe Cake

    1 (2-layer) package white cake mix
    1 (4-ounce) package vanilla instant pudding mix
    ½ cup orange juice
    ½ cup vegetable oil
    4 large eggs
    ¼ cup water
    ¼ cup green crème de menthe
    ¼ teaspoon vanilla extract
    1 (5-ounce) can chocolate syrup
    ¼ cup confectioners' sugar

Combine the cake mix, pudding mix, orange juice, vegetable oil, eggs, water, crème de menthe and vanilla in a large mixer bowl. Beat for 4 minutes or until well blended. Pour ⅔ of the batter into a greased and floured bundt pan. Stir the chocolate syrup into the remaining cake batter. Pour evenly over the batter in the pan. Do not stir. Bake at 350 degrees for 35 to 45 minutes or until a wooden pick inserted into the center comes out clean. Remove to a wire rack. Cool for 10 minutes. Invert the cake onto the rack; remove the pan. Cool completely. Dust lightly with the confectioners' sugar. Yield: 16 servings

Jack Lunn

Prune Cake

    1 cup vegetable oil
    1 (8-ounce) jar baby food prunes with tapioca
    3 eggs
    2 cups each self-rising flour and sugar
    1 teaspoon each cinnamon, nutmeg and allspice
    1 cup chopped pecans or walnuts (optional)

Combine the vegetable oil, prunes and eggs in a large mixer bowl. Mix the dry ingredients in a large bowl. Blend into the prune mixture gradually. Stir in the pecans. Pour into a greased and floured 10-inch tube pan. Bake at 325 degrees for 55 minutes or until the cake tests done. Cool on a wire rack for 10 minutes. Remove from the pan; cool completely. Note: May drizzle with a confectioners' sugar glaze. Yield: 16 servings

Josie Wood (Mrs. Allen Wood)

Desserts

Hummingbird Cake

3 cups flour
2 cups granulated sugar
1 teaspoon each baking soda and cinnamon
1/2 teaspoon salt
3 eggs, lightly beaten
3/4 cup vegetable oil
1 (8-ounce) can crushed pineapple packed in unsweetened juice
1 3/4 cups mashed ripe bananas (about 3 medium bananas)
1 cup finely chopped pecans
1 1/2 teaspoons vanilla extract
1/2 cup unsalted butter or margarine, softened
8 ounces cream cheese, softened
1 (1-pound) box confectioners' sugar, sifted (3 1/2 to 4 cups)
1 teaspoon vanilla extract
1/2 cup finely chopped pecans

Mix the flour, granulated sugar, baking soda, cinnamon and salt in a large bowl. Add the eggs and vegetable oil, stirring until moistened. Stir in the undrained pineapple, bananas, 1 cup pecans and 1 1/2 teaspoons vanilla. Pour the batter evenly into 3 greased and floured 9-inch round cake pans. Bake at 350 degrees for 30 minutes or until the layers test done. Cool on wire racks for 10 minutes. Remove from the pans; cool completely. Cream the butter and cream cheese in a mixer bowl. Add the confectioners' sugar gradually, beating well. Blend in 1 teaspoon vanilla. Spread the frosting between the layers and over the top and side of the cake. Sprinkle with 1/2 cup pecans. Yield: 12 servings

Nancy Cathcart (Mrs. Foster Cathcart)

Good and Easy Lemon Cake

1 (2-layer) package lemon cake mix
1/2 cup melted butter
1 egg
8 ounces cream cheese, softened
2 eggs
1 (1-pound) box confectioners' sugar

Blend the cake mix, butter and 1 egg in a large bowl. Press onto the bottom of a greased 9x13-inch baking pan. Beat the cream cheese and 2 eggs in a large mixer bowl. Blend in the confectioners' sugar gradually. Pour over the crust in the pan. Bake at 350 degrees for 40 minutes or until set. Yield: 15 to 18 servings

Nancy M. Bennett (Mrs. George Bennett)

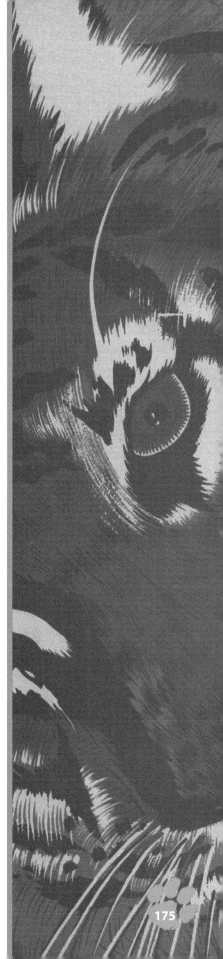

Desserts

Pecan Cake

½ cup margarine, softened
½ cup shortening
2 cups granulated sugar
5 egg yolks
2 cups flour
1 teaspoon baking soda
1 cup buttermilk
1 teaspoon vanilla extract
1 cup chopped pecans
1 (3-ounce) can flaked coconut
5 egg whites, stiffly beaten
½ cup margarine, softened
1 (1-pound) box confectioners' sugar
8 ounces cream cheese, softened
1 teaspoon vanilla extract
1 cup chopped pecans
¼ cup flaked coconut

Cream ½ cup margarine, shortening and granulated sugar in a large mixer bowl. Beat in the egg yolks. Sift together the flour and baking soda. Add to the sugar mixture alternately with the buttermilk, beating well after each addition. Blend in 1 teaspoon vanilla. Stir in 1 cup pecans and 3-ounce can coconut. Fold in the egg whites. Pour into 3 greased and floured 8-inch round cake pans. Bake at 350 degrees for 25 minutes or until the layers test done. Cool on wire racks for 10 minutes. Remove from the pans; cool completely. Cream ½ cup margarine and confectioners' sugar in a large mixer bowl. Blend in the cream cheese and 1 teaspoon vanilla. Stir in 1 cup pecans and ¼ cup coconut. Spread between the layers and over the top and side of the cake. Yield: 12 servings

Young Pecan Company

Rennie's Red Velvet Cake

1½ cups vegetable oil
1 cup buttermilk
2 large eggs
¼ cup (2 ounces) red food coloring
1 teaspoon each vanilla extract and vinegar
2½ cups self-rising flour
1½ cups granulated sugar
1 teaspoon each baking soda and baking cocoa
⅔ cup butter, softened
1 (1-pound) box confectioners' sugar
10 ounces cream cheese, softened

Mix the oil, buttermilk, eggs, food coloring, vanilla and vinegar in a bowl. Combine the flour, granulated sugar, baking soda and cocoa in a bowl. Add to the buttermilk mixture gradually, mixing well. Pour into three 9-inch cake pans sprayed with nonstick baking spray. Bake at 350 degrees for 20 minutes or until layers test done. Cool on wire racks for 10 minutes. Remove from the pans; cool completely. Cream the butter and confectioners' sugar in a mixer bowl. Blend in the cream cheese. Spread between the layers and over the top and side of the cake. Sprinkle with chopped pecans. Yield: 12 servings

Rennie Newman

Scuppernong Wine Cake

½ cup chopped pecans or walnuts
1 (2-layer) package butter-flavor yellow cake mix
1 (4-ounce) package vanilla instant pudding mix
½ cup each water and vegetable oil
½ cup scuppernong or other grape wine
4 eggs
½ cup confectioners' sugar
2 to 3 tablespoons scuppernong or other grape wine

Sprinkle the pecans into a greased and floured 10-inch tube pan. Beat the cake mix, pudding mix, water, oil, ½ cup wine and eggs in a mixer bowl for 2 minutes. Pour into the prepared pan. Bake at 325 degrees for 50 to 60 minutes or until the cake tests done. Invert onto a wire rack; cool for 10 minutes. Remove the cake from the pan; cool completely. Blend the confectioners' sugar and 2 tablespoons wine in a small bowl. Add the remaining 1 tablespoon wine if needed. Drizzle over the cake. Yield: 16 servings

Sarah Wilhelm (Mrs. Bill Wilhelm)

Sarah Wilhelm tells us, "I was given this recipe during a tour of Southland Estate Winery in North Carolina while Bill was on the program of a baseball coach's clinic in Goldsboro. Bill retired July 2, 1993, after coaching the Clemson University baseball team for 36 years, 1958-1993."

Bill and Sarah have two sons. Michael works for CNN in Atlanta. Randall has an art degree from Winthrop and a master's in English from Clemson. While Randall was at Clemson, he did numerous paintings for the Athletic Department, including a portrait of Banks McFadden in his football uniform from 1939. These paintings are in the Jervey Athletic Center, Tennis Center, and McFadden Building.

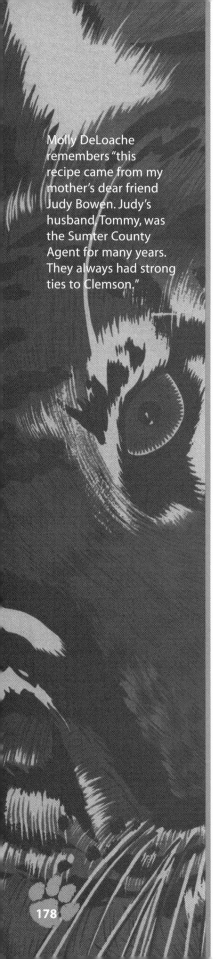

Walnut Rum Cake

½ cup finely chopped black walnuts
½ cup finely chopped pecans
1 (2-layer) package yellow cake mix
1 (4-ounce) package vanilla instant pudding mix
½ cup rum
½ cup vegetable oil
½ cup water
4 eggs
¼ cup rum
¼ cup water
½ cup margarine
1 cup sugar

Sprinkle the walnuts and pecans onto the bottom of a greased and floured 10-inch bundt pan. Combine the cake mix, pudding mix, ½ cup rum, oil and ½ cup water in a large mixer bowl. Beat until well blended. Add the eggs, 1 at a time, beating well after each addition. Pour the batter into the prepared pan. Bake at 325 degrees for 50 to 60 minutes or until a wooden pick inserted halfway between the center and outside edge of the cake comes out clean. Remove to a wire rack. Combine ¼ cup rum, ¼ cup water, margarine and sugar in a medium saucepan. Bring to a boil; simmer for 2 minutes. Pour over the warm cake (still in the pan), while gently pulling the cake away from the side of the pan with a knife to allow the glaze to run to the bottom of the pan. Let stand for about 10 minutes. Invert the cake onto the wire rack; remove the pan. Cool completely. Note: You may substitute 2 miniature bundt pans for the larger bundt pan. Yield: 16 servings

Molly A. DeLoache (Mrs. Bill DeLoache)

Mollie and Bill were reunited with Banks McFadden at a reunion dinner for Coach McFadden's former basketball players.

Desserts

Chocolate Pound Cake

1 cup butter, softened
3 cups granulated sugar
5 eggs
3 cups flour
5 tablespoons baking cocoa
1/2 teaspoon baking powder
1/4 teaspoon salt
1 cup milk
2 teaspoons vanilla extract
1/2 cup butter, softened
1 (1-pound) box confectioners' sugar
1/2 cup baking cocoa
1/4 cup hot brewed coffee
1 teaspoon vanilla extract

Cream 1 cup butter and granulated sugar in a mixer bowl. Beat in the eggs, 1 at a time. Sift together the flour, 5 tablespoons cocoa, baking powder and salt. Add to the butter mixture alternately with the milk, beating well after each addition. Blend in 2 teaspoons vanilla. Pour into a greased and floured 10-inch tube pan. Place in a cold oven. Bake at 300 degrees for 1 to 1 1/2 hours or until the cake tests done. Cool on a wire rack for 10 minutes before removing the cake from the pan to cool completely. Cream 1/2 cup butter, confectioners' sugar and 1/2 cup cocoa in a mixer bowl. Add the coffee and 1 teaspoon vanilla gradually, beating until well blended. Spread on the cooled cake. Yield: 16 servings

Anne H. Marchant (Mrs. Seabrook Marchant)

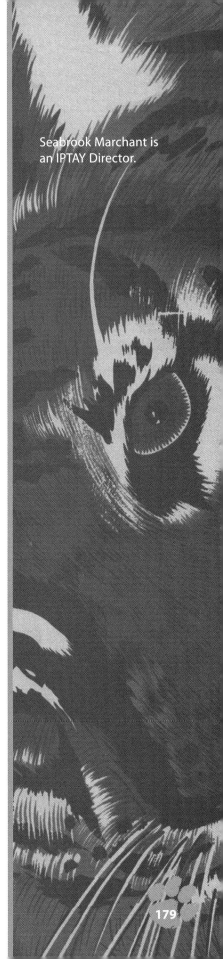

Seabrook Marchant is an IPTAY Director.

Old-Fashioned Chocolate Pound Cake

½ cup butter or margarine, softened
1 cup shortening
3 cups granulated sugar
5 eggs
3 cups flour
5 tablespoons baking cocoa
1 teaspoon salt
½ teaspoon baking powder
1 cup milk
1 tablespoon vanilla extract
1 (1-pound) box brown sugar
¼ cup baking cocoa
⅛ teaspoon salt
½ cup milk
6 tablespoons shortening

Cream the butter, 1 cup shortening and granulated sugar in a mixer bowl. Beat in the eggs, 1 at a time. Combine the flour, 5 tablespoons cocoa, 1 teaspoon salt and baking powder in a large bowl. Add to the butter mixture alternately with 1 cup milk, beating until blended. Beat in the vanilla. Pour into a greased 10-inch tube pan. Bake at 325 degrees for 1 hour 15 minutes or until the cake tests done. Cool on a wire rack for 10 minutes; remove the cake from the pan. Cool completely. Combine the brown sugar, ¼ cup cocoa, ⅛ teaspoon salt, ½ cup milk and 6 tablespoons shortening in a saucepan. Bring to a boil; simmer for 2 minutes. Remove from the heat; beat until cooled. Spread over the cake. Yield: 16 servings

Betty Turner (Mrs. Jim Turner)

Cold Oven Pound Cake

1 cup margarine, softened
¼ cup shortening
3 cups sugar
5 eggs
3 cups flour
⅛ teaspoon salt
1 cup milk
1 teaspoon vanilla extract
1 teaspoon lemon extract

Cream the margarine, shortening and sugar in a large mixer bowl until light and fluffy. Add the eggs, 1 at a time. Sift together the flour and salt twice. Add to the sugar mixture alternately with the milk, mixing well after each addition. Blend in the extracts. Pour into a greased and floured 10-inch tube pan. Place in a cold oven. Bake at 300 degrees for 1½ hours or until the cake tests done. Remove to a wire rack. Cool for 10 minutes; remove the cake from the pan. Cool completely. Yield: 16 servings

Pat Sullivan Rhoden (Mrs. Ken Rhoden)

Whipped Cream Pound Cake

1 cup butter, softened
3 cups sugar
6 eggs
3 cups flour
1 cup whipping cream
1 teaspoon vanilla extract
½ teaspoon almond extract

Cream the butter and sugar in a large mixer bowl until light and fluffy. Add the eggs, 1 at a time, beating well after each addition. Add the flour alternately with the whipping cream, beating until well blended. Add the extracts; mix well. Pour the batter into a greased and floured 10-inch tube pan. Place in a cold oven. Bake at 325 degrees for 1 hour 30 minutes or until a wooden pick inserted halfway between the center and outside edge of the cake comes out clean. Remove the cake to a wire rack. Cool for 10 minutes; remove the cake from the pan. Cool completely. Yield: 16 servings

Ruth M. Crawford

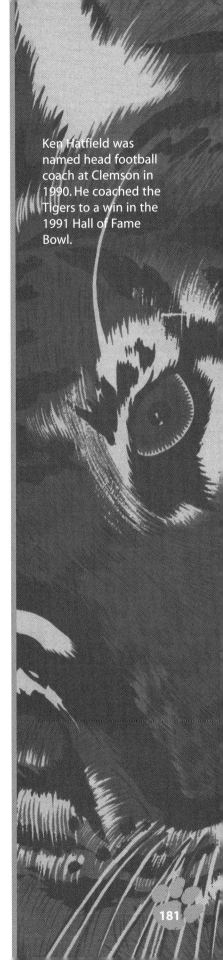

Ken Hatfield was named head football coach at Clemson in 1990. He coached the Tigers to a win in the 1991 Hall of Fame Bowl.

Mama's Pound Cake

1 cup butter, softened
3 cups sugar
6 large eggs
3 cups flour
1 cup whipping cream
1 teaspoon vanilla extract
1 teaspoon lemon extract

Cream the butter and sugar in a large mixer bowl until light and fluffy. Add the eggs, 1 at a time, beating well after each addition. Add the flour alternately with the whipping cream, beating until well blended. Add the extracts; mix well. Pour into a greased and floured 10-inch tube pan. Place in a cold oven. Bake at 325 degrees for 1 hour 30 minutes or until a wooden pick inserted halfway between the center and outside edge of the cake comes out clean. Remove the cake to a wire rack. Cool for 10 minutes; remove the cake from the pan. Cool completely. Yield: 16 servings

Nancy B. Bell (Mrs. T. James Bell, Jr.)

Quarterback Jimmy Bell

Coach Howard's Peach Brandy Pound Cake

1 cup butter, softened
3 cups sugar
6 large eggs
3 cups flour
1/4 teaspoon baking soda
1/8 teaspoon salt
1 cup sour cream
1/2 cup peach brandy
2 teaspoons rum
1 teaspoon vanilla extract
1 teaspoon orange extract
1/2 teaspoon lemon extract
1/4 teaspoon almond extract

Beat the butter in a large mixer bowl until creamy. Add the sugar gradually, beating until light and fluffy. Add the eggs, 1 at a time, beating well after each addition. Combine the flour, baking soda and salt in a large bowl. Add to the sugar mixture alternately with the sour cream, beating until well blended. Blend in the brandy, rum and extracts. Pour into a greased and floured 10-inch bundt pan. Bake at 325 degrees for 1 hour 20 minutes or until the cake tests done. Remove to a wire rack. Cool for 10 minutes; remove the cake from the pan. Cool completely. Yield: 16 servings

Alice Howard McClure (Mrs. Bob McClure),
daughter of Coach Frank Howard

Coach Frank Howard with Howard's Rock

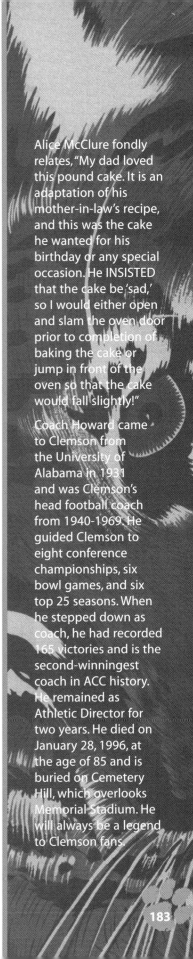

Alice McClure fondly relates, "My dad loved this pound cake. It is an adaptation of his mother-in-law's recipe, and this was the cake he wanted for his birthday or any special occasion. He INSISTED that the cake be 'sad,' so I would either open and slam the oven door prior to completion of baking the cake or jump in front of the oven so that the cake would fall slightly!"

Coach Howard came to Clemson from the University of Alabama in 1931 and was Clemson's head football coach from 1940-1969. He guided Clemson to eight conference championships, six bowl games, and six top 25 seasons. When he stepped down as coach, he had recorded 165 victories and is the second-winningest coach in ACC history. He remained as Athletic Director for two years. He died on January 28, 1996, at the age of 85 and is buried on Cemetery Hill, which overlooks Memorial Stadium. He will always be a legend to Clemson fans.

Harold Cheatham is Dean of the College of Health, Education and Human Development.

7-Up Pound Cake

1½ cups butter or margarine, softened
3 cups sugar
5 eggs
2 tablespoons lemon extract
3 cups sifted flour
¾ cup 7-Up or ginger ale, at room temperature

Cream the butter and sugar in a large mixer bowl until light and fluffy. Add the eggs, 1 at a time, beating well after each addition. Blend in the lemon extract. Add the flour alternately with the 7-Up, mixing until well blended. Bake at 325 degrees for 1 hour and 15 minutes or until a wooden pick inserted halfway between the center and outside edge of the cake comes out clean. Remove to a wire rack. Cool for 10 minutes; remove the cake from the pan. Cool completely. Yield: 16 servings

Arlene Cheatham (Mrs. Harold Cheatham)

Professor's Pound Cake

2 cups butter, softened
3¼ cups sugar
10 large eggs
1 teaspoon vanilla extract
1 teaspoon lemon extract
1 teaspoon cream of tartar
4 cups flour

Cream the butter and sugar in a large mixer bowl until light and fluffy. Add the eggs, 1 at a time, beating well after each addition. Blend in the extracts and cream of tartar. Gradually add the flour, mixing until well blended. Pour into a greased and floured 10-inch tube pan. Place in a cold oven. Bake at 275 degrees for 2 hours or until a wooden pick inserted halfway between the center and outside edge of the cake comes out clean. Remove the cake to a wire rack. Cool for 10 minutes; remove the cake from the pan. Cool completely. Yield: 16 servings

Elizabeth M. Gage (Mrs. Gaston Gage)

Desserts

Easy Sour Cream Pound Cake

½ cup butter, softened
1 cup sugar
3 eggs
1 cup sour cream
1 (2-layer) package butter-flavor yellow cake mix
1 cup flour
1 cup milk

Cream the butter and sugar in a large mixer bowl until light and fluffy. Add the eggs, 1 at a time, beating well after each addition. Blend in the sour cream. Combine the cake mix and flour in a large bowl. Add to the butter mixture alternately with the milk, mixing until well blended. Pour into a greased and floured 10-inch bundt pan. Bake at 350 degrees for 1 hour or until a wooden pick inserted halfway between the center and outside edge of the cake comes out clean. Remove to a wire rack. Cool for 10 minutes; remove the cake from the pan. Cool completely. Yield: 16 servings

Brenda Rabon

Sour Cream Pound Cake

1 cup butter, softened
3 cups sugar
6 eggs
1 cup sour cream
1 teaspoon vanilla extract
3 cups cake flour
1 teaspoon baking powder
⅛ teaspoon salt

Cream the butter and sugar in a large mixer bowl until light and fluffy. Add the eggs, 1 at a time, beating well after each addition. Blend in the sour cream and vanilla. Sift together the flour, baking powder and salt. Gradually add to the sour cream mixture, mixing until well blended. Pour into a well-greased and floured 10-inch tube pan. Bake at 325 degrees for 1 hour 30 minutes or until a wooden pick inserted halfway between the center and outside edge of the cake comes out clean. Remove to a wire rack. Cool for 10 minutes; remove the cake from the pan. Cool completely. Yield: 16 servings

Ann Coleman (Mrs. Dean Coleman)

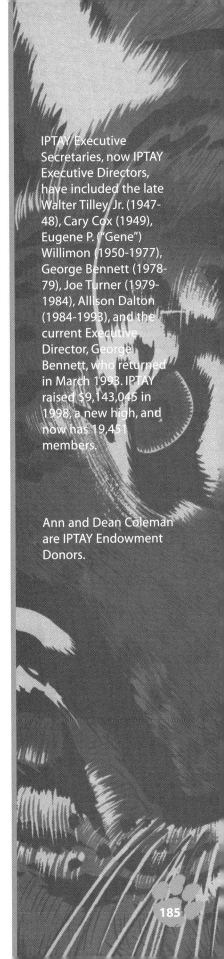

IPTAY Executive Secretaries, now IPTAY Executive Directors, have included the late Walter Tilley, Jr. (1947-48), Cary Cox (1949), Eugene P. ("Gene") Willimon (1950-1977), George Bennett (1978-79), Joe Turner (1979-1984), Allison Dalton (1984-1993), and the current Executive Director, George Bennett, who returned in March 1993. IPTAY raised $9,143,045 in 1998, a new high, and now has 19,451 members.

Ann and Dean Coleman are IPTAY Endowment Donors.

Don's Favorite Banana Cupcakes

1 teaspoon baking soda
⅓ cup warm water
½ cup shortening
1 cup sugar
1 egg, beaten
4 large ripe bananas, mashed (about 1½ cups)
1 teaspoon vanilla extract
1 teaspoon banana extract
1½ cups flour
¼ teaspoon nutmeg

Combine the baking soda and warm water in a small bowl; stir until the baking soda is dissolved. Cream the shortening and sugar in a large mixer bowl until light and fluffy. Beat in the egg and the bananas. Blend in the extracts. Sift together the flour and nutmeg twice. Add to the banana mixture gradually, mixing well. Blend in the baking soda mixture. Spoon the batter evenly into paper-lined or greased and floured muffin cups, filling each cup ½ full. Bake at 400 degrees for 10 to 12 minutes or until golden brown. Remove to wire racks to cool. Yield: 15 to 18 cupcakes

Gale W. Golightly (Mrs. Don Golightly)

Grandmother's Frosting

2 eggs, lightly beaten
1 cup sugar
2 tablespoons plus 1 teaspoon cornstarch
1 cup chopped walnuts
1 cup milk

Combine the eggs, sugar, cornstarch and walnuts in the top of a double boiler; mix well. Stir in the milk. Cook over boiling water until thickened, stirring frequently. Note: You may substitute ⅓ cup firmly packed brown sugar for ⅓ cup of the granulated sugar. Yield: enough to frost three 9-inch round cake layers

Mrs. Fred P. Guerry

Desserts

Peanut Butter Candy

1 (1-pound) box confectioners' sugar
½ cup butter
1 teaspoon vanilla extract
1 (18-ounce) jar creamy peanut butter

Sift the confectioners' sugar into a large bowl. Melt the butter in a large saucepan. Stir in the vanilla. Add to the confectioners' sugar gradually, mixing until well blended. Shape the mixture into a ball. Sprinkle additional confectioners' sugar onto a large sheet of foil or waxed paper. Using a rolling pin coated with additional confectioners' sugar, roll out the dough to ¼-inch thickness. Spread evenly with the peanut butter. Starting at one short end, roll up the dough, jelly roll fashion, using the edge of the foil to help roll the dough. Cut into thin slices. Place on trays with sheets of waxed paper between the layers of the slices. Refrigerate, covered, until well chilled. Store, covered, in the refrigerator. Yield: 10 servings

Marsha Y. Nobles (Mrs. Pat Nobles)

Sugared Pecans

2 cups pecan pieces
1 cup sugar
5 tablespoons water
1 teaspoon vanilla extract
1 teaspoon cinnamon
¼ teaspoon salt

Spread out the pecans on a 1x10x15-inch jelly-roll pan. Bake at 250 degrees for 8 minutes or until lightly toasted, stirring once. Remove to a wire rack. Combine the sugar, water, vanilla, cinnamon and salt in a large saucepan. Cook until the mixture reaches the soft ball stage (240 degrees), stirring frequently. Add the pecans; stir until well coated. Spread out onto a waxed paper-covered baking sheet to cool. Break into bite-size pieces. Store in a tightly covered container. Yield: 1 to 1¼ pounds

Clarice Lake

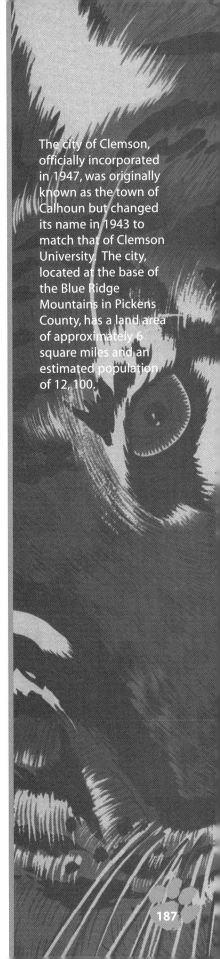

The city of Clemson, officially incorporated in 1947, was originally known as the town of Calhoun but changed its name in 1943 to match that of Clemson University. The city, located at the base of the Blue Ridge Mountains in Pickens County, has a land area of approximately 6 square miles and an estimated population of 12,100.

Blonde Brownies

5⅓ cups sifted flour
5 teaspoons baking powder
1 teaspoon salt
1½ cups melted butter
2 (1-pound) boxes brown sugar
6 extra-large eggs
2 cups chopped pecans

Sift together the flour, baking powder and salt; set aside. Combine the butter and brown sugar in a large mixer bowl. Add the eggs, 1 at a time, beating well after each addition. Stir in the flour mixture and pecans. Spread the dough in a greased 12x17-inch baking pan. Bake at 350 degrees for 30 to 35 minutes or until the center springs back when lightly touched with your finger. Remove to a wire rack to cool. Cut into squares to serve. For large crowds, ARAMARK uses 7 pounds cake flour, 2 ounces baking powder, 2 ounces salt, 4 pounds butter, 12 pounds brown sugar, ½ gallon eggs and 6 pounds pecans and bake the brownies in batches. Yield: 6 dozen

ARAMARK Corporation—Clemson Catering

Beacon Hill Cookies

1 cup semisweet chocolate chips
2 egg whites
⅛ teaspoon salt
½ cup sugar
½ teaspoon vanilla extract
½ teaspoon vinegar
¾ cup chopped walnuts

Place the chocolate chips in the top of a double boiler. Cook, stirring frequently, until melted. Set aside to cool. Beat the egg whites with the salt in a large mixer bowl at high speed until foamy. Add the sugar gradually, beating until stiff peaks form. Blend in the vanilla and vinegar. Stir in the melted chocolate and walnuts. Drop teaspoonfuls of dough, 2 inches apart, onto greased cookie sheets. Bake at 350 degrees for 10 minutes or until lightly browned. Remove to wire racks to cool. Yield: 4 dozen

Joyce M. Bussey (Mrs. Charlie Bussey)

Desserts

Miss Bonnie's Chocolate Chip Cookies

1 cup oats, rolled
¾ cup butter-flavored shortening
1¼ cups firmly packed brown sugar
1 egg
1 tablespoon vanilla extract
2 tablespoons milk
2 cups flour
1 teaspoon salt
¾ teaspoon baking soda
2 cups semisweet chocolate chips

Place the oats in a blender and blend until finely ground. Set aside. Cream the shortening and brown sugar in a large mixer bowl. Add the egg; beat until blended. Add the extract and milk; mix well. Combine the oats, flour, salt and baking soda in a large bowl. Add to the sugar mixture gradually, mixing until well blended. Stir in the chocolate chips. Shape the dough into 1-inch balls. Place, 2 inches apart, on nonstick cookie sheets. Bake at 375 degrees for 8 minutes or until golden brown. Cool on cookie sheets. Yield: 2 dozen

Bonnie Bennett Dixon (Mrs. David Dixon)

Bonnie, Bennett, Brooks, Augusta and David Dixon

Bonnie, '84, and her husband, David, '85, live in Greenville, where David works as an architect. They have three children, Bennett, 8, Brooks, 6, and Augusta, 4. Bonnie bakes these cookies for her children and her friends' children. They all call her "Miss Bonnie."

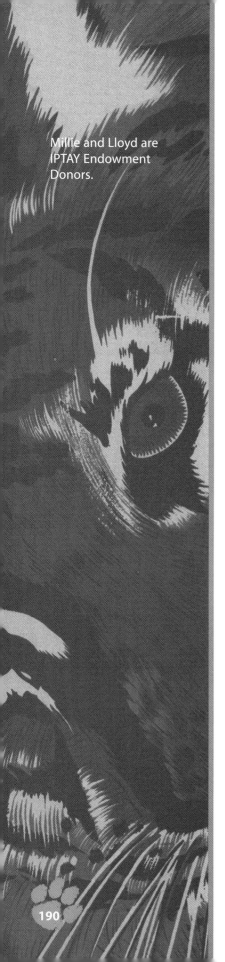

Chocolate Mini Squares

2 cups each flour and granulated sugar
1/4 teaspoon salt
1/2 cup each butter and shortening
1/4 cup baking cocoa
1 cup water
1/2 cup buttermilk
2 eggs, lightly beaten
1 teaspoon each vanilla extract and baking soda
1/2 teaspoon cinnamon
1/2 cup butter
1/4 cup baking cocoa
6 tablespoons milk
1 (1-pound) box confectioners' sugar
1 teaspoon vanilla extract
1 cup chopped pecans or walnuts

Sift the flour, granulated sugar and salt into a large bowl. Combine 1/2 cup butter, shortening, 1/4 cup cocoa and water in a saucepan. Bring to a boil, stirring constantly. Pour over the flour mixture; mix well. Blend in the buttermilk, eggs and 1 teaspoon vanilla. Stir in the baking soda and cinnamon. (Batter will be thin.) Pour into a greased and floured 10x15-inch jelly-roll pan. Bake at 400 degrees for 20 minutes. Remove to a wire rack. Combine 1/2 cup butter, 1/4 cup cocoa and milk in a saucepan. Bring to a boil, stirring constantly. Remove from the heat. Add the confectioners' sugar gradually, beating well. Stir in the vanilla. Pour over the warm cake. Sprinkle with the pecans. Cool completely. Cut into squares to serve. Note: You may use a wooden pick to poke holes all over the top of the cake before topping it with the frosting. Yield: 54 squares

Millie Gurley (Mrs. Lloyd Gurley)

Desserts

Irresistible Peanut Butter Cookies

½ cup butter, softened
¾ cup peanut butter
1¼ cups firmly packed brown sugar
1 egg
3 tablespoons milk
1 tablespoon vanilla extract
1¾ cups flour
¾ teaspoon baking soda
¾ teaspoon salt

Combine the butter, peanut butter and brown sugar in a mixer bowl. Beat until well blended. Add the egg; mix well. Blend in the milk and vanilla. Combine the flour, baking soda and salt in a large bowl. Add to the peanut butter mixture gradually, beating until well blended. Drop heaping teaspoonfuls of dough, 2 inches apart, onto ungreased cookie sheets. Flatten in a criss-cross pattern with the tines of a fork. Bake at 375 degrees for 8 minutes or until golden brown. Remove to wire racks to cool. Note: To prevent sticking, dip the fork into a glass of cold water before pressing it into the cookie dough. Yield: 3 dozen

Richard (Dick) L. Sobocinski

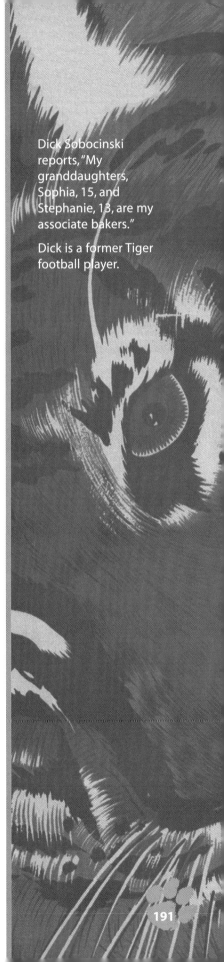

Dick Sobocinski reports, "My granddaughters, Sophia, 15, and Stephanie, 13, are my associate bakers."

Dick is a former Tiger football player.

Dick Sobocinski

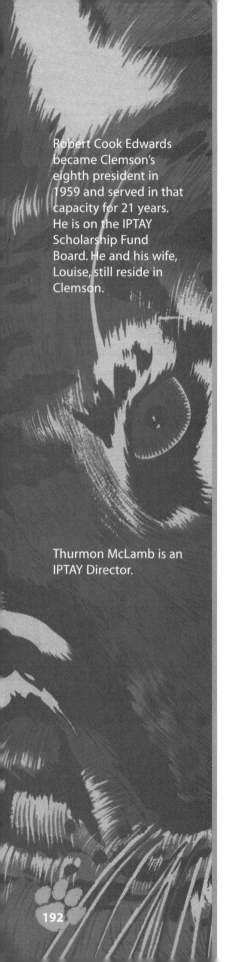

Pecan Pie Squares

3 cups flour
1/4 cup plus 2 tablespoons sugar
3/4 cup butter or margarine, softened
3/4 teaspoon salt
4 eggs, lightly beaten
1 1/2 cups sugar
1 1/2 cups light corn syrup
3 tablespoons melted butter or margarine
1 1/2 teaspoons vanilla extract
2 1/2 cups chopped pecans

Beat the flour, 1/4 cup plus 2 tablespoons sugar, 3/4 cup butter and salt in a large mixer bowl until crumbly. (Mixture will be dry.) Press firmly onto the bottom of a greased 9x13-inch baking pan. Bake at 350 degrees for 20 minutes or until lightly browned. Remove to a wire rack. Combine the eggs, 1 1/2 cups sugar, corn syrup, 3 tablespoons melted butter and vanilla in a medium bowl until well blended. Stir in the pecans. Pour over the baked layer; spread to cover evenly. Bake at 350 degrees for 25 minutes or until the filling is set. Remove to a wire rack to cool. Cut into 1 1/2-inch squares. Yield: 4 1/2 dozen

Louise Stone (Mrs. Herbert Stone)

Grandmother Colson's Old-Fashioned Tea Cakes

4 cups flour
1 teaspoon baking soda
1 cup lard
3 cups sugar
3 eggs
2 teaspoons vanilla extract
1 cup buttermilk

Sift the flour and measure. Sift together the 4 cups flour with the baking soda; set aside. Cream the lard and sugar in a mixer bowl until light and fluffy. Add the eggs, 1 at a time, beating well after each addition. Blend in the vanilla. Add the flour mixture alternately with the buttermilk, mixing until well blended. Shape the dough into a ball. Add water, if necessary, to make a stiff dough. Place the dough on a lightly floured surface; roll out to a 1/4-inch thickness. Cut with a lightly floured biscuit cutter. Place on a baking sheet. Bake at 350 degrees for 10 to 12 minutes or until golden brown. Remove to wire racks to cool. Note: You may substitute 1/2 cup butter for 1/2 cup of the lard. Yield: 5 dozen

Diane McLamb (Mrs. Thurmon McLamb)

Desserts

Treasure Chest Bars

2 cups flour
1 ½ teaspoons baking powder
½ teaspoon salt
½ cup margarine, softened
½ cup firmly packed brown sugar
½ cup granulated sugar
2 eggs
1 teaspoon vanilla extract
¾ cup milk
1 cup chopped pecans or walnuts
1 cup semisweet chocolate chips

Sift together the flour, baking powder and salt; set aside. Cream the margarine, brown sugar and granulated sugar in a large mixer bowl. Add the eggs, 1 at a time, beating well after each addition. Blend in the vanilla. Add the flour mixture alternately with the milk, mixing until well blended. Stir in the pecans and chocolate chips. Spread the dough onto the bottom of a greased and floured 9x13-inch baking pan. Bake at 325 degrees for 25 to 30 minutes or until a wooden pick inserted into the center comes out clean. (Do not overbake.) Remove to a wire rack to cool. Note: May drizzle the cooled bars with white icing or dust with confectioners' sugar. Yield: 24 bars

Sharon Match (Mrs. Tim Match)

"Miss" Clara's Sugar Cookies

½ cup butter, softend
1 (1-pound) box brown sugar
3 eggs
1 teaspoon vanilla extract
1 cup self-rising flour
1 cup all-purpose flour
⅛ teaspoon salt
1 cup chopped pecans or walnuts

Beat the butter and brown sugar in a large mixer bowl until well blended. Add the eggs, 1 at a time, beating well after each addition. Blend in the vanilla. Combine the self-rising flour, all-purpose flour and salt in a large bowl. Add to the brown sugar mixture gradually, mixing well. Stir in the nuts. Drop tablespoonfuls of the dough, 2 inches apart, onto greased cookie sheets. Bake at 300 degrees for 12 minutes or until lightly browned. (Do not overbake; these cookies burn easily.) Remove to wire racks to cool. Yield: 2 dozen

Claudia Paulling (Mrs. Robert Paulling)

Tim Match is the Associate Athletic Director for Public Relations.

Desserts

World's Most Delicious Cookies

1 cup margarine or butter, softened
1 cup granulated sugar
1 cup firmly packed brown sugar
1 egg
1 cup vegetable oil
2 teaspoons vanilla extract
3½ cups flour
1 teaspoon baking soda
1 teaspoon salt
1 cup crushed cornflakes
1 cup rolled oats
½ cup flaked coconut
½ cup chopped pecans

Cream the margarine, granulated sugar and brown sugar in a large mixer bowl until light and fluffy. Add the egg; mix well. Blend in the oil and vanilla. Add the flour gradually, mixing until well blended. Add the baking soda and salt; mix well. Add the cornflakes, oats and coconut. Stir in the pecans. Shape the dough into 1-inch balls. Place on ungreased cookie sheets; flatten with a fork. Bake at 325 degrees for 10 to 12 minutes or until lightly browned. (Do not overbake.) Let cool a few minutes on the cookie sheet before removing the cookies to wire racks to cool. Note: Sprinkle the baked cookies with additional granulated sugar, if desired. Yield: 6 dozen

Billy and Beverly O'Dell

Billy and Beverly O'Dell enjoy living in Madison, Georgia. They see the Tigers play as often as they can.

Desserts

Cheesecake Bars

1/3 cup margarine
1 (12-ounce) package butterscotch morsels
2 cups graham cracker crumbs
1 cup chopped pecans
8 ounces cream cheese, softened
1 egg
1 (14-ounce) can sweetened condensed milk
1 teaspoon vanilla extract

Combine the margarine and butterscotch morsels in a medium saucepan. Stir over low heat until melted. Combine the graham cracker crumbs and pecans in a large bowl. Press 1/2 the mixture onto the bottom of a greased 9x13-inch baking pan; set aside. Beat the cream cheese in a small mixer bowl until creamy. Beat in the egg. Mix in the sweetened condensed milk and vanilla. Spread evenly over the crumb mixture in the baking pan. Top with the remaining crumb mixture. Bake at 350 degrees for 30 minutes or until the filling is set. Remove to a wire rack to cool. Refrigerate, covered, until chilled. Note: If using a glass baking dish, reduce the oven temperature to 325 degrees. Yield: 12 to 15 servings

Joann West (Mrs. Joe West)

My Mammy's Peach Cobbler

3 cups peeled fresh peach slices
1 tablespoon lemon juice
1 cup self-rising flour
1 cup sugar
1 egg
6 tablespoons melted butter

Place the peach slices in the bottom of a 9x13-inch baking dish. Sprinkle with the lemon juice. Combine the flour, sugar and egg in a medium bowl; mix with a fork until well blended. (Mixture will be dry and crumbly.) Sprinkle over the peaches. Drizzle with the butter. Bake at 375 degrees for 35 minutes or until the topping is golden brown. Remove to a wire rack to cool. Note: Drained canned peach slices can be substituted for the fresh peaches. Yield: 6 to 8 servings

Zane Lake (Mrs. Robbie Lake)

Clemson's presidents

1890—Henry Aubrey Strode

1893—Edwin Boone Craighead

1897—Henry Simms Hartzog

1902—Patrick Hues Mell

1911—Walter Merritt Riggs

1925—Enoch Walter Sikes

1940—Dr. Robert Poole, Sr.

1959—Robert Cook Edwards

1979—Bill Lee Atchley

1985—Walter Thompson Cox

1986—Max Lennon

1993—Phil Prince

1995-Dr. Constantine Curris

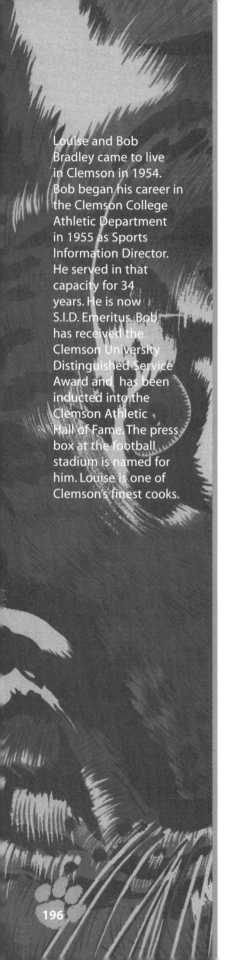

Blackberry Cobbler

1 cup water
1 cup sugar
3 tablespoons all-purpose flour
3 to 4 cups blackberries
2 tablespoons butter
¼ teaspoon cinnamon
1 cup self-rising flour
3 tablespoons sugar
3 tablespoons shortening
½ cup milk

Bring the water to a boil over high heat in a medium saucepan. Combine 1 cup sugar and all-purpose flour in a small bowl. Add to the boiling water. Boil for 1 minute, stirring constantly. Add the blackberries; stir until evenly coated. Pour into a 2-quart baking dish. Dot with 2 tablespoons butter. Sprinkle with the cinnamon. Combine the self-rising flour and 3 tablespoons sugar in a medium bowl. Cut in the shortening with a pastry blender or 2 forks until the mixture resembles coarse crumbs. Add the milk; stir until the mixture forms a soft dough. (Do not overstir.) Drop tablespoonfuls of dough over the blackberries. Bake at 400 degrees for 30 minutes or until the top is golden brown. Note: When using very sweet berries, you may decrease the 1 cup sugar to ⅔ cup.
Yield: 6 servings

Louise Bradley (Mrs. Bob Bradley)

Bob and Louise Bradley

Desserts

Bobby's Favorite Banana Pudding

4 cups milk
4 eggs, lightly beaten
1 1/3 cups sugar
1 teaspoon vanilla extract
1 (11-ounce) box vanilla wafers
6 bananas, sliced
3 egg whites
3 tablespoons sugar

Heat the milk in the top of a double boiler, but do not let it come to a boil. Combine the eggs and 1 1/3 cups sugar in a medium bowl; mix well. Stir in the vanilla. Add to the milk mixture gradually, mixing well. Cook, stirring constantly, until the mixture coats a spoon. Remove from the heat; set aside to cool. Place a layer of 1/3 of the wafers in a 2-quart baking dish. Cover with a layer of 1/3 of the bananas and a layer of 1/3 of the pudding. Repeat the layers, ending with the pudding. Beat the egg whites and 3 tablespoons sugar in a small mixing bowl until stiff peaks form. Spoon over the pudding. Bake at 325 degrees for 10 minutes or until the meringue is lightly browned. Remove to a wire rack to cool. Yield: 10 to 12 servings

Carolyn Robinson (Mrs. Robert Robinson),
mother of Athletic Director Bobby Robinson

Bobby Robinson, ready to eat his mother's
Banana Pudding

Carolyn Robinson

Grandma Keating's Rice Pudding

5 tablespoons long grain white rice
2 egg yolks, lightly beaten
4 cups milk
3 tablespoons sugar
2 tablespoons butter
1 teaspoon vanilla extract
⅛ to ¼ teaspoon nutmeg
2 egg whites
2 tablespoons sugar

Rinse the rice under cold running water; drain. Combine the rice and egg yolks in a large saucepan. Add the milk; mix well. Cook over low heat, stirring occasionally, for 1 to 1½ hours or until the rice is tender and the milk is absorbed. Remove a small amount of the rice mixture. Place in a small bowl; stir in 3 tablespoons sugar. Return to the saucepan. Add the butter; stir until melted. Remove from the heat. Let cool. Stir in the vanilla. Spoon into individual dessert dishes. Sprinkle with the nutmeg. Beat the egg whites and 2 tablespoons sugar with an electric mixer at high speed until stiff peaks form. Spoon over the pudding; swirl with the back of the spoon to form peaks. Bake at 425 degrees for 3 to 4 minutes or until lightly browned. Yield: 4 servings

Helen S. Golan

Brownie Ice Cream Dessert

1 box brownie mix
½ gallon ice cream, any flavor, slightly softened
2 cups confectioners' sugar
⅔ cup semisweet chocolate chips
1½ cups evaporated milk
½ cup butter or margarine
1½ cups chopped pecans
1 teaspoon vanilla extract

Prepare and bake the brownies in a 9x13-inch baking pan according to the package directions. Let cool. Spread the ice cream over the top of the brownies. Freeze, covered, until firm. Mix the confectioners' sugar, evaporated milk and butter in a medium saucepan. Bring to a boil over medium heat, stirring constantly. Stir in the pecans and vanilla. Remove from the heat; cool completely. Spread over the ice cream. Freeze, covered, until ready to serve. Cut into squares. Serve immediately. Note: To serve warm, place the dessert squares on a microwave-safe dessert dish and microwave until heated. Yield: 12 servings

Marie L. Staedeli

Desserts

Ice Cream Delight

9 or 10 ice cream sandwiches
16 ounces whipped topping
6 to 8 toffee candy bars, crushed

Place the ice cream sandwiches in a single layer on the bottom of an 11x13-inch baking dish. Cover with the whipped topping. Sprinkle with the candy bars. Freeze, covered, until firm. Cut into squares to serve. Yield: 12 servings

Cathy Turner (Mrs. Joe Turner)

Joe Turner and his partner, Kelly Durham

Joe Turner, '71, worked as a Clemson alumni field representative and also as Executive Secretary of IPTAY from 1979 to 1984.

Robert Ricketts is Associate Athletic Director and Chief Financial Officer for Athletics.

Punch Bowl Cake

1 (2-layer) package yellow cake mix
1 (6-ounce) package vanilla instant pudding mix
1 (20-ounce) can crushed pineapple
2 (10-ounce) packages frozen strawberries
1 package frozen coconut
20 ounces whipped topping
½ cup chopped pecans, toasted

Prepare and bake the cake in a 10x15-inch jelly roll pan according to the package directions. Remove to a wire rack to cool completely. Prepare the pudding mix according to the package directions. Refrigerate, covered, until thickened. Crumble ½ the cake into the bottom of a punch bowl. Top with ½ each of the undrained pineapple, undrained strawberries, coconut and whipped topping. Repeat the layers, ending with the whipped topping. Sprinkle with the pecans. Yield: 16 to 20 servings

Kathy B. Ricketts (Mrs. Robert Ricketts)

Krispie Ice Cream Delight

½ cup melted margarine
1 cup firmly packed brown sugar
2 cups crisp rice cereal
1 cup chopped pecans or walnuts
1 cup flaked coconut
½ gallon vanilla ice cream, softened

Combine the margarine and brown sugar in a large bowl; mix well. Add the cereal, nuts and coconut; mix lightly until all the ingredients are evenly coated with the brown sugar mixture. Spread the mixture in a jelly roll pan. Bake at 350 degrees for 20 minutes, stirring occasionally. Remove to a wire rack to cool. Spread ½ the cereal mixture onto the bottom of a 9x13-inch baking pan. Cover with a layer of the ice cream and the remaining cereal mixture. Freeze, covered, until firm. Cut into squares to serve. Note: Top individual servings with fudge topping, if desired. Yield: 6 servings

Catherine (Kitty) Cutler

Ma's Cheesecake

40 ounces cream cheese, softened
1³/₄ cups sugar
3 tablespoons flour
5 eggs
3 egg yolks
1 teaspoon vanilla extract
1 cup whipping cream
Juice of ¹/₂ medium orange
Juice of ¹/₂ medium lemon

Combine the cream cheese, sugar and flour in a large mixer bowl; beat with an electric mixer until well blended. Add the 5 eggs, 1 at a time, beating well after each addition. Add the egg yolks; mix well. Blend in the vanilla. Add the whipping cream, orange juice and lemon juice gradually, mixing until well blended. Pour the batter into a 10-inch springform pan. Bake at 350 degrees for 1 hour. Turn the oven off. Partially open the oven door. Let the cheesecake set in the oven for 1 hour. Remove to a wire rack. Cool for 10 minutes before loosening the side of the pan. Cool the cheesecake completely. Refrigerate, covered, until ready to serve.
Yield: 8 to 10 servings

Jeanne Bisaccia, wife of football Coach Richard Bisaccia

Carolyn Hendrix says, "When my son, Bill, '63, was 10 years old, he asked if he could have three pecan pies instead of a birthday cake. I have been baking them for him since then."

Bill's Favorite Pie

¼ cup butter or margarine, softened
1¼ cups firmly packed brown sugar
2 large eggs
1 tablespoon corn syrup
1¼ cups pecan pieces
1 unbaked (9-inch) pie shell

Combine the butter and brown sugar in a large bowl. Mix with a pastry blender or fork until the mixture forms coarse crumbs. Add the eggs and corn syrup; mix well. Stir in the pecans. Pour into the pie shell. Bake at 350 degrees for 10 to 15 minutes or until the filling is set. Note: Serve topped with scoops of vanilla ice cream, if desired. Yield: 6 servings

Carolyn O. Hendrix (Mrs. L.J. Hendrix)

Carolyn Hendrix and family

Evelyn Moore's Blueberry Pie

3 cups sifted flour
1¼ cups shortening
½ teaspoon salt
1 egg
5 tablespoons ice water
2 teaspoons vinegar
4 cups fresh blueberries
1 cup sugar
¼ cup flour
¼ teaspoon cinnamon
⅛ teaspoon salt
3 tablespoons lemon juice
2 tablespoons butter

Combine 3 cups flour, shortening and ½ teaspoon salt in a large bowl. Mix with a pastry blender or 2 forks until the mixture resembles coarse crumbs. Beat together the egg, ice water and vinegar in a small bowl. Add to the flour mixture; mix with a fork until the mixture forms a ball. Divide the ball in half. Roll out each half on a lightly floured surface to a ⅛-inch thickness. Place 1 crust in the bottom of a 10-inch pie plate. Cover and set aside the remaining pie crust. Mix the blueberries, sugar, ¼ cup flour, cinnamon and salt in a large bowl. Add the lemon juice; toss lightly. Place in the pie shell; dot with the butter. Top with the remaining pie crust. Cut slits in the top crust. Seal and flute the edges. Cover the edge with foil to prevent the crust from browning too quickly. Bake at 425 degrees for 35 to 45 minutes or until the crust is golden brown and the berry juice is bubbling through the slits in the crust. Remove the foil for the last 15 minutes of baking. Yield: 6 to 8 servings

Coach Larry and
Pam Shyatt

Geoff, Philip, Jeremy,
Larry and
Pam Shyatt

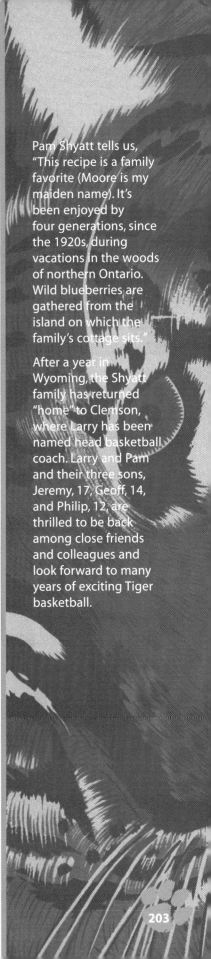

Pam Shyatt tells us, "This recipe is a family favorite (Moore is my maiden name). It's been enjoyed by four generations, since the 1920s, during vacations in the woods of northern Ontario. Wild blueberries are gathered from the island on which the family's cottage sits."

After a year in Wyoming, the Shyatt family has returned "home" to Clemson, where Larry has been named head basketball coach. Larry and Pam and their three sons, Jeremy, 17, Geoff, 14, and Philip, 12, are thrilled to be back among close friends and colleagues and look forward to many years of exciting Tiger basketball.

Desserts

Tiger Sweet Brown Sugar Pie

2 eggs
2 cups firmly packed brown sugar
3 tablespoons melted butter
2 tablespoons flour
1 teaspoon vanilla extract
¾ cup milk
1 (9-inch) pie shell

Lightly beat the eggs in a medium bowl. Add the brown sugar, butter, flour and vanilla. Stir in the milk gradually. Pour into the pie shell. Bake at 300 degrees for 35 to 45 minutes or until the filling is set. Remove to a wire rack to cool. Yield: 6 to 8 servings

Carolyn Dalton (Mrs. Allison Dalton)

California Tarts

3 ounces cream cheese, softened
½ cup butter, softened
1 cup flour
½ cup butter
1 cup sugar
2 egg yolks
1 tablespoon vanilla extract
1 cup chopped dates
1 cup chopped pecans
2 egg whites

Beat the cream cheese and ½ cup butter in a large mixer bowl until creamy. Add the flour; mix well. Press the dough into 36 miniature muffin cups; set aside. Cream ½ cup butter with the sugar in a large mixer bowl. Blend in the egg yolks and vanilla. Stir in the dates and pecans. Beat the egg whites in a small mixer bowl at high speed with an electric mixer until stiff peaks form. Fold into the date mixture. Spoon evenly into the unbaked tart shells. Bake at 300 degrees for 25 minutes or until the filling is set. Remove to wire racks to cool. Yield: 3 dozen

Rebecca C. Horton (Mrs. S. F. Horton)

Chess Pie

5 eggs
1½ cups sugar
Juice of 1½ lemons
Grated rind of 1 lemon
½ cup melted butter
1 (9- or 10-inch) pie shell

Lightly beat the eggs in a medium bowl. Add the sugar, lemon juice and lemon rind; mix well. Stir in the butter. Pour into the pie shell. Bake at 400 degrees for 35 to 45 minutes or until the filling is set. Remove to a wire rack to cool. Yield: 6 to 8 servings

Hazel C. Poe (Mrs. H. Vernon Poe)

Chocolate Coconut Chess Pies

½ cup butter or margarine, softened
4 cups sugar
5 eggs
½ cup baking cocoa
1 (12-ounce) can evaporated milk
1 tablespoon vanilla extract
1 cup flaked coconut
1 cup chopped pecans
3 (9-inch) pie shells
Whipped cream or whipped topping

Cream the butter and sugar in a large mixer bowl until light and fluffy. Add the eggs, 1 at a time, beating well after each addition. Add the cocoa; mix well. Add the evaporated milk gradually, mixing until well blended. Blend in the vanilla. Stir in the coconut and pecans. Pour evenly into the pie shells. Bake at 350 degrees for 50 minutes or until the filling is set. Remove to wire racks to cool. Top with dollops of whipped cream. Yield: 18 to 24 servings

Ava P. Campbell (Mrs. Lynn Campbell)

Hazel Poe shares with us, "In 1917 my Virginia-born father brought his bride to Clemson College. He taught agronomy courses there for some 45 years, becoming known, sometimes affectionately, to hundreds of students as 'The Lord.' When we visited my grandmother in Virginia, she would have the cook prepare pies or tarts from this recipe, a particular favorite. It is very rich, but simple and delicious. While I have occasionally found recipes for something called Chess Pie in cookbooks, generally the ingredients will include such items as cornmeal, raisins, or nuts, which make an entirely different type of pie."

Marbled Chocolate Rum Pie

    1 envelope unflavored gelatin
    ¼ cup sugar
    ⅛ teaspoon salt
    2 egg yolks, beaten
    1 cup milk
    ¼ cup rum
    1 (12-ounce) package semisweet chocolate chips
    2 egg whites
    ½ cup sugar
    1 cup whipping cream
    ¼ cup sugar
    1 teaspoon vanilla extract
    1 (9-inch) pie shell, baked, cooled

Combine the gelatin, ¼ cup sugar and salt in the top of a double boiler. Add the egg yolks, milk and rum; mix well. Cook over boiling water until thickened, stirring occasionally. Remove from the heat. Add the chocolate chips; stir until melted. Refrigerate until thickened, but not set. Beat the egg whites and ½ cup sugar in a small mixer bowl until stiff peaks form. Fold into the chocolate mixture. Combine the whipping cream, ¼ cup sugar and vanilla in a small mixer bowl. Beat at high speed with an electric mixer until stiff peaks form. Spoon the chocolate and whipped cream mixtures alternately into the pie shell; swirl with a knife to marbleize. Refrigerate, covered, until firm. Yield: 6 to 8 servings

Joan S. Kennerty (Mrs. Bill Kennerty)

Coconut Pies

    ½ cup melted margarine
    2 cups sugar
    4 eggs
    1 teaspoon lemon juice
    1 teaspoon vanilla extract
    1 cup milk
    1 cup evaporated milk
    1 (3-ounce) can flaked coconut
    2 (9-inch) pie shells

Cream the margarine and sugar in a large bowl. Add the eggs, 1 at a time, beating well after each addition. Blend in the lemon juice and vanilla. Stir in the milk, evaporated milk and coconut. Pour evenly into the pie shells. Bake at 350 degrees for 30 minutes or until the filling is set and lightly browned. Yield: 12 to 16 servings

Jean Holladay

Desserts

Aunt Lottie's Pineapple Coconut Pies

2 cups flour
1 teaspoon salt
⅔ cup shortening or lard
3 to 4 tablespoons cold water
5 medium eggs
2½ cups sugar
1 (8-ounce) can crushed pineapple
1 cup flaked coconut
½ cup melted margarine or butter

Combine the flour and salt in a large bowl. Cut in the shortening with a pastry blender or 2 forks until the mixture resembles coarse crumbs. Sprinkle ⅓ of the flour mixture with 1 tablespoon water; mix lightly with a fork until the flour mixture is moistened. Repeat with 2 tablespoons water and flour mixture. Shape the dough into a ball. Add the remaining 1 tablespoon water, if necessary. Divide the dough in half. Roll each half out on a lightly floured surface to a ⅛-inch thickness. Place in 9-inch pie plates; trim and flute the edges. Lightly beat the eggs in a medium bowl. Add the sugar, undrained pineapple, coconut and margarine. Pour ½ of the filling into each pie crust. Bake at 350 degrees for 30 to 35 minutes or until a wooden pick inserted into the centers comes out clean. Note: You may substitute 4 large eggs for the 5 medium eggs, or 1 (3-ounce) can flaked coconut for the 1 cup coconut. Yield: 16 servings

Lee Ann Henderson (Mrs. Bert Henderson)

Bert Henderson

Bert Henderson works as an Associate Director of IPTAY. He and Lee Ann have two daughters, Amy Lee and Kimberly.

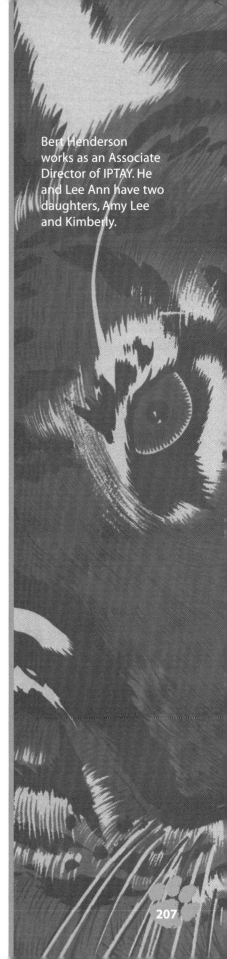

Desserts

Sara Lee's Tang Pies

1 (14-ounce) can sweetened condensed milk
2 cups sour cream
1/2 cup Tang
8 ounces whipped topping
2 (8- or 9-inch) prepared graham cracker crumb pie shells

Combine the sweetened condensed milk, sour cream and Tang in a large bowl. Fold in the whipped topping. Spoon evenly into the pie shells. Freeze, covered, for 1 hour or until firm. Note: Serve topped with dollops of additional thawed frozen whipped topping, if desired. Yield: 16 servings

Robin Mahony (Mrs. Bob Mahony)

Bob Mahony

Lemon Angel Pie

1 (9-inch) pie shell
4 egg whites
1 cup sugar
¼ teaspoon cream of tartar
4 egg yolks, lightly beaten
1 tablespoon grated lemon rind
6 teaspoons lemon juice
½ cup sugar
⅛ teaspoon salt
12 ounces whipped topping

Bake the pie shell according to the recipe or package directions; cool completely. Beat the egg whites in a medium bowl with an electric mixer at high speed until stiff peaks form. Gradually beat in 1 cup sugar and cream of tartar. Spoon into the pie shell; smooth the top to make it even. Bake at 275 degrees for 1 hour. Remove to a wire rack to cool. Combine the egg yolks, lemon rind, lemon juice, ½ cup sugar and salt in a medium saucepan. Cook over low heat, stirring constantly, until thickened. Remove from the heat; cool. Fold 1 cup of the whipped topping into the lemon mixture. Prick the meringue shell all over with a fork. Fill with the lemon filling. Top with the remaining whipped topping. Refrigerate, covered, overnight. Note: You can substitute drained sweetened strawberries for the lemon juice and rind. Yield: 8 servings

Betty J. Robinson (Mrs. Ed Robinson)

Ed and Betty Robinson

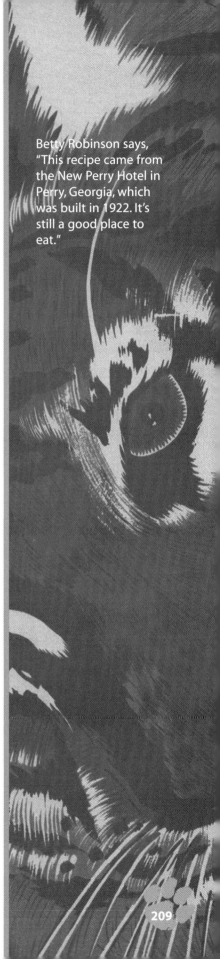

Betty Robinson says, "This recipe came from the New Perry Hotel in Perry, Georgia, which was built in 1922. It's still a good place to eat."

Rosie's Lemon Ice Box Pie

2 (14-ounce) cans sweetened condensed milk
½ cup lemon juice
1 egg yolk
1 purchased or prepared graham cracker crumb pie shell
2 egg whites
¼ cup sugar

Combine the sweetened condensed milk, lemon juice and egg yolk in a medium bowl; mix well. Pour into the pie shell. Beat the egg whites and sugar in a small mixing bowl with an electric mixer at high speed until stiff peaks form. Spread over the filling. Bake at 250 degrees for 10 minutes or until lightly browned. Remove to a wire rack to cool. Refrigerate, covered, until ready to serve.
Yield: 6 to 8 servings

Charlie and Rosie Waters

Clemson Ice Cream Pie

1 (16-ounce) package chocolate creme-filled sandwich cookies, crushed
½ cup melted butter
½ gallon vanilla ice cream, softened
12 ounces whipped topping
1 (12-ounce) jar chocolate and/or caramel ice cream topping
1 cup chopped pecans or walnuts

Spray a 9x13-inch baking dish with nonstick cooking spray. Combine the cookie crumbs and butter in a medium bowl. Press onto the bottom of the prepared dish to form a crust. Top with layers of ½ of the ice cream and ½ of the whipped topping. Drizzle with ½ of the ice cream topping. Sprinkle with ½ of the pecans. Repeat the layers. Freeze, covered, overnight. Cut into squares to serve. Yield: 12 to 15 servings

Angie Alexander (Mrs. Mike Alexander)

Nutty Pie

½ cup butter
1 cup light corn syrup
1 cup sugar
3 eggs
1 teaspoon vanilla extract
1½ cups chopped pecans
1 (9-inch) pie shell

Combine the butter, corn syrup and sugar in a medium saucepan. Cook over medium heat, stirring constantly, until the butter is melted. Lightly beat the eggs in a medium bowl. Add the corn syrup mixture gradually, stirring constantly. Blend in the vanilla. Stir in the pecans. Pour into the pie shell. Bake at 350 degrees for 45 minutes or until the filling is set. Yield: 6 to 8 servings

Elva Hoover (Mrs. Fred Hoover)

Fred and Elva Hoover

Elva Hoover remembers, "This recipe was sent to us, along with a Christmas gift of pecans, about 38 years ago. I use it for our Thanksgiving and Christmas dessert."

Fred Hoover has been head trainer at Clemson for over 3 decades.

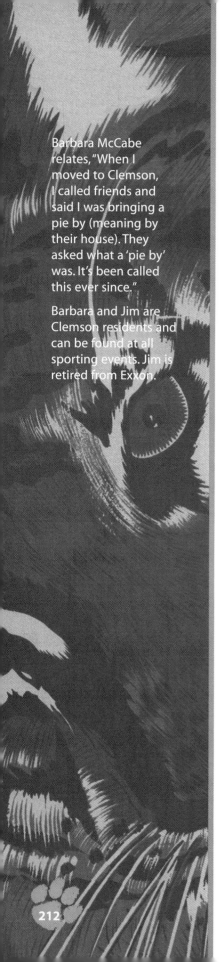

Pecan "Pie By"

3 eggs, lightly beaten
1 cup sugar
1 cup light corn syrup
2 tablespoons melted butter
1 teaspoon vanilla extract
1¼ cups chopped pecans
1 (9-inch) deep-dish pie shell

Combine the eggs, sugar, corn syrup, butter and vanilla in a medium bowl; mix well. Stir in the pecans. Pour into the pie shell. Bake at 350 degrees for 55 minutes or until a knife inserted into the center comes out clean. Remove to a wire rack to cool. Yield: 8 servings

Jim and Barbara McCabe

Pecan Sand Tarts

1 cup butter, softened
½ cup granulated sugar
2 teaspoon vanilla extract
2 cups flour
2 cups finely chopped pecans
Confectioners' sugar

Cream the butter and granulated sugar in a large mixer bowl until light and fluffy. Blend in the vanilla. Add the flour gradually, mixing until well blended. Add the pecans; mix well. Refrigerate, covered, for 1 hour or until well chilled. Shape the dough into tiny crescents or half-moon shapes. Place on ungreased cookie sheets. Bake at 275 degrees for 35 to 45 minutes or until lightly browned. Remove to wire racks to cool completely. Sprinkle with the confectioners' sugar and store in an airtight container. Yield: 5 to 5½ dozen

Nancy Cathcart (Mrs. Foster Cathcart)

Desserts

Hayes Star Brand Pinto Bean Pies

1 cup cooked Hayes Star Brand Pinto Beans
4 eggs, lightly beaten
1 cup melted butter or margarine
1 tablespoon vanilla extract
3 cups sugar
1 (3-ounce) can flaked coconut
1 cup chopped pecans
3 (9-inch) pie shells

Mash the beans well, using any liquid from the cooked beans. Blend in the eggs. Stir in the butter and vanilla. Add the sugar; mix well. Stir in the coconut and pecans. Pour the filling evenly into the pie shells. Bake at 300 degrees for 45 minutes to 1 hour or until the filling is set. Remove to wire racks to cool completely. Note: These baked pies freeze well. Cool completely before wrapping tightly to freeze. Yield: 24 servings

Joe and Eleanor Hayes

Eleanor and Joe Hayes own Hayes Star Brand Beans Company. They developed this pie recipe, and most people can't guess what kind of pie it is. Some think it's a pecan or apple pie. The Hayeses are long-time Clemson IPTAY supporters.

Les and Mae Tindal were among the guests helping Eleanor and Joe Hayes celebrate their 50th wedding anniversary.

Desserts

"Proud Products" for Every Occasion

A proud ACC Tiger team

Cream Cheese and Sun-Dried Tomato Fondue

16 ounces cream cheese, softened
1 cup **Naturally Fresh**® Lite Peppercorn Ranch Dressing
½ cup grated Parmesan cheese
½ cup sliced sun-dried tomatoes
½ cup roasted corn niblets
2 tablespoons finely chopped roasted red pepper
2 tablespoons finely chopped green onions
1 teaspoon kosher salt
¾ teaspoon crushed black pepper
1 cup finely chopped pecans

Beat the cream cheese, **Naturally Fresh** Lite Peppercorn Ranch Dressing, Parmesan cheese, sun-dried tomatoes, corn, red pepper, green onions, salt and pepper in a bowl for about 1 minute or until well mixed. Form the mixture into a wedge shape on a piece of wet cheesecloth. Refrigerate, covered, overnight. Roll in the pecans. Serve with toasted pita chips. Yield: 72 (1-tablespoon) servings

Sesame Cheese Ball

8 ounces cream cheese, softened
8 ounces shredded sharp Cheddar cheese
1 cup chopped pecans
¼ cup milk
1 clove of garlic, minced
½ cup toasted sesame seeds

Combine the cream cheese, Cheddar cheese, pecans, milk and garlic in a bowl. Form the cream cheese mixture into a ball. Wrap in waxed paper. Refrigerate for at least 2 hours. Roll the cheese ball in the sesame seeds before serving. Serve with crackers.
Yield: 64 (1-tablespoon) servings

Naturally Fresh®
Dressings, Sauces & Dips

Crab Meat Pita Sandwiches

1 pound crab meat
1 bunch asparagus tips, cooked and chilled
1 red bell pepper, sliced
½ cup chopped celery
½ teaspoon cracked peppercorns
1 cup **Naturally Fresh**® Lite Peppercorn Ranch Dressing
6 whole-wheat pita bread shells
1 bunch arugula (rocket greens)
¼ cup very thinly sliced onion
6 slices Lorraine Swiss cheese

Combine the crab meat, asparagus tips, red pepper, celery, peppercorns and **Naturally Fresh** Lite Peppercorn Ranch Dressing in a bowl. Refrigerate, covered, for 30 minutes. Stir the mixture and spoon into the pita bread shells. Top with the arugula, onion and Lorraine Swiss cheese. Serve with chips or your favorite pasta salad. Yield: 6 servings

Bill Bellamy, Bob Brooks' uncle, in the Naturally Fresh lab

Naturally Fresh®
Dressings, Sauces & Dips

Garlic and Tomato Bread

1 pound loaf French or Italian bread
1 cup **Naturally Fresh**® Classic Caesar Dressing
½ cup marinated sun-dried tomatoes, chopped
3 tablespoons grated Parmesan cheese
1 teaspoon chopped fresh parsley

Cut the bread into 1-inch slices. Combine the **Naturally Fresh** Caesar Dressing and the sun-dried tomatoes in a bowl. Spread over the bread slices. Sprinkle with the Parmesan cheese. Bake at 350 degrees for 10 minutes or until golden. Sprinkle with the parsley. Yield: 20 servings

Gourmet Olé Burgers

1½ pounds ground beef
¼ cup **Naturally Fresh** Lite Ranch Dressing
1 (1-ounce) package taco seasoning mix
6 slices Monterey Jack cheese
6 hamburger buns
6 avocado slices
Naturally Fresh Picante Salsa

Combine the ground beef, **Naturally Fresh** Lite Ranch Dressing and taco seasoning mix in a medium bowl. Shape the ground beef mixture into 6 patties. Grill for 5 to 7 minutes on each side or until cooked through. Top each burger with a cheese slice. Grill until the cheese is melted. Top the burgers with the avocado slices and **Naturally Fresh** Picante Salsa; serve on buns. Yield: 6 servings

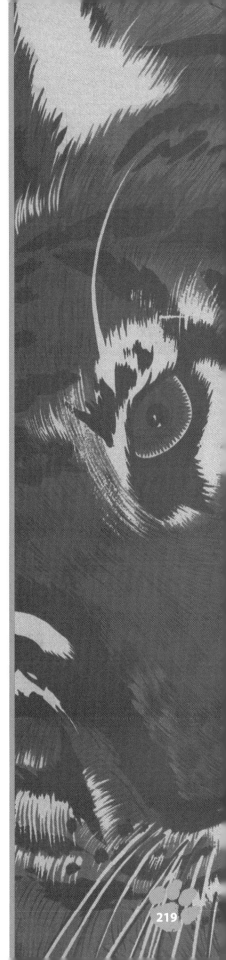

Pesto Ranch Croutons

2 cups **Naturally Fresh**® Pesto Ranch Dressing
³/₄ cup melted butter
¹/₂ cup grated Parmesan cheese
12 cups ¹/₂-inch bread cubes

Combine the **Naturally Fresh** Pesto Ranch Dressing, butter and Parmesan cheese in a large bowl. Add the bread cubes and toss to coat. Spread out on a baking sheet. Bake at 250 degrees for 30 to 45 minutes or until the bread is browned and crisp.
Yield: 12 cups croutons

Stuffed Potato Skins

4 medium baking potatoes, baked
2 cups **Naturally Fresh** Bleu Cheese Dressing
8 ounces bacon bits
¹/₂ cup sliced green onions

Cut the baked potatoes in half lengthwise. Scoop out the center of each potato leaving a ¹/₄-inch shell. Reserve the potato pulp for another use. Fill the potato shells with **Naturally Fresh** Bleu Cheese Dressing. Place the potatoes on a baking sheet. Bake at 300 degrees for 25 minutes. Top with the bacon bits and onions. Yield: 8 servings

NaturallyFresh®
Dressings, Sauces & Dips

Half Moon Bay Artichoke Salad

    6 cups mixed salad greens
    9 ounces artichoke hearts, cooked
    8 ounces cooked green beans
    ½ red onion, sliced
    8 cherry tomatoes, halved
    1 cup **Naturally Fresh**® Bleu Cheese Dressing
    ½ cup bacon bits
    2 hard-cooked eggs, cut into wedges

Combine the salad greens, artichoke hearts, green beans, red onion, cherry tomatoes and **Naturally Fresh** Bleu Cheese Dressing in a salad bowl. Toss well. Top with the bacon bits and eggs. Refrigerate, covered, until chilled. Yield: 4 to 6 servings

Balsamic Layered Slaw

    1 medium sweet onion, thinly sliced
    1 small head cabbage, shredded
    2 tomatoes, cut into thin wedges
    1 cucumber, halved lengthwise and sliced
    1 small yellow bell pepper, thinly sliced
    1 (4-ounce) can sliced black olives, drained
    ¾ cup crumbled feta cheese
    1 cup **Naturally Fresh** Olive Oil and Balsamic Vinegar Dressing

Cut each onion slice in half and separate into half rings. Layer the onion, cabbage, tomatoes, cucumber, yellow pepper, black olives and feta cheese in a salad bowl. Pour the **Naturally Fresh** Olive Oil and Balsamic Vinegar Dressing over the salad. Refrigerate, covered, for 8 hours. Toss the salad just before serving. Yield: 4 to 6 servings

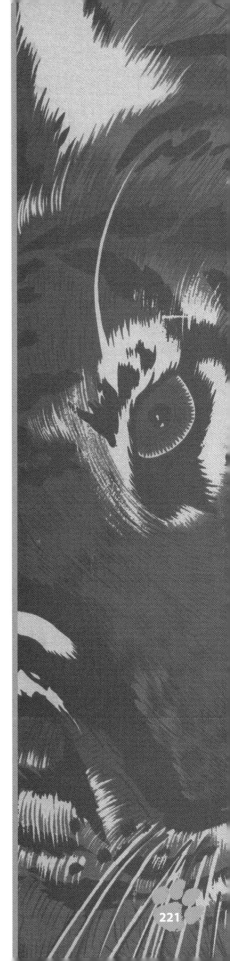

Naturally Fresh®
Dressings, Sauces & Dips

Cantaloupe and Chicken Salad

> 4 cups cubed cooked chicken
> 2 cups cantaloupe balls
> 1 (15-ounce) can pineapple chunks, drained
> 1 cup thinly sliced celery
> ½ cup chopped green bell pepper
> 1 cup **Naturally Fresh**® Poppy Seed Dressing
> 1 (3-ounce) can chow mein noodles
> ⅓ cup honey-roasted peanuts

Combine the chicken, cantaloupe, pineapple, celery, green pepper and **Naturally Fresh** Poppy Seed Dressing in a salad bowl. Sprinkle the chow mein noodles and peanuts over the top. Yield: 4 servings

Country Garden Chicken Salad

> 4 boneless skinless chicken breast halves, cooked
> ½ cup chopped pecans
> ¼ cup thinly sliced celery
> 1 cup **Naturally Fresh** Country Garden Dip

Chop the chicken into ¼-inch chunks. Combine the chicken chunks, pecans, celery and **Naturally Fresh** Country Garden Dip in a bowl. Serve the salad on a bed of lettuce, in pita pockets or stuffed into fresh tomato halves. Yield: 4 servings

Chick-Pea Salad

2 cups diced tomatoes
1 cup canned chick-peas, rinsed and drained
1 cup diced cucumber
1 cup diced yellow onion
1 cup **Naturally Fresh**® Fat Free Thousand Island Dressing

Combine the tomatoes, chick-peas, cucumber, onion and **Naturally Fresh** Fat Free Thousand Island Dressing in a salad bowl. Toss well. Refrigerate, covered, until chilled. Yield: 4 servings

Southwest Corn and Black Bean Salad

2 cups grilled or roasted corn kernels
2 cups peeled seeded diced tomatoes
1 cup canned black beans, rinsed and drained
1 cup chopped grilled red onion
1 cup chopped roasted green bell pepper
1 cup chopped roasted red bell pepper
1 cup thinly sliced grilled celery
³/₄ cup **Naturally Fresh** Fat Free Italian Dressing
¹/₃ cup **Naturally Fresh** Raspberry Vinaigrette
³/₄ cup chopped fresh cilantro
1 teaspoon cumin
1 teaspoon chili powder

Combine the corn, tomatoes, black beans, red onion, green pepper, red pepper and celery in a salad bowl. Combine the **Naturally Fresh** Fat Free Italian Dressing, **Naturally Fresh** Raspberry Vinaigrette, cilantro, cumin and chili powder in a bowl. Pour over the vegetables and toss to mix well. Refrigerate, covered, until serving time. Serve over iceberg lettuce leaves, if desired. Yield: 8 servings

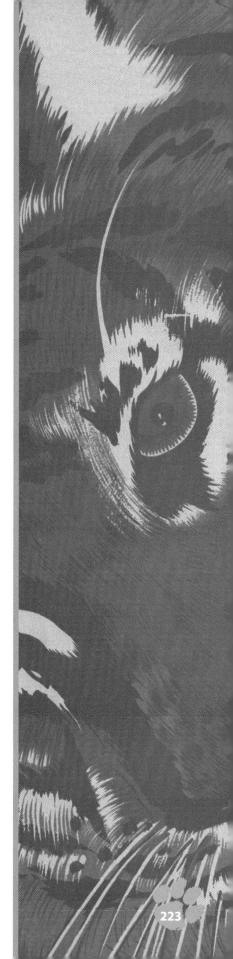

Layered Lettuce Salad

1 small head iceberg lettuce, torn into pieces
1 (10-ounce) package frozen green peas, thawed and drained
4 hard-cooked eggs, sliced
8 slices bacon, cooked and crumbled (optional)
1 small onion, chopped
½ cup diced celery
1 green bell pepper, diced
2 teaspoons sugar
Salt and pepper to taste
1½ cups **Naturally Fresh**® Mayonnaise
4 ounces Cheddar cheese, shredded

Layer the lettuce, peas, eggs, bacon, onion, celery, green pepper, sugar, salt, pepper, **Naturally Fresh** Mayonnaise and Cheddar cheese in a 9x13-inch baking dish. Refrigerate, covered, overnight.
Yield: 6 to 8 servings

Anchorage Pasta Salad

1 pound canned salmon, flaked
1 pound penne pasta, cooked
10 ounces mushrooms, sliced
1 large red onion, thinly sliced
½ cup toasted bread crumbs
½ cup chopped celery
2 tablespoons drained capers
2 cloves of garlic, minced
1 cup **Naturally Fresh** Tartar Sauce

Mix the salmon, pasta, mushrooms, red onion, bread crumbs, celery, capers, garlic and **Naturally Fresh** Tartar Sauce in a bowl. Refrigerate, covered, until chilled. Yield: 6 servings

Bob Brooks, CEO of Eastern Foods, Inc.

Naturally Fresh®
Dressings, Sauces & Dips

Chilled Orecchiette Pasta and Shrimp Salad

2 pounds sugar snap peas, cooked and chilled
1 pound orecchiette pasta, cooked and chilled
8 ounces baby shrimp, peeled, deveined and cooked
1 cup diced roasted red bell pepper
1/2 cup roasted corn niblets
1/2 cup sliced green onions
1/2 cup diced cooked carrots (1/4-inch dice)
1 cup **Naturally Fresh**® Pesto Ranch Dressing
3 ounces pine nuts, toasted

Combine the peas, pasta, shrimp, red pepper, corn, green onions, carrots and **Naturally Fresh** Pesto Ranch Dressing in a salad bowl. Toss to mix. Top with the toasted pine nuts. Yield: 6 servings

Naturally Fresh Pasta Salad

3 cups Marrichetti penne pasta (baby penne)
Vegetable oil
3/4 cup **Naturally Fresh** Lite Ranch Dressing
1/2 cup **Naturally Fresh** Sour Cream & Herb Dressing or Dip
1/4 teaspoon dillweed
1 1/2 cups fresh peas, parboiled and chilled
3/4 cup shredded reduced-fat Cheddar cheese
1/2 cup chopped celery
1/3 cup diced yellow bell pepper
1/3 cup diced red bell pepper
1/2 cup pine nuts, toasted

Cook the pasta according to the package directions. Drain and rinse under cold water. Toss with just enough oil to lightly coat. Combine the **Naturally Fresh** Lite Ranch Dressing, **Naturally Fresh** Sour Cream & Herb Dressing or Dip and dillweed in a large bowl; stir well. Add the pasta, peas, cheese, celery, yellow pepper and red pepper. Toss to coat. Refrigerate, covered, until chilled. Stir and sprinkle with the pine nuts before serving. Yield: 4 to 6 servings

Naturally Fresh®
Dressings, Sauces & Dips

Stir-Fry Beef

    1 pound flank steak, thinly sliced
    ½ cup cooking sherry
    2 teaspoons minced garlic
    2 tablespoons vegetable oil
    1 green or red bell pepper, sliced
    1 onion, sliced
    1 yellow squash, sliced
    1 cup broccoli florets
    1 cup **Naturally Fresh**® Sweet & Sour Sauce
    2 cups hot cooked rice

Combine the steak slices, sherry and garlic in a bowl. Refrigerate, covered, for 30 minutes. Heat the oil in a large skillet. Remove the steak from the marinade and add to the oil. Stir-fry for 1 minute. Add the green pepper, onion, squash and broccoli. Stir-fry until the meat is cooked through and the vegetables are tender. Stir in the **Naturally Fresh** & Sour Sauce and heat through. Serve over the rice. Yield: 4 servings

Savory BBQ Pork Ribs

    3 pounds country-style pork ribs
    1 envelope onion soup mix
    1 bottle **Jackaroo**® Meat Sauce

Rinse the ribs and place in a Dutch oven. Add enough water to cover the ribs. Bring to a boil. Boil until the ribs are almost cooked, adding an additional cup of water to keep the ribs covered. Stir in the onion soup mix. Cook until almost all of the liquid is evaporated. Reduce the heat to low. Add the **Jackaroo** Meat Sauce. Simmer, covered, for 10 minutes. Yield: 4 servings

Stir-Fry Pork

1 pound pork tenderloin, thinly sliced
1 egg, beaten
½ cup cornstarch
2 tablespoons vegetable oil
1 green or red bell pepper, sliced
1 onion, sliced
1 yellow squash, sliced
1 cup broccoli florets
1 cup **Naturally Fresh**® Sweet & Sour Sauce
1 (8-ounce) can pineapple chunks, drained
2 cups hot cooked rice

Dip the pork tenderloin slices in the beaten egg and then in the cornstarch to coat. Heat the oil in a skillet. Add the pork. Cook until browned on both sides. Add the green pepper, onion, squash and broccoli. Cook until the vegetables are tender-crisp and the pork is cooked through. Stir in the **Naturally Fresh** Sweet & Sour Sauce and the pineapple. Cook until heated through. Serve over the rice.
Yield: 4 servings

Naturally Fresh refrigerated trucks, ready to deliver their wonderful products

Naturally Fresh®
Dressings, Sauces & Dips

Creamed Tuscan Pork with Peppers

2 pounds boneless pork, cut into 1-inch cubes
4 cloves of garlic, minced
2 cups chopped tomatoes
½ cup dry white wine
1 cup **Naturally Fresh**® Pesto Ranch Dressing
1 medium onion, chopped
1 red bell pepper, sliced
1 green bell pepper, sliced

Brown the pork with the garlic in a large nonstick skillet. Stir in the tomatoes, wine and **Naturally Fresh** Pesto Ranch Dressing. Bring to a boil; reduce the heat. Simmer until the pork is tender and cooked through. Sauté the onion, red pepper and green pepper in a nonstick sauté pan until tender. Stir into the pork mixture. Simmer for 5 minutes. Serve with rice. Yield: 8 servings

Chicken Caesar Casserole

1 cup crushed cornflakes
½ cup melted butter or margarine
2 cups cubed cooked chicken
1 cup cooked white rice
1 cup chopped celery
1 (10-ounce) can cream of chicken soup
1 (8-ounce) can water chestnuts, drained and chopped
2 tablespoons chopped onion
¾ cup **Naturally Fresh** Caesar Dressing

Combine the crushed cornflakes and butter in a small bowl; set aside. Mix the chicken, rice, celery, chicken soup, water chestnuts, onion and **Naturally Fresh** Caesar Dressing in a bowl. Pour into a greased 2-quart casserole. Top with the cornflake mixture. Bake at 350 degrees for 30 minutes or until bubbly. Yield: 6 to 8 servings

NaturallyFresh®
Dressings, Sauces & Dips

Chicken Italian

3 pounds boneless skinless chicken pieces
1½ cups **Naturally Fresh**® Italian Herb Vinaigrette Dressing
1 cup flour
3 eggs, beaten
1 cup bread crumbs
2 cups canola oil
4 ounces sliced prosciutto
1½ cups **Naturally Fresh** Tomato Basil Vinaigrette
3 ounces tomato paste (5 tablespoons)
4 ounces sliced provolone cheese

Combine the chicken pieces and **Naturally Fresh** Italian Herb Vinaigrette Dressing in a baking dish. Refrigerate, covered, overnight. Remove the chicken from the marinade; discard the marinade. Rinse the chicken and pat dry. Pound the chicken between 2 pieces of plastic wrap until slightly flattened. Place the flour, eggs and bread crumbs in 3 separate bowls. Coat the chicken with flour. Dip into the egg and then roll in the bread crumbs to coat. Heat the oil in a skillet. Add the chicken and cook until golden brown on both sides. Transfer to a greased 9x13-inch baking dish. Top the chicken with the prosciutto. Combine the **Naturally Fresh** Tomato Basil Vinaigrette and tomato paste in a bowl. Pour over the chicken and prosciutto. Top with the provolone cheese. Bake at 350 degrees for 30 minutes or until bubbly and the cheese is melted.
Yield: 8 servings

Naturally Fresh®
Dressings, Sauces & Dips

Sweet and Sour Chicken Stir-Fry

3 boneless skinless chicken breast halves, diced (about 2 cups)
¾ cup **Naturally Fresh®** Honey French Dressing
1 tablespoon brown sugar
2 teaspoons soy sauce
2 tablespoons vegetable oil
1 cup each thinly sliced carrots and snow peas
1 small green bell pepper, sliced
1 (8-ounce) can sliced water chestnuts, drained
¼ cup sliced green onions
1 tablespoon each minced garlic and minced gingerroot
2 teaspoons cornstarch
½ cup water
1 medium tomato, cut into wedges
½ cucumber, halved, sliced
1 cup **Naturally Fresh** Classic Oriental Dressing
¼ cup sesame seeds, toasted
2 cups hot cooked rice

Combine the diced chicken, **Naturally Fresh** Honey French Dressing, brown sugar and soy sauce in a bowl. Refrigerate, covered, for 30 minutes. Heat the oil in a wok or large skillet over high heat. Add the chicken. Stir-fry until slightly browned. Remove from the wok and set aside. Add the carrots, snow peas, green pepper, water chestnuts, green onions, garlic and gingerroot to the wok. Stir-fry until tender-crisp. Stir in a mixture of the cornstarch and water. Add the chicken, tomato, cucumber and **Naturally Fresh** Classic Oriental Dressing. Cook until heated through and the chicken is cooked. Top with the sesame seeds. Serve over the rice. Yield: 4 servings

BBQ Deep-Fried Turkey

1 (12-pound) turkey
1 bottle **Jackaroo®** Meat Sauce
Vegetable oil for deep-frying

Loosen the turkey's skin gently, but do not remove. Spread the **Jackaroo** Meat Sauce over the turkey's surface under the skin. Heat enough oil to 375 degrees in a deep-fryer or stockpot to completely cover the turkey. Lower the turkey carefully into the hot oil. Cook for 35 minutes or until the internal temperature reaches 180 degrees. Remove the turkey carefully from the hot oil. Drain thoroughly. Cover and let stand for 10 minutes before carving. Yield: 12 to 14 servings

Naturally Fresh®
Dressings, Sauces & Dips

Clemson Orange Roughy and Garden Vegetables

1 cup sliced carrots
1 cup sliced zucchini
1 cup sliced yellow squash
½ cup chopped green onions
2 tablespoons vegetable oil (optional)
Salt and pepper to taste
1 (8-ounce) orange roughy fillets
½ cup teriyaki sauce
½ cup **Naturally Fresh**® Classic Oriental Dressing

Steam the carrots, zucchini, yellow squash and green onions or stir-fry in a wok or large skillet in the oil until tender-crisp. Season the vegetables lightly with salt and pepper; set aside. Brush the fish fillets lightly with teriyaki sauce. Place in a fish grill basket. Grill for 10 to 15 minutes or until the fish is cooked through. Place the vegetables on a serving plate. Top with the grilled fish. Drizzle with the **Naturally Fresh** Classic Oriental Dressing. Yield: 2 servings

One of the **Naturally Fresh** race cars

Dressings, Sauces & Dips

Cajun Catfish

    1½ pounds catfish fillets
    ½ cup plain bread crumbs
    2 cups **Naturally Fresh**® Cajun Sauce
    4 cups hot cooked rice

Coat the fish fillets in the bread crumbs. Place in a single layer in a greased baking dish. Bake at 400 degrees for 8 minutes. Pour the **Naturally Fresh** Cajun Sauce over the fillets. Bake for 5 minutes or until the fish is cooked through. Serve over the rice. Yield: 6 servings

Lemon Butter Shrimp

    ¼ cup melted margarine
    2 teaspoons parsley flakes
    ½ teaspoon garlic powder
    1 teaspoon **Naturally Fresh** Lemon Vinaigrette Dressing
    12 ounces cooked shrimp
    1 (7-ounce) package pasta shells, cooked
    ¼ cup **Naturally Fresh** Wine and Cheese Dressing

Combine the margarine, parsley flakes, garlic powder and **Naturally Fresh** Lemon Vinaigrette Dressing in a bowl and set aside. Combine the cooked shrimp, cooked pasta shells and **Naturally Fresh** Wine and Cheese Dressing in a serving bowl. Add the margarine mixture and mix well. Yield: 3 servings

Naturally Fresh®
Dressings, Sauces & Dips

Oriental Chicken Vermicelli

12 ounces boneless skinless chicken breasts
¼ cup **Naturally Fresh**® Classic Oriental Dressing
Dash of Tabasco sauce
½ cup cooked vermicelli
3 tablespoons **Naturally Fresh** Classic Dressing
4 cups romaine lettuce leaves
1 cup thinly sliced Chinese or red cabbage
1 cup cucumber slices
1 cup red bell pepper strips
1 cup sliced carrots
½ cup sliced green onions (¼ inch thick)
¼ cup chopped fresh cilantro leaves

Grill the chicken over medium-hot coals for 15 to 20 minutes or until cooked through. Slice into strips. Toss with ¼ cup **Naturally Fresh** Classic Oriental Dressing and Tabasco sauce in a bowl. Refrigerate, covered, until ready to serve. Toss the cooked vermicelli with 3 tablespoons **Naturally Fresh** Classic Oriental Dressing in a bowl. Combine the lettuce, cabbage, cucumber, red pepper, carrots, green onions and cilantro in a bowl. Arrange on individual plates or a serving platter. Top with the vermicelli and chicken. Serve with extra Classic Oriental Dressing on the side. Yield: 3 servings

Pasta with Tomatoes and Spinach

1 cup **Naturally Fresh** Tomato Basil Vinaigrette
8 ounces cooked pasta shells
8 ounces cherry tomatoes, halved
2 ounces fresh spinach leaves
2 tablespoons olive oil
2 ounces grated Parmesan cheese

Combine the **Naturally Fresh** Tomato Basil Vinaigrette, cooked pasta shells, cherry tomatoes and spinach in a bowl. Heat the oil in a large skillet. Add the pasta mixture. Sauté for 5 minutes. Top with the Parmesan cheese. Serve immediately. Yield: 4 servings

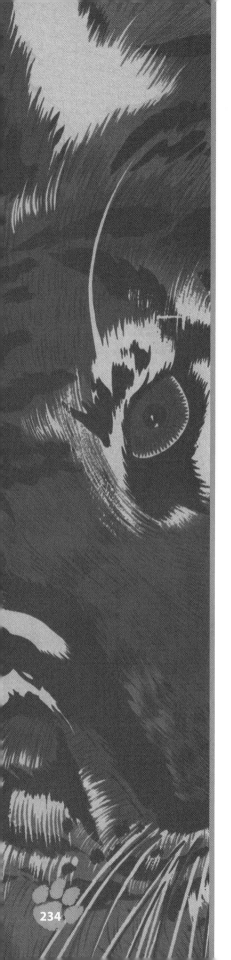

Rotini Pasta with Vegetables and Smoked Turkey

1 bunch broccoli florets
2 to 3 carrots, sliced
2 tablespoons **Naturally Fresh**® Olive Oil
2 red bell peppers, chopped
1 (16-ounce) package rotini or fusilli pasta, cooked
6 to 8 ounces smoked turkey, julienned
1 bunch green onions, chopped
2 tablespoons chopped fresh basil
1 teaspoon black pepper
1 cup **Naturally Fresh** Fat Free Italian Dressing
¼ cup grated Romano cheese

Steam the broccoli and carrots until tender-crisp; cool and set aside. Heat the **Naturally Fresh** Olive Oil in a skillet. Add the red peppers. Cook until heated through; cool. Place the cooked rotini in a serving bowl. Add the broccoli, carrots, red peppers, smoked turkey, green onions, basil, pepper and **Naturally Fresh** Fat Free Italian Dressing and toss to mix. Top with the Romano cheese. Yield: 4 to 6 servings

Grilled Asparagus Tips Oriental

2 pounds asparagus, trimmed
2 tablespoons sesame oil
1 tablespoon soy sauce
½ cup chopped navel orange
¼ cup cashews, toasted
1 green onion, thinly sliced diagonally
1 cup **Naturally Fresh** Classic Oriental Dressing

Combine the asparagus, sesame oil and soy sauce in a baking dish. Marinate, covered, for 1 hour. Grill the asparagus until tender; cool. Toss the grilled asparagus, orange, cashews, green onion and **Naturally Fresh** Classic Oriental Dressing in a bowl. Refrigerate, covered, until chilled. Yield: 8 servings

Dressings, Sauces & Dips

Jackaroo® Baked Beans

4 slices bacon, chopped
½ cup minced onion
1 clove of garlic, minced
1 (28-ounce) can baked beans
1 cup **Jackaroo®** Meat Sauce
¼ cup packed brown sugar

Brown the bacon with the onion and garlic in a large skillet, stirring until the bacon is crisp and the onion is browned. Drain most of the drippings from the skillet. Stir in the baked beans, **Jackaroo** Meat Sauce and brown sugar. Pour into a greased 1-quart baking dish. Bake at 350 degrees for 20 minutes or until bubbly. Yield: 6 to 8 servings

The **Jackaroo** tent

Naturally Fresh®
Dressings, Sauces & Dips

Baked Eggplant with Rice Stuffing

2 eggplants
1 tablespoon **Naturally Fresh**® Olive Oil
1 cup cooked rice
1 tomato, diced
1 green bell pepper, chopped
½ cup chopped onion
¼ cup chopped ham or prosciutto
¾ cup **Naturally Fresh** Fat Free Tomato Basil Vinaigrette
1 tablespoon grated Parmesan cheese

Cut the eggplants in half lengthwise. Brush the cut surfaces with the **Naturally Fresh** Olive Oil. Place in a baking dish. Bake at 350 degrees until tender. Sauté the rice, tomato, green pepper, onion, ham and **Naturally Fresh** Fat Free Tomato Basil Vinaigrette in a skillet until the green pepper and onion are tender. Scoop out the centers of the eggplant halves leaving a ¼-inch shell. Chop the removed eggplant and stir into the rice mixture. Fill the eggplant shells with the rice mixture. Place on a baking sheet and cover lightly with foil. Bake at 350 degrees for 20 minutes. Uncover and bake for 10 minutes or until browned. Sprinkle with Parmesan cheese and serve.
Yield: 4 servings

Okra Creole

¼ cup minced onion
3 tablespoons minced green bell pepper
2 tablespoons butter
8 ounces sliced okra
2 cups chopped tomatoes
1 tablespoon sugar
Salt and pepper to taste

Sauté the onion and green pepper in the butter in a large skillet for 2 minutes. Add the okra. Cook for 5 minutes, stirring constantly. Stir in the tomatoes and sugar. Simmer over low heat for about 20 minutes or until the okra is tender. Season with salt and pepper.
Yield: 4 servings

Naturally Fresh®
Dressings, Sauces & Dips

Garden Vegetable Casserole (Ghiveci)

4 medium tomatoes, quartered
2 medium carrots, thinly sliced
2 small potatoes, cut into cubes
3 small yellow squash, sliced
3 small zucchini, sliced
1 Bermuda onion, sliced
1 small head cauliflower, separated into florets
1 cup fresh sliced green beans
1 rib celery, sliced
$\frac{1}{2}$ cup julienned red bell pepper
$\frac{1}{2}$ cup julienned green bell pepper
$\frac{1}{2}$ cup green peas
1 clove of garlic, minced
1 cup beef bouillon
$\frac{1}{2}$ cup olive oil
2 teaspoons salt
$\frac{1}{2}$ bay leaf, crumbled
$\frac{1}{2}$ teaspoon savory
$\frac{1}{4}$ teaspoon tarragon

Combine the tomatoes, carrots, potatoes, yellow squash, zucchini, onion, cauliflower, green beans, celery, red pepper, green pepper, peas and garlic in an ungreased 11x13-inch baking dish. Combine the bouillon, oil, salt, bay leaf, savory and tarragon in a saucepan. Bring to a boil. Pour over the vegetables. Cover with heavy-duty foil. Bake at 350 degrees for 1 hour or until the vegetables are tender.
Yield: 8 to 10 servings

Naturally Fresh®
Dressings, Sauces & Dips

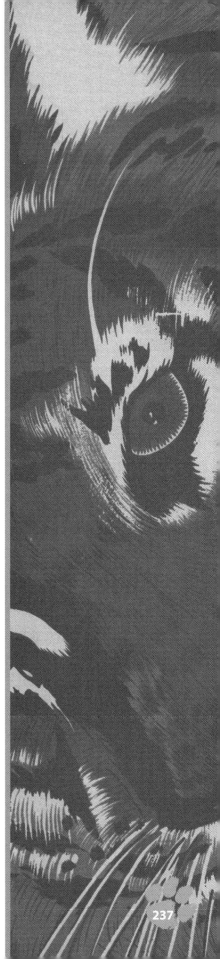

Pineapple Casserole

2 (15-ounce) cans pineapple chunks
1 cup sugar
2 tablespoons flour
1 egg
2 cups shredded sharp Cheddar cheese
35 butter crackers, crushed
½ cup melted butter

Drain the pineapple, reserving 2 tablespoons juice. Place the pineapple in a greased 7x11-inch baking dish. Combine the 2 tablespoons reserved pineapple juice, sugar, flour and egg in a saucepan. Cook and stir until thickened. Pour over the pineapple. Top with the cheese and crushed crackers. Drizzle the melted butter over the crackers. Bake at 350 degrees for 25 minutes or until heated through. Yield: 4 to 6 servings

Naturally Fresh®
Dressings, Sauces & Dips

Reuben Baked Potatoes

6 baking potatoes, baked
1 pound julienned corned beef
8 ounces sauerkraut
¾ cup **Naturally Fresh**® Fat Free Thousand Island Dressing
½ cup shredded Swiss cheese
4 ounces shredded asiago cheese

Cut the baked potatoes in half lengthwise. Scoop out the center of each potato leaving a ¼-inch shell. Combine the potato pulp, corned beef, sauerkraut and **Naturally Fresh** Fat Free Thousand Island Dressing in a bowl. Fill the potato shells with the corned beef mixture. Top with the Swiss and asiago cheeses. Place the potatoes on a baking sheet. Bake at 350 degrees for 20 minutes or until heated through. Yield: 6 servings

Vegetarian Delight

2 cups broccoli florets
2 cups cauliflower florets
1 medium zucchini, sliced ½ inch thick
1 small yellow squash, cut into ½-inch chunks
1 carrot, sliced ¼ inch thick
1 medium onion, quartered
Pinch of lemon salt
8 ounces cooked pasta
2 cups **Naturally Fresh** Bleu Cheese Dressing

Steam the broccoli, cauliflower, zucchini, yellow squash, carrot and onion until tender-crisp. Season with the lemon salt. Toss the vegetables with the cooked pasta and **Naturally Fresh** Bleu Cheese Dressing in a serving bowl. Yield: 6 servings

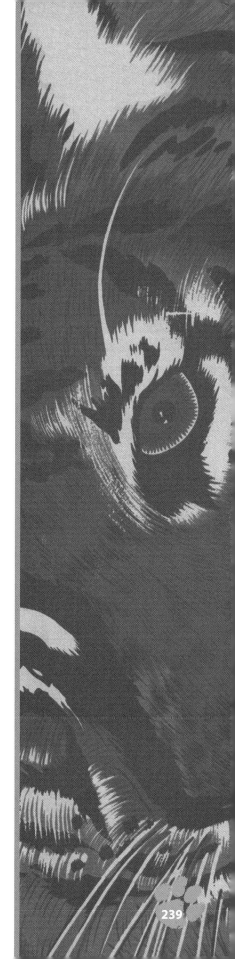

Naturally Fresh®
Dressings, Sauces & Dips

Marinated Grilled Vegetables

1 cup **Naturally Fresh**® Italian Herb Vinaigrette Dressing
¼ cup chopped fresh basil
2 teaspoons chopped fresh oregano
1 teaspoon chopped fresh chives
1 clove of garlic, minced
¼ teaspoon black pepper
1½ cups new potatoes, parboiled and diced
1 cup sliced yellow squash
1 cup sliced zucchini
1 cup cauliflower florets
2 medium onions, coarsely chopped
½ cup chopped green bell pepper
½ cup chopped red bell pepper
1 cup diced smoked mozzarella cheese (½ inch dice)

Combine the **Naturally Fresh** Italian Herb Vinaigrette Dressing, basil, oregano, chives, garlic and black pepper in a large bowl. Add the potatoes, yellow squash, zucchini, cauliflower, onions, green pepper and red pepper. Toss to mix. Marinate for 1 to 2 hours. Remove the vegetables from the marinade and place in a grill basket. Grill for 5 to 10 minutes on each side or until tender-crisp. Sprinkle with the smoked mozzarella. Note: To hold the grilled vegetables for later serving, brush them with the marinade and pour into a greased baking dish. Keep warm in a 200 degree oven until serving time. Top with the cheese just before serving.
Yield: 8 to 10 servings

Naturally Fresh® Vegetable Ranch Medley

1 cup baby carrots or sliced carrots
1 cup cauliflower florets
1 cup broccoli florets
1 cup sliced yellow squash or zucchini
⅓ cup **Naturally Fresh** Lite Ranch Dressing
Salt and pepper to taste

Steam the carrots for 2 minutes. Add the cauliflower, broccoli, and yellow squash to the carrots. Steam for 8 to 10 minutes or until the vegetables are tender-crisp. Place the vegetables on a serving platter. Drizzle with the **Naturally Fresh** Lite Ranch Dressing. Season with salt and pepper. Serve immediately. Yield: 6 to 8 servings

One of the Naturally Fresh race cars

Naturally Fresh®
Dressings, Sauces & Dips

Zucchini Casserole

2 large zucchini, sliced
½ cup sliced water chestnuts
Salt and pepper to taste
1 (10-ounce) can cream of chicken soup
½ cup bread crumbs
¼ cup melted butter
¼ cup grated Parmesan cheese

Layer the zucchini and water chestnuts in a greased 7x11-inch baking dish. Season with salt and pepper. Spread the chicken soup over the vegetables. Combine the bread crumbs and butter in a bowl. Sprinkle the crumb mixture and Parmesan cheese over the top. Bake, covered, at 350 degrees for 30 minutes. Uncover. Bake for 30 minutes or until bubbly. Yield: 4 to 6 servings

Curried Fruit

1 (16-ounce) can sliced pineapple
1 (16-ounce) can pear halves
1 (16-ounce) can peach halves
1 (16-ounce) can apricot halves
1 (16-ounce) jar maraschino cherries
½ cup butter, melted
½ cup packed brown sugar
1 tablespoon cornstarch
2 teaspoons curry powder
½ cup sliced almonds

Drain the pineapple, pears, peaches, apricots and cherries, reserving all the juices. Pour the melted butter into a 9x13-inch baking dish. Stir in the brown sugar, cornstarch and curry powder until smooth. Add all the fruit. Pour in enough of the reserved juices to cover the fruit. Top with the almonds. Bake at 350 degrees for 1 hour. Note: This tastes better if made a day ahead of time and reheated before serving. Yield: 10 to 12 servings

Impossible Coconut Pies

1 cup flour
1½ cups sugar
2 cups milk
4 eggs, beaten
½ cup melted butter
1 (7-ounce) can flaked coconut
1 teaspoon vanilla extract

Combine the flour and sugar in a large bowl. Stir in the milk, eggs, butter, coconut and vanilla until well blended. Pour into 2 well-buttered 8-inch pie pans. Bake at 350 degrees for 35 minutes.
Yield: 12 servings

Pecan Pie Katrina

1 cup light corn syrup
½ cup packed brown sugar
3 eggs
2 teaspoons melted butter
1 cup pecan halves
½ teaspoon vanilla extract
1 (9-inch) unbaked pie shell

Beat the corn syrup, brown sugar, eggs and butter in a bowl. Stir in the pecans and vanilla. Pour into the pie shell. Bake at 350 degrees for 45 minutes or until a knife inserted near the center comes out clean. Yield: 6 servings

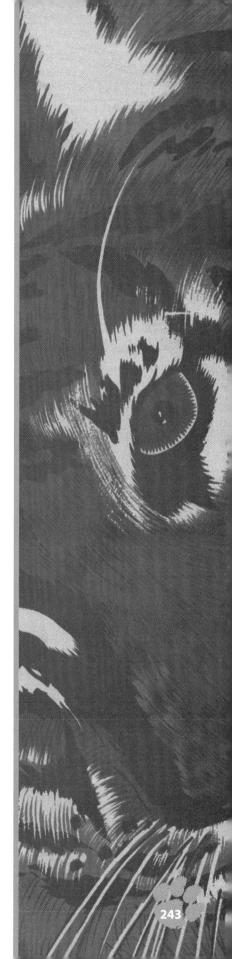

NaturallyFresh®

Dressings, Sauces & Dips

Piña Colada Cake

  1 (2-layer) package white cake mix
  1 cup **Classic**® Piña Colada Mix
  1 (12-ounce) container frozen whipped topping, thawed
  2 cups flaked coconut
  1 (16-ounce) jar maraschino cherries, drained

Prepare the cake mix according to the package directions. Pour the batter into a greased and floured 9x13-inch cake pan. Bake according to the package directions. Poke 10 to 15 holes over the surface of the hot cake with the handle of a wooden spoon. Pour the **Classic** Piña Colada Mix over the hot cake. Let stand for 3 to 4 hours. Spread the whipped topping over the cake. Sprinkle with the coconut. Garnish with the cherries. Yield: 15 servings

These **Naturally Fresh**® products are available at your local supermarket.

Regular & Lite Dressings
Honey French
Russian
Thousand Island
Caesar
Poppy Seed
Lite Peppercorn Ranch
Lite Bleu Cheese
Bleu Cheese
Wine & Cheese
Creamy Italian
Italian Herb Vinaigrette
Olive Oil & Vinegar
Lite Ranch
Slaw Dressing
Creamy Oriental
Honey Mustard
Lite Honey Mustard

Fat-Free Dressings
FF Bleu Cheese
FF Burgundy Wine
FF Balsamic Vinaigrette
FF Honey French
FF Raspberry Vinaigrette
FF Thousand Island
FF Lemon Vinaigrette
FF Italian
FF Ranch
FF Tomato Basil Vinaigrette
FF Honey Mustard

Vegetable Dips
FF Bacon, Tomato, Chive
French Onion
Bleu Cheese
Lite Ranch
Country Garden
Sour Cream & Herb
Picante Salsa
Dijon Horseradish
Honey Mustard

Fruit Dips
Fat Free Caramel
Fat Free Chocolate
Chocolate Peanut Butter

Meat Sauces
Sweet & Sour Sauce
BBQ Sauce
Mesquite BBQ Sauce
Cajun Sauce
Jackaroo® Gold Meat Sauce
Jackaroo® Buffalo Wing
Jackaroo® Meat Sauce

Seafood Sauces
Tartar Sauce
Seafood Cocktail Sauce

Classic® Bar Mixers
Grenadine
Whiskey Sour
Margarita
Bloody Mary
Pina Colada
Strawberry Daiquiri

Oils & Vinegars
Marl Vinegar
White Wine Vinegar
Red Wine Vinegar
Lemon Butter Oil
Mandarin Garlic Oil
Salad Oil
Olive Oil

Naturally Fresh Mountain Spring Water

If you cannot find your favorite **Naturally Fresh** product, please ask your store manager or write us at:

Naturally Fresh Foods
1000 Naturally Fresh Blvd.
Atlanta, GA 30349
1-800-765-1950
www.naturallyfresh.com

NaturallyFresh®
Dressings, Sauces & Dips

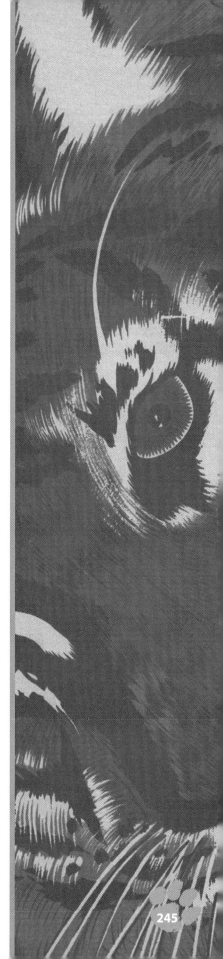

The Wren House

The Wren House, the *Southern Living* showcase home in the South Carolina Botanical Garden at Clemson University, is complete. The house opened to the public June 1, 1998. Hours are 9 a.m. to 6 p.m. Monday through Saturday and 1 p.m. to 6 p.m. Sunday. The house will be closed on Wednesday. Admission is $5.00 during the week and $8.00 Friday through Sunday.

Construction of the house and the adjacent Bob Campbell Geology Museum began in April 1997. In addition, construction of the nearby Betsy Campbell Carriage House began in the spring of 1998. It opened in the fall of 1998. The carriage house includes an open-air market café serving fresh produce, coffees, and teas. It also includes administrative and educational offices for the Garden staff. The 3,800-square-foot home and its landscape and furnishings will be on public display for about a year as a *Southern Living* home. The building will then be dedicated as the Fran Hanson Visitor Center for the Garden and a "Discovery Center" for the Heritage Corridor.

The garden design was created by Ryan Gainey of Atlanta. Gainey, author of *The Well-Placed Weed* and principal of the Ryan Gainey Companies, is a Clemson horticultur alumnus. Joining him to create the award-winning home and garden design are nationally recognized architect Keith Summerour and interior designer Ann Platz, both of Atlanta. Robby Newton of Southern Homes & Remodeling, Inc., was the builder.

More than 75 pieces of original artwork by some 50 South Carolina artists are included in the house, as well as handmade ceramic lavatory and fireplace tiles. In addition, a 90-foot canvas mural in the dining room features South Carolina landscapes from Table Rock to Charleston.

While the house is on display as a *Southern Living* home, an admission fee will be charged. This money will be placed in an endowment to help fund operating costs. Plans for the house will be featured in *Southern Living* magazine and will be available for purchase through the magazine, with part of the proceeds to be placed in the operating fund endowment.

The 3,400-square-foot museum will house the university's extensive geology collection, as well as rotating exhibits from other university collections, such as natural history and entomology. The geology collection is valued at more than $2 million and includes meteorites, minerals, dinosaur fossils, and the largest faceted stone collection in the Southeast. Betty Newton, now deceased, is recognized as the person who organized the collection and made it the magnificent collection it is today.

Index

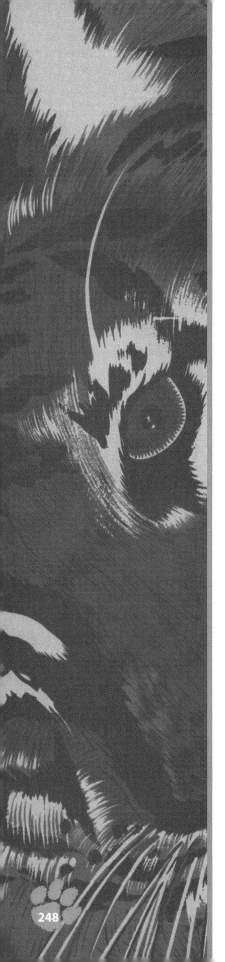

Trevor Adair, head coach of Clemson's men's soccer team

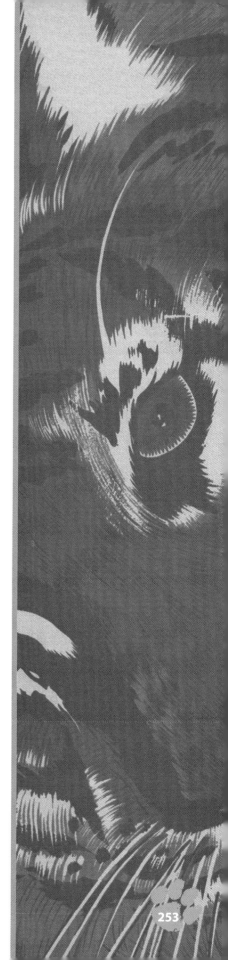

Tiger baseball players Kris Benson, Matthew LeCroy, and Billy Koch all played on the 1996 U.S. Olympic team and were later drafted to play pro baseball.

Pawsitively Clemson
Tastes of the Tigers

YOUR ORDER	QTY	TOTAL
Pawsitively Clemson $19.95 per book		$
South Carolina residents add $1.20 sales tax per book		$
Shipping and handling $5.00 per book		$
TOTAL		$

Method of payment: [   ] VISA   [   ] MasterCard
[   ] Check enclosed

_____

Account Number   Expiration Date
_____

Signature

Make checks payable to IPTAY Scholarship Fund, "Pawsitively Clemson"

_____

Name
_____

Street Address
_____

City   State   Zip
_____

Telephone

To order by mail, send to:
IPTAY Scholarship Fund, "Pawsitively Clemson"
Clemson University • P.O. Box 1529 • Clemson, South Carolina 29633

Photocopies will be accepted.

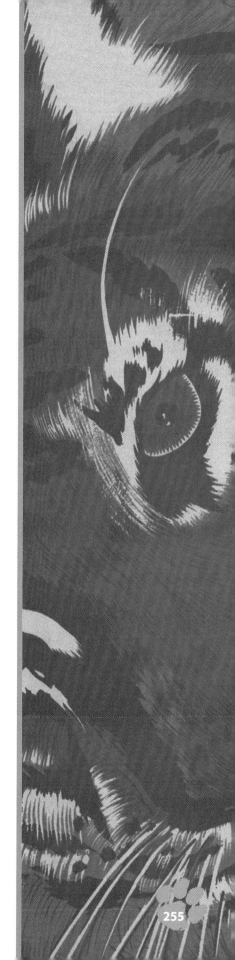